Against
Their Will

Against Their Will

Sadistic Kidnappers and the Courageous
Stories of Their Innocent Victims

Nigel Cawthorne

 Ulysses Press

Published in the United States by
ULYSSES PRESS
P.O. Box 3440
Berkeley, CA 94703
www.ulyssespress.com

ISBN13: 978-1-61243-066-9
Library of Congress Catalog Number: 2012931326

Printed in the United States by Bang Printing

10 9 8 7 6 5 4 3 2 1

Acquisitions: Keith Riegert
Managing Editor: Claire Chun
Editor: Barbara Schultz
Proofreader: Elyce Berrigan-Dunlop
Production: Judith Metzener
Cover design: what!design @ whatweb.com
Front cover photo: © spxChrome/istockphoto.com
Back cover photos: Phillip Garrido © Rich Pedroncelli/Associated Press;
 Josef Fritzl © Associated Press; Brian David Mitchell © Douglas C. Pizac/
 Associated Press

Distributed by Publishers Group West

Contents

Introduction

THIS BOOK IS FULL OF SOME of the vilest criminals imaginable. They take people, mainly young girls and boys, away from their families and subject them to unspeakable abuse and torture. The kidnappers do this for their own sexual and sadistic satisfaction, raping and tormenting at will. They do not, by and large, kill their victims. Instead, those that fall into their hands are forced to endure suffering seemingly without end.

The self-confessed monsters who commit these crimes attempt to rob their young and defenseless victims of all hope. They tell them that their parents do not want them back. No one is looking for them. No one cares. Victims are even told that their religion sanctions what is happening to them. They must suffer cruelty, neglect, maltreatment, squalor, and exploitation without complaint.

With no one to turn to, victims often become dependent on their captors for fear of something worse. Their kidnappers have at least kept them alive, though they make life a living hell. Others out there, victims are told, would be happy to torture them to death.

The perpetrators are mainly men, though some kidnappers have used female accomplices. The victims are usually young women, held naked as sex toys; they are defiled and humiliated, damaged both physically and psychologically. In many cases, they never fully recover.

Nothing can be said in defense of the offenders. No amount of psychiatric probing can explain or excuse their crimes. These are often individuals that medical science has already given up on. Morally, they are depraved.

Many kidnappers are persuaded to plead guilty on all charges brought against them to spare their victims the horror of reliving the details of their captivity, or so it is said. But the real reason they plead guilty seems to be that they don't want the world to know the true depths of their depravity.

But even in this dark corner of human experience, there is a spark of hope. You cannot but admire the strength, resilience, resourcefulness, and sheer courage of the victims. Somehow, no matter what they have been though, the human spirit survives. Often, in the end, the victims find a way to outsmart their captors, even while feeling compassion for them. It seems, in the end, good can triumph over evil.

This book is not for the squeamish. The victims have been to the very limits of what human beings can endure. It is best read as the story of these survivors, each a tribute to guts, nerve, determination, and tenacity against all the odds. The survivors—many do not want to be considered victims—have endured the worst privations and made it through. They have been into the abyss, many literally held underground, only to fight their way back into the light of day.

Nigel Cawthorne
Bloomsbury, London
March 2012

Chapter 1

Jaycee Lee Dugard—
The Backyard Prisoner

ON JUNE 10, 1991, ELEVEN-YEAR-OLD Jaycee Lee Dugard woke to hear the front door close. Her mother, Terry Probyn, had left without giving her a kiss good-bye. Jaycee lingered in bed, then hurried to get herself ready for school. She wanted to catch the school bus and not annoy her stepfather Carl Probyn by asking him for a ride.

She dressed quickly in pink stretch pants and her favorite kitty shirt, though she could not find the ring she wanted to wear, which she had bought at the craft fair the day before. Although she felt a little queasy, she did not want to ask to take the day off school in case it provoked an argument with her stepdad. Instead, she scarfed some oatmeal. Luckily, Carl was outside. He often scolded her for her table manners. She decided that when she became a parent, she would not be so mean to her children.

Jaycee made a peanut butter and jelly sandwich for her lunch and packed an apple and a box of juice. Then she went to say good-bye to her baby sister, Shayna, but she was not awake yet. She had to make do with saying good-bye to her cat, a black Manx named Monkey who was outside on the deck. He had been separated from his mother at young age and loved to snuggle up to Jaycee's fuzzy blanket. It was as if he thought she was his mom. Jaycee did not like leaving him outside because her mom's cat, Bridget, had been eaten by wild animals after they had moved to South Lake Tahoe the previous September.

The family had left Anaheim after their apartment had been broken into. Although at the age of ten, Jaycee had already been considered old enough to walk to school by herself, one time when she had been walking home a group of guys in a car shouted at her and gestured for her to come over, and she ran away and hid. Since the move to Tahoe, she felt safe.

On her way to catch the school bus, she was often accompanied by a neighbor's dog named Ninja. But the dog was nowhere to be seen that morning, so Jaycee started walking up Washoan Boulevard toward the bus stop on her own.

Back at the house, Carl Probyn watched his stepdaughter walk up the hill. He noticed a gray sedan with a couple in it drive past the girl. Then it did a U-turn and came back. The driver rolled down his window as if to ask the girl for directions, then he leaned out of the door and grabbed her. Jaycee screamed and tried to get away, but she heard a cracking sound. She had been paralyzed with a stun gun and was dragged into the back of the car. A blanket was thrown over her. Someone sat on her, and the car took off.

Carl had just seen his stepdaughter be abducted in broad daylight, but she was too far away for him to stop it. He jumped on his bike and cycled after the car. There was no way he could keep up, and the car had lost him before he could get the license number. He returned home and called the police. When they arrived, he gave them a description of the car and the couple in it. By then they were long gone.

Some way out of town, the car stopped. The woman who had been sitting on top of Jaycee got out and moved into the front of the car. Jaycee had been stifling under the blanket and had peed herself due to the effects of the stun gun. The man who had grabbed her offered her a drink. She was thirsty and took it.

Suddenly, the man was laughing. He said he could not believe that they'd gotten away with it. Jaycee was scared.

The next thing she remembered was the car stopping. The man said they were home. He threw the blanket back over Jaycee's head and warned her to keep quiet; otherwise, she would disturb his very aggressive dogs. Inside, he zapped her with his stun gun again. Then he took her to the bathroom and made her take her clothes off. He stripped off as well and asked whether she had ever seen a naked man before. Jaycee said she hadn't and was very afraid.

He made her touch him, then forced her to take a shower with him while he shaved what little hair she had in her armpits and around her pubic region. She cried. He offered to comfort her, but she did not want that. She said that, while her family did not have much money, they would pay to get her back. Then he wrapped her in a towel and, putting her back under a blanket, led her out into the back garden. When he took the blanket off, she found herself in a small room with carpet under her feet. There were blankets and egg crates he said she could use as a bed. As Jaycee stood shaking with fatigue from her ordeal, the man said he would come back later. He handcuffed her and warned her to keep quiet, and he locked the door behind him as he left. Jaycee cried herself to sleep. She was still crying when she woke up the following morning. She worried whether she would be in trouble at school and whether her parents were out looking for her.

When the sun came up it was hot in the room where she was being held. Eventually her abductor arrived with some food and drink, and he took the handcuffs off so she could eat. He also brought a bucket that she could use as a toilet. But before he left, he put the handcuffs back on again. She managed to pull a towel that was covering the window down with her teeth, but all she could see outside was a tree.

Whenever her abductor came to see her, he tried to make her smile and win her trust. She resisted at first. But soon she began to look forward to seeing him, as his company was the only human contact she got. All the time her heart was breaking. To pass the time, she made up a story about a boy who would come from the stars, take her by the hand and fly around the world with her—though he would eventually return her to her prison. Even in her imagination there was no escape.

Within hours of Jaycee's abduction, the media descended on South Lake Tahoe. Over the following days, dozens of volunteers searched the area. Tens of thousands of fliers and posters were mailed to businesses across the United States, to no avail. At one stage, Carl Probyn was considered a suspect, though he was eventually ruled out. Meanwhile the Probyns' marriage fell apart.

About a week after the kidnapping, Jaycee's abductor again came with some food and a milkshake. But this time, when he undid her handcuffs, he fastened them again behind her back. Then he took off his clothes and raped her. Afterward she was bleeding. He brought her a washcloth and a bucket of warm water to wash herself. Jaycee was in shock. She knew something terrible had happened to her, though she did not really realize what it was. She had not heard the word rape and did not know what it meant.

This was the first of many times he would rape her. She learned to distance herself from the experience and think about something else until he had finished.

At first she did not even know his name, but gradually she got to know that it was Phillip, though she did not know how she knew. She even admitted to enjoying his company, when he was not using her for sex.

He installed an air-conditioning unit to keep her cool that summer. But she had to wash from a bucket. Unable to have a shower, she found she was attracting ants. With her hands cuffed, it was impossible to flick them away. They made her skin itch and even got in her mouth.

After a while, he left off the cuffs, saying he trusted her. But she still had to cope with the boredom and longed to go outside, or even brush her teeth. She tried the door. It was firmly locked. Some days he would come with a guitar and play for her, saying that one day he was going to be famous. He showed her his mixing desk and brought her a small black-and-white TV. It had few channels, but at least it provided the sound of the human voice and gave her some way to relieve the boredom. Then he bought her a cat for companionship.

Unable to go out, the cat peed everywhere, so he took it away again. The room was no place for a cat, he said, though it seems it was good enough for a little girl. If she didn't cry, he said, one day she may be able to see the cat again.

Jaycee wondered, in passing, whether Phillip was her real father, whom she did not know. He said he wasn't. She began to wonder why her biological father had never bothered to see her. This made her feel even lonelier. As always, she took refuge in sleep. When she dreamt, at least, she could be at home with her mother and sister.

Phillip mentioned that the woman with him when he abducted her was his wife, Nancy. He then told the eleven-year-old that he had a "problem" with sex. She was there to help him with it. Apparently, his sexual problem was that he hurt other people. She was there so that he would not hurt anyone else. Jaycee even found herself feeling sympathetic, though she was well aware that he was hurting her.

Eventually, he brought her some clothes—underwear and a pink jump suit. She hated having to take them off for sex. Then one night he took her into a larger room with a couch, a desk, a small fridge, a TV, and a partition dividing it into two. Quickly she realized that there was a price to be paid for her new surroundings. He said that he was going to take drugs and he explained all the terrible things that she was going to have to do to fulfill his depraved fantasies. She began to cry, but he was not to be denied. He threatened her with the stun gun. Then, he took a cocktail of drugs and plunged her into a nightmare of sexual abuse. She was used in every way imaginable.

Phillip Garrido, then forty, was a registered sex offender. Born in 1951 in Antioch, California, he was brought up in Brentwood. By the time he graduated from Liberty High School in 1969, he had grown his hair long and played in a psychedelic rock band. His high school sweetheart was Christine Perreira, a popular girl and the daughter of a prominent local family. The story circulated that he had raped a girl, but Christine believed Garrido when he said that the girl was lying.

During his teens, Garrido had a motorcycle accident which, his father said, changed him. Within a month of graduating, he was arrested for the possession of cannabis and LSD. In 1972, he gave a fourteen-year-old girl drugs and took her to a motel where he raped her. He was arrested, but when his victim refused to testify, the charges were dropped.

The following year, Garrido had a falling out with some local drug dealers and fled to South Lake Tahoe. Christine went with him. They married. She supported them as a blackjack dealer in a casino while he struggled to make a career as a musician playing bass guitar.

For years he took LSD every day, up to ten hits a day. This made his sexual urges irresistible, he said. He turned violent with Christine, beating her when she refused to go along with his plans to have sex with multiple partners. When another man flirted with Christine, Garrido tried to stab her in the eye with a safety pin. She tried to run away, but he drove after her, grabbed her, and threw her in the car.

In the fall of 1976, he stalked a woman and made meticulous plans to kidnap her. He rented a mini storage locker and set up a small apartment at the back. The entrance was hung with a maze of thick carpet to deaden any sound. On November 26, he dropped four tabs of acid and tried to abduct the woman he had been stalking. But he only managed to get the handcuffs around one of her wrists. She fought him off, leapt from the car and eventually persuaded him to unlock the handcuffs, setting her free.

Garrido drove to the casino where Christine worked. Outside, he approached another blackjack dealer, twenty-five-year-old Katherine Callaway. Pointing at a Mercedes-Benz parked there, he said he could not get his car to start and asked her for a ride. When she stopped where he said he lived, which was across the state line in Nevada, she found they were at an empty lot. Before she knew what was happening, he smashed her head into the steering wheel and handcuffed her.

"If you do everything I say, you won't get hurt," he said. "I'm serious."

Then he tied her head to her knees, covered her with a coat, and drove off.

"Don't worry," he told her. "I've got it all planned."

On the way, he told her about his sexual fantasies and preached about Jesus.

When they arrived at his lockup, he bundled her inside. Behind some heavy plastic sheeting, there was a mattress with a "red, old satin, holey, old sheet," she said. There were red, blue, and yellow stage lights set up around the mattress, a movie projector, and a stack of pornographic magazines, along with marijuana, hashish, and some cheap wine. There was also an old kerosene can that Garrido indicated she could use as a toilet.

He insisted that she drink some wine and smoke some hash. Then for five and a half hours, he raped her repeatedly. Katherine kept track of the time from the radio Garrido had left switched on. Soon after 2:38 a.m., someone began banging on the door. Garrido went out and returned saying that it was "just the guy next door."

Not long after that, there was another bang on the door.

"I think it is the heat," Garrido said. "Are you going to be good?"

Outside was Reno cop Clifford Conrad. He began questioning Garrido. Then Katherine came running out naked and bruised, crying, "Help me!"

In court, Garrido said, "I had this fantasy that was driving me to do this, inside of me, something that was making me want to do it without—no way to stop it."

He blamed the LSD, saying it increased his sexual powers. It came out that his libido was so high that he would masturbate in drive-in theaters, restaurants, bars, public restrooms, and outside the windows of people's homes. More disturbingly, he would watch girls aged from seven to ten outside elementary schools and expose himself to them, or sit in his car and masturbate at the sight of them.

Garrido was sentenced to fifty years and sent to the federal penitentiary at Leavenworth, Kansas. Christine seized the opportunity to divorce him. He used his time in jail to study psychology and theology. As he was clearly unhinged, he was offered a transfer to a mental health facility, but he elected to stay in Leavenworth to complete his religious training. He became a Jehovah's Witness, and prison psychologist J. B.

Kielbauch saw Garrido's renewed religious zeal as an indication that he would be unlikely to commit further crimes. So after just eleven years, Garrido was paroled.

But Garrido was the same pervert that he was when he went to jail. Just three years after he was released, he kidnapped Jaycee Dugard. This time, he inflicted his depravity on an eleven-year-old girl. The horrors she went through are indescribable, but as part of her therapy, she detailed them in her book *A Stolen Life*. When the first night of drug-fueled depravity was over, she was bleeding again. This time she was having her first period.

Jaycee had difficulty understanding her feelings for her tormentor. Sometimes he could be amusing and kind. Other times he would scare her, even with the words he used. He promised to make her the best sex slave ever. When she cried, he threatened to give her to other men who were even worse than he was. They would keep her in a cage. She was so frightened that she begged him not to do that, saying she would do anything he wanted.

In small ways, she kept the spirit of rebellion alive though. She quickly learned the way he liked things done and to not quite do it that way, but not in a manner that would seem deliberate. She would forget to put her lipstick on, not masturbate him quite as fast as he liked, or pretend to be asleep when he was engrossed in TV.

The drug-fueled "runs" continued. He would tie her up or videotape her doing degrading things. Sometimes, after sex, he would beg her to forgive him. At times, she was even sympathetic to his "problem," but eventually realized that he was a selfish man, concerned only with his own gratification.

After one "run"—a daylong session of drug-fueled sex—he let her remain in the larger room. He began to call her Snoopy as she snooped through the things he had in there. At first, he would handcuff her to a pullout bed in there. But after a few months, he left her unshackled. But although she could walk around, she could not go anywhere. The door was securely locked and there were iron bars on the windows.

Even though Jaycee now lived in a bigger room she still did not have proper bathroom facilities. There was no running water and she still had to use a bucket as a toilet. Sometimes it would get filled up and there was often a shortage of toilet paper.

Eventually, Garrido introduced Jaycee to Nancy, saying that he wanted them to be good friends. He had met Nancy Bocanegra when she came to visit her uncle in jail. Garrido and Bocanegra wrote to each other and, in 1981, they were married by the prison chaplain. When Garrido was paroled in 1988, the two moved in with Garrido's mother who lived just outside Antioch in a modest home with a large, secluded backyard. Together, they looked after Garrido's mother when she began to exhibit the early stages of dementia.

According to Garrido's brother, Nancy was a "robot" under Phillip's control. Ron Garrido said his brother, over the subsequent years, spoke of his plans to get rich and start a church of his own. But he never spoke of the girl he was keeping in the backyard. When he learned what his brother had done, Ron said: "It just seems so bizarre, but I can believe it. I know my brother, and I can believe he did that... He's a fruitcake."

Nancy started bringing Jaycee her food, but Jaycee could not understand why Nancy had helped Garrido abduct her, or why he had to have sex with her instead of his wife. But these were not topics they could address. Instead they got to talking about Nancy's job in a nearby convalescent home. Nancy gave Jaycee a teddy bear and some magazines she asked for. Jaycee was also given a Nintendo to pass the time, and Phillip and Nancy sometimes slept in the larger room with her.

Phillip said he was trying to persuade Nancy to join in one of their "runs." Jaycee prayed she would not agree. They were bad enough—humiliating enough—as it was. At one time, he even wanted Jaycee to have sex with a dog.

On Jaycee's twelfth birthday, Phillip and Nancy said they had a surprise for her. The surprise was that Nancy had had her hair high-lighted. However, a few days later, Nancy gave her a Birthday Barbie, after Jaycee had figured out how to make Barbie furniture out of empty milk cartons. Jaycee did this because it reminded her of her mother, who had made her Barbie clothes, and her Aunt Tina, who had taught her how to put Barbie's hair in a ponytail.

Jaycee's family certainly had not forgotten about her. Her mother, Terry, founded a group called Jaycee's Hope that raised money to keep her case in the public eye. Her kidnapping also appeared several times on *America's Most Wanted*. But there was no clue to her whereabouts and, as in all such cases, people soon found it hard to believe that she was still alive.

After the first year, Phillip, Nancy, and Jaycee spent more time together, eating fast food and watching movies Phillip rented. Nancy brought her books and crayons. Jaycee got the impression that Nancy even liked her. The situation was tough for a twelve-year-old to figure out. How must Nancy feel about

Jaycee having sex with her husband? She must also have felt guilty for her part in the abduction, Jaycee surmised. They managed a relationship of sorts, though. On special occasions, Nancy would bring home-cooked food for Jaycee that had been prepared by Phillip's mother. They talked about music and movies. Nancy explained that Garrido was sweet and nice to her most of the time, but admitted that they smoked weed and crystal meth together.

Then for four weeks, Jaycee was spared having to give Garrido sex. In April 1993, the police had found drugs in the house and he had been sent back to jail for violating the conditions of his parole. During that time, Nancy looked after Jaycee. They slept in the same bed when Jaycee was frightened. But Jaycee recalled being happy to see Garrido when he returned because while he was gone, Nancy did not say much and cried a lot. When he came back, he had an electronic tag on his ankle.

Jaycee learned that Garrido was on parole for rape. He was constantly afraid that his parole agent would show up unexpectedly. But she did not understand why the agent who came to the house did not investigate what was happening in the backyard.

Soon the sexual abuse started again. But the "runs" were shorter and Garrido spent more time reading the Bible. Jaycee managed to get through the sex and the accompanying pain by reminding herself that he became a nice person again once it was over. However, he was getting weird. He said he had begun to hear voices and spent hours listening to the walls.

Sometimes, Jaycee was sent back into the smaller room, which Garrido called the studio. This was because Garrido's friends came over and they smoked weed and played music in the large room all night.

Garrido bought Jaycee a tent and a sleeping bag. Jaycee considered this ironic as she was not allowed outside. He also bought her a kitten, but it proved a distraction during their "runs" and he got rid of it. Later he bought her another cat, but again took it away after month. This made Jaycee sad, as the various cats reminded her of the one she had had at home.

To pass the time, Jaycee wrote a journal about the cat, but Garrido grew concerned when he saw Jaycee had written her name in it. As a result, she tore off the corner with her name on it and did not write her name on anything again while she was in captivity. Later, she kept a secret journal where she could express her thoughts and feelings, and what she could recall of her previous life. She also speculated about a future away from Garrido. She decided she would like to live in a little cottage that overlooked the ocean. And she wondered whether she would ever be able to bear a man touching her in a sexual way, after what she had been through. She kept this journal hidden, knowing that Garrido would not approve.

On Easter Sunday 1994, Jaycee was moved back into the studio. Garrido said that there were police in the area and she had to be very quiet. Soon after Jaycee began to put on weight, and Phillip and Nancy said they thought she was pregnant. Jaycee was just fourteen. All she knew about babies was that they were born in the hospital. She knew that Garrido would not let her go to the hospital. How was she going to have one there in the backyard? And how could she raise it there in the backyard? She wondered whether they would make her give it up for adoption. But then when she felt the baby kick, she knew she could not give it away. In fact, Garrido seemed happy about her pregnancy, and giving the baby away was never mentioned. At last, Jaycee felt less alone in the world.

She was moved back into the larger room, which was now partitioned. She had the part with no windows. Then Garrido said that he had heard that the house was going to be raided. She would have to be moved. He put a blanket over her again and led her out through the house to his van where Nancy was waiting. Jaycee was hidden under the backseat, then Garrido drove off.

When the van stopped, Jaycee was led to a trailer. As she was pregnant, she needed to go to the bathroom—and she found herself in an actual bathroom for the first time in years. It had running water and a flushing toilet. The next morning, Phillip and Nancy said they had to go back to the house to see what was happening. Jaycee cried when she was left alone and was happy when they came back. The next night after driving around to make sure it was safe, they returned to what Jaycee was now calling home.

Garrido began to watch videos about giving birth and tried to assure Jaycee that he knew what he was doing. Besides, Nancy was a nurse's aide. But when Jaycee had the first contractions, she was alone and there was no one she could call. When they eventually came to check on her, they found her doubled up in pain. During the birth, Garrido found that the umbilical cord was wrapped around the baby's neck. He freed it, and Jaycee gave birth to a baby girl.

Garrido's sexual demands lessened after Jaycee gave birth, but did not go away completely. Also, Nancy sometimes took the baby away to sleep with her and Phillip in the studio as if it were her own, plunging Jaycee back into the depths of loneliness.

Jaycee was provided with a microwave oven so she could heat the water he bought in large containers. She was also given diapers, wipes, toys, and the other things that she needed for the baby. Later, Garrido installed a sink so they could have running water. Nancy bought a cockatiel in a cage. During the day, she would take it outside in the sunshine to give it some air. However, she did not do the same for Jaycee and her child. They were still not allowed out. At first the bird was mean, but Jaycee slowly tamed it. Then Nancy left it out late one cold fall evening and it died.

Garrido's drug intake lessened and there were fewer "runs." Jaycee hated them and told Garrido, but he insisted that one day she would enjoy them. Her only consolation was that she was saving someone else from going through the same ordeal. There was always that danger. Nancy told her that they drove around school playgrounds and parks where he would secretly videotape little girls. Sometimes he would get Nancy to play with them in the back of the van and get them to do the splits or sit with their legs open. Later, after he had smoked weed and crystal meth, he would watch the videotapes and masturbate.

Jaycee's first daughter was three and still breast feeding when Jaycee became pregnant again. Garrido bought her a new bed, with bunks for the kids. Her second child, another daughter, was born with a growth above her eye. Garrido said that, if it got any bigger, he would figure out a way to get it examined by a doctor.

He picked names for both girls. Jaycee has never released their names. The U.S. media respected this and has also declined to publish the names, though the names of the children have been published in the foreign press.

Garrido erected a tall fence around the yard, so Jaycee and her children could go outside. Phillip and Nancy said that they could have barbecues out there and be a real family. Eventually, Jaycee was allowed to roam outside in the backyard unsupervised. But escape was still not a possibility. Now that she had children, she was tied to her captors by invisible bonds. Garrido painted a picture of the outside world as a scary place, full of rapists and pedophiles. The only place she and her girls were safe, he said, was with their dad. At least, she would not have to worry about them being abducted as she had been.

With a growing family, Garrido needed to make money, so he set up a printing business, turning the studio into an office. He was against sending children to school. They were better off being taught at home, he said, claiming that he had created the perfect environment for raising children. So Jaycee used the office computer to teach the children the alphabet and numbers. Later, with the help of the Internet and the printing equipment, Jaycee made worksheets and set about educating her children with "class" from ten to two every day.

She also did some design work for Garrido's business and was grateful to have something useful to do to fill up her time. However, Garrido warned her that he monitored everything she did on the computer, so she did not dare to try to contact her mother via the Internet.

Jaycee even met the business's customers. When client Ben Daughdrill drove to Garrido's home outside Antioch, he said he met a polite young woman with blonde hair whom Garrido said was his daughter.

"She was the design person," said Daughdrill. "She did the art work; she was the genius."

Daughdrill later said that he had regularly exchanged e-mails with her and they had even spoken on the phone, but that she had never hinted at her real identity or her secret life.

Nancy quit her job and stayed at home. She encouraged Jaycee to flatter Garrido and build up his ego. He had been diagnosed with Attention Deficit Disorder and was on new medication. She did not want him slipping back into his old ways. He and Nancy had seen a therapist just days before abducting Jaycee and a few days after. The therapist had even made excuses for him to the parole board when his drug test proved positive.

Garrido then insisted that Jaycee's daughters call Nancy "Mommy," while Jaycee herself would be the "big sister." He decided, in that case, Jaycee needed a new name too. She chose "Allissa."

As the girls grew bigger, they were allowed to climb on the roof to watch the fireworks on the Fourth of July. The following day, they went to the beach. The girls played in the water while Garrido sat on the beach reading the Bible. A few weeks later, Garrido gave Jaycee $100 to go to a nail salon with Nancy. They stopped for fast food on the way back. Soon after that, Jaycee and Nancy went to Walmart together.

More outings followed, but only after Garrido got Nancy to cut Jaycee's hair short and dye it brown. She had been missing for six years and had put on weight after her pregnancies. Who was going to recognize her? Jaycee was of two minds about being discovered anyway. She longed to shout out her name "Jaycee!" But in public she was now Allissa. She stuck close to Nancy in case someone asked her a question she could not answer. She thought they would say, "Aren't you that missing girl?" No one ever did. She began to feel as if she was invisible. Garrido said there were angels protecting them. And always there was the backyard to go back to.

Garrido had added a few more tents to accommodate the growing family. They took in stray cats. When high on drugs, Garrido would empty a bucket of urine over a cat that cried because he kept it tied up. Jaycee begged him not to. She was devastated when two dogs from next door broke through the fence and killed her favorite cats. The neighbors must have heard her crying, she thought. Next time she went out shopping with Nancy, she bought two kittens.

They also inherited two dogs from an elderly neighbor who had been taken into nursing care. To stop the dogs from chasing the cats, a dog run was built, and Jaycee would take them for a walk on a leash around the backyard once a day. The animals were a great comfort to her.

A newborn kitten had an eye infection. Garrido allowed Jaycee to take it to the vet, provided she pretended to be his daughter. It was another opportunity to escape. She often thought about escaping, but she knew she could not leave her girls behind.

In December 2003, Jaycee saw on TV that people speculated that Richard Allen Davis, who had been convicted of killing twelve-year-old Polly Klaas in California in 1993, had also killed her. This was a trailer for a news program that Jaycee feared would upset her mom. Jaycee avoided watching the show too.

"Why can't they just leave it in the past?" she wrote in her journal.

When Garrido's mother became very ill, he let the two girls stay in the house to keep her company. Then Jaycee was allowed into the house too, to help Nancy look after his mother. Around the same time, the laws on parole were tightened. This meant that Jaycee's outings were curtailed. A new parole agent was assigned to Garrido. He even saw one of the girls asleep in the house. Nothing was said, and he, too, was soon replaced. Later, Jaycee even got to talk to a visiting parole agent. She asked him whether he was the agent who had walked into her daughter's bedroom. He said he was not, took Garrido's urine sample, and left.

Although Jaycee found that being in the house was better than being in the backyard, the house itself was falling apart. The drains backed up, making it impossible to keep things clean.

The print business was not going well and Garrido talked about setting up a church called "God's Desire," which would provide a remedy for rapists and pedophiles. The nation needed to know. On August 24, 2009, he went to the FBI office in San Francisco to deliver a rambling four-page essay called "Schizophrenia Revealed." He said it showed how sexual predators like him could be cured by ideas about religion and sexuality which had been vouchsafed to him by mysterious voices he had picked up via a "black box" of his own devising. This turned out to be nothing but a cassette recorder with random recordings on it inside a black case. In the essay, he described how having sex with his wife had turned from an act of anger to an act of love, though it was not clear whether, by his "wife," he meant Nancy or Jaycee.

He took the girls with him on his visit to the FBI, believing that people were more likely to listen to him if they were there. He also visited the University of California in Berkeley to ask for permission to stage a "God's Desire" event on the campus. The events manager, Lisa Campbell, felt that there was something odd about the two girls he brought with him, whom he introduced as his daughters. She asked campus police officer Ally Jacobs to do a background check on Garrido. When they discovered that Garrido had a rape conviction, she contacted the parole office and registered her concern.

The parole office had not been informed about the two girls, so two parole agents were sent to Garrido's house. They handcuffed him and searched the place. They found only Nancy and his mother, but they did not look out in the backyard. Then they took Garrido to the parole office. On the way, he explained that the two girls who had accompanied him to UC Berkeley "were the daughters of a relative, and he had permission from their parents to take them to the university."

When Jaycee heard that Garrido had been arrested, she was worried. After all, she had been with him for eighteen years. He was a staple of her life. But after a few hours, Garrido was returned. A month earlier, Garrido had been barred from being around minors; the parole agents were prepared to overlook the violation of his new parole conditions on the condition that he return to the parole office the following day.

When she thought about it, Jaycee could not believe that he had been returned. Garrido now believed he was above the law. He was protected by angels, he said. He even thought that the angels had been with him when he had kidnapped her. That's how he got away with it. They had allowed him to kidnap Jaycee to keep him occupied and out of their realm. She was confused about this, as angels were supposed to be good. Did she count for nothing?

The next day Garrido, in his hubris, took Nancy, Jaycee, and the girls with him to the parole office. The parole officer could not understand what Jaycee and the girls were doing there and led them away to a separate office. When Jaycee looked back at Garrido, he winked at her.

When she was questioned, Jaycee gave her name as Allissa. Garrido had told her to say that she was the girls' mother and she had given him permission to take them with him the previous day, even though she knew he was a sex offender. If they asked anything else, she should demand a lawyer.

Jaycee did as she was told and, after about twenty minutes, she was released. She and the girls walked back to the car where Nancy was waiting. Jaycee said that, together, they willed Phillip to return. Instead two parole agents came out of the building. One of them took Jaycee aside and accused her of lying to him. Garrido had said that she and the two girls were the daughters of his brother. She was their older sister. Jaycee could not understand this. He had told her to tell a different story and she felt betrayed. Then she grew scared that, if there was trouble, her daughters might be taken away from her. She told the agent that Garrido had lied for her sake. She had run away from an abusive husband with the children and Garrido did not want their father to know where they were.

A woman officer asked Jaycee her name. Jaycee did not know what to do. For the last eighteen years Garrido had made all the decisions. She asked to see Garrido. He was brought in, in handcuffs, and he told her to get a lawyer. But why did she need a lawyer if she had done nothing wrong, the woman officer asked.

Jaycee was left on her own to think things over. Then the woman officer returned and told her that Garrido had confessed to kidnapping her. She asked Jaycee for her name again. Jaycee replied she could not say it after not saying it for eighteen years. But she could write it down. With a shaky hand, she wrote: "JAYCEELEEDUGARD."

Suddenly she felt free, she said. The spell was broken.

Immediately she was reunited with her girls and they were taken to the police station where they would be more comfortable. Was there anything they wanted? Their first concern was for the animals left at the house. Then the tears she had been holding back for eighteen years began to fall.

The police got on the phone to contact Jaycee's mother. They located her at her work and the first thing that Jaycee said to her mother after eighteen years was: "Hi, Mom, I have babies." Only they weren't babies any longer. There was a tearful reunion the following day. Then she began down the long road to recovery.

As part of that, Jaycee visited Nancy, who said she had done what she did for love of Phillip. And she still loved him. Jaycee explained that what they had done was unforgivable.

Garrido became a person of interest in the cases of other missing girls, but a thorough search of the house and back garden yielded nothing. What the searchers did find was a scene of squalor. Before, those who had been to 1554 Walnut Avenue had only seen a small area of the backyard. Beyond a tarpaulin, there was a second compound surrounded by tall trees and a six-foot-high fence. In it, there was a barn and sheds, one of which was soundproofed. It had been used as a recording studio. Garrido recorded religious-themed and romantic country songs there. It had also been used as a makeshift prison.

Electricity was supplied to the compound by extension cords, which none of the officials who had visited the house seemed to have noticed. There were also two tents and a camping-style shower and toilet, which Garrido had provided later, as well as an old car similar to the one used in the abduction. Searchers also found childhood possessions, including books and toys.

Although Garrido had made a confession to the police, in jail, he was unrepentant.

"In the end, this is going to be a powerful, heartwarming story," he told Walt Gray of KCRA-TV in the telephone interview and he directed him to the documents he had given to the FBI, "because what you are going to have in your hands will take world news immediately…

"Wait till you hear the story of what took place at this house," he went on. "And you're going to be absolutely impressed. It's a disgusting thing that took place with me in the beginning. But I turned my life completely around."

On August 28, 2009, Garrido and Nancy pleaded not guilty to charges that included kidnapping, rape, and false imprisonment. They persisted in this, though they had both made full confessions. But when the case finally came to trial on April 28, 2011, they both pleaded guilty to kidnapping and sexual assault. This relieved Jaycee and her daughters of the ordeal of testifying. Not that Jaycee would have shrunk from that.

"Jaycee's courage and willingness to confront her abductors in court directly led to the defendants' plea and life sentences," said the district attorney.

Jaycee did not attend court for the sentencing, but she did send a written statement to be read aloud in court. In it she said:

> I chose not to be here today because I refuse to waste another second of my life in your presence. I've chosen to have my mom read this for me. Phillip Garrido, you are wrong. I could never say that to you before, but I have the freedom now and I am saying you are a liar and all of your so-called theories are wrong. Everything you have ever done to me has been wrong, and someday I hope you can see that. What you and Nancy did was reprehensible. You always justified everything to suit yourself, but the reality is and always has been that to make someone else suffer for your inability to control yourself, and for you, Nancy, to facilitate his behavior and trick young girls for his pleasure, is evil. There is no God in the universe that would condone your actions. To you, Phillip, I say that I have always been a thing for your own amusement. I hated every second of every day of eighteen years because of you and the

sexual perversion you forced on me. To you, Nancy, I have nothing to say. Both of you can save your apologies and empty words. For all the crimes you have both committed I hope you have as many sleepless nights as I did. Yes, as I think of all of those years I am angry because you stole my life and that of my family. Thankfully I am doing well now and no longer live in a nightmare. I have wonderful friends and family around me. Something you can never take from me again. You do not matter any more.

Phillip Garrido was sentenced to 431 years, Nancy 36 years to life. By the time the Garridos were convicted, Jaycee and her family had already been awarded a $20 million settlement in 2009 through the state's victim's compensation fund.

Meanwhile an investigation was under way to discover how Garrido, a registered sex offender on parole, was able to keep Jaycee Dugard captive for eighteen years without being found out.

At least twice a month, Garrido's home was visited by parole agents, but they never ventured beyond the house, even though a neighbor complained that children were living in a complex of tents in the backyard. Even when they had seen Jaycee and one of her daughters there, the parole agents made no further inquiries.

Neighbors knew Garrido was a registered sex offender, and kids on the block called him "Creepy Phil" and kept their distance. Though the compound was arranged so that people could not see in easily, the next-door neighbor reported that children were living there. Another neighbor recalled that when he was a child, he met Jaycee through the fence. He said that she had called herself Jaycee. He asked whether she lived there or was just visiting. She said that she lived there. Then Garrido came and took her back inside. Later, Garrido built a tall fence around the property. However, Jaycee does not mention meeting a neighbor boy through the fence in her book *A Stolen Life*.

Ten months after Jaycee had been abducted, a girl with her description was seen staring at a picture of herself on a "missing" poster in a gas station in Oakley, not two miles from the house outside Antioch where Garrido lived. A witness called the Contra Costa County sheriff's office from the pay phone there and reported seeing the girl return to a yellow van, possibly a Dodge. A deputy was sent to the gas station, but the yellow van was gone—as was the caller, who did not leave his name and never came forward. In *A Stolen Life* Jaycee does not mention leaving the backyard compound until shortly before her first child was born in August 1994. However, when the police searched the backyard of 1554 Walnut Avenue they unearthed a dilapidated yellow Dodge Ram van with flat tires that was half-buried in dirt behind the house.

In June 2002, the fire department was called to Garrido's house after it was reported that a juvenile had injured her shoulder in the swimming pool in the backyard. However, this incident did not get passed to the parole officer, who had no record of juveniles living at 1554 Walnut Avenue.

Law enforcement officers visited the residence at least twice, but did not give the backyard more than a quick inspection. In November 2006, a neighbor called 911, saying that Garrido, a sex addict, had people living in his backyard and there were children there. An officer investigating the complaint spent half an hour interviewing Garrido on his front porch, but did not enter the house or search the backyard. The officer did not even know that Garrido was a registered sex offender, though the police department had that information. Before leaving, he warned Garrido that the tents in the backyard could be a building code violation.

The California Office of the Inspector General issued a special report on the failure of the California Department of Corrections and Rehabilitation's supervision of parolee Phillip Garrido. It said that many warning signs were overlooked or ignored. Agents failed to spot the utility cables that led to the hidden backyard compound, and data from the satellite tracking device the state made him wear could have alerted his parole agent to his presence in that area, had it been reviewed.

Federal parole records, not obtained by the state, noted that Garrido had a soundproof room in his yard. Agents had failed to speak to neighbors or other local agencies. Jaycee was seen in the house and even answered the front door, though no further investigation was made concerning her background. And agents failed to act when Garrido had violated the terms of his parole

In 2008, the report says, Garrido's parole agent met a twelve-year-old girl at Garrido's house and accepted his explanation that she was his brother's daughter without doing anything to verify it.

"No one can know, had the parole agents done everything right, whether we would have discovered Jaycee and her children any sooner," said the Inspector General David R. Shaw. "However, our investigation revealed that there were missed clues and opportunities to discover their existence sooner than they did."

Though Jaycee's childhood had been stolen, her daughters' had not. As a proud mother, Jaycee went on to enjoy watching them go to high school.

Chapter 2

Elisabeth Fritzl and the Father from Hell

ON THE NIGHT OF AUGUST 28, 1984, eighteen-year-old Elisabeth Fritzl was awoken by her father. He asked her to come down to the cellar with him. Over the years, he had been building a nuclear air-raid shelter down there. The Fritzls lived at 40 Ybbsstrasse in Amstetten, a small town in northern Austria, some thirty miles from the Czech border. It was on the front line if the Cold War heated up. Elisabeth's father wanted her to help him install a heavy steel door. It was a strange request, but she was afraid of her father and knew it was best to do what he said.

After the two of them wrestled the heavy door into place, Elisabeth's father grabbed her from behind and rendered her unconscious with ether. When she came to, she found herself in the dark, handcuffed to a metal pole. The bunker in the basement was not intended to be an air-raid shelter after all. It was a prison.

The room was insulated and soundproofed. Elisabeth screamed herself hoarse, but no one could hear her. People in the town who knew her were told that she had run off to join a religious sect. This was all too believable. She had run away from her abusive father before. Some neighbors were, no doubt, relieved that she had sought safety.

After a couple of days, Elisabeth was put on a long leash so that she could reach a makeshift lavatory. Then the real ordeal began. Her father started raping her. This was no surprise. He had been sexually abusing her since she was a child. And fighting back was not an option.

"I faced the choice of being left to starve or being raped," she said. It was no choice at all.

This ordeal would not just go on for one day, or one week, or one month, or one year, but 8,516 days—just a few months short of twenty-four years.

Josef Fritzl has made no attempt to explain the incarceration and rape of his daughter. However, he has claimed to be a victim of Austria's Nazi past. Born on April 9, 1935, he was nearly three when the people of Amstetten lined the road with their arms raised to greet Hitler (himself an Austrian by birth) as he drove into Austria on March 12, 1938, to annex the country as part of the Greater German Reich. Born in Braunau am Inn on the Bavarian border just eighty-five miles from Amstetten, Hitler spent most of his childhood in Linz, less than thirty miles from Fritzl's home town. After the 1938 *Anschluss*, Hitler was made an honorary citizen of Amstetten.

Fritzl did not know his father. It seems he was killed in the war, but his mother had already caused a scandal in the small Austrian town by divorcing him, apparently for infidelity.

"My father was somebody who was a waster; he never took responsibility and was just a loser who always cheated on my mother," Fritzl said. "When I was four she quite rightly threw him out the house. After that my mother and I had no contact with this man; he did not interest us. Suddenly there were only us two."

After Hitler invaded the Soviet Union in 1941, the rail line through Amstetten was used to move men and material to the front. It was repeatedly bombed by the RAF and the U.S. Eighth Air Force, so Fritzl would have spent much of his childhood in the cellar. He would also have known about captivity from an early age. In town, there was a camp for the slave laborers who were used to rebuild the railroad after the bombing raids. There was also a concentration camp for five hundred women. Many Austrians were enthusiastic supporters of the Holocaust, and inmates of the nearby Amstetten-Mauer Landesklinikum Clinic, where Elisabeth and her children would later recuperate, were killed in the Nazi euthanasia program. Fritzl would almost certainly have been a member of the Hitler Youth. Membership was compulsory after the age of ten. Indeed, Fritzl called the cellar of his home in Ybbsstrasse his "Reich." Down there, he called himself the "Führer."

"I have always placed a great deal of value on discipline and good behavior," he said. "I admit that. My behavior comes from my generation. I am from the old school. I was brought up during the time of the Nazis, that meant discipline and self-control. I admit that took over me to a certain extent."

In April 1945, Soviet tanks rolled into Amstetten and Russian troops embarked on an orgy of pillage and rape. Reports in the Austrian media say that, as a child, Fritzl "suffered badly" during this post-war occupation, a period marked by the high incidence of sexual assaults perpetrated by Russian soldiers on German and Austrian women. The Red Army stayed in Austria until 1955.

Times were hard, and Fritzl's mother was strict. He was in awe of her and she beat him regularly. He did well at school, though he was seen as something of a loner. At the age of sixteen, he went to college to study electrical engineering and took an apprenticeship at a steel works company. He had a number of affairs with women.

At twenty-one, he met seventeen-year-old Rosemarie, who became his wife. They had seven children. Having been an only child, he had wanted a big family. While he held down a good job, Fritzl began to exhibit a tendency toward sexual deviancy. At the age of twenty-four, he came to the attention of the police for exposing himself. He seems to have raped at least two women in Linz, though only one pressed charges. She was a nurse, and Fritzl broke into her apartment to attack her. He was convicted of rape and spent eighteen months in jail. As a result, he lost his job. But he was a talented and inventive engineer, so he quickly found employment when he was released.

He bought property, including a guesthouse and camping ground, on the shores of Lake Mondsee near Salzburg. He also extended the house in Ybbsstrasse to take in tenants. They lived directly over the cellar that Fritzl also extended into the back garden. Though some of his business ventures failed and he ran up debts of $2.7 million, he was considered a pillar of the community.

Fritzl also ruled the roost over his wife. She was frightened of him, and he mocked and humiliated her in public. Her sister thought that he beat his wife as well as the children. A friend said that Fritzl would hit and slap Rosemarie. She wanted to leave him, but could not take all seven children with her and dared not leave them in his care. However, in 1973 she made an excuse to stay at the guesthouse at Mondsee to take care of business there. Fritzl insisted that the children stay with him on Ybbsstrasse, only allowing her to see them occasionally. She moved home after the guesthouse burned down. Fritzl was arrested for arson, but was acquitted due to lack of evidence.

Of his five girls and two boys, Elisabeth was Fritzl's favorite. He was a strict father who would not stand for dissent. His sister-in-law compared him to a drill sergeant. She said the children married young to leave home. They called him a tyrant. One son apparently had learning difficulties; he remained at home, and Fritzl used him as a drudge. The other son told a friend that he was afraid his father would kill him. Even though Elisabeth was his favorite, Fritzl brutalized her too. She was a shy, sad child and was never known to laugh. She sometimes had bruises on her body, though she took care to hide them from her school friends.

Elisabeth was also the prettiest of Fritzl's daughters. From the age of eleven, he began abusing her after allowing her mother to take the other children on vacation. After that, his treatment of her grew worse. He was brutally strict with her in public and then, when they were alone, he would rape her without warning—in his car, on walks in the woods, even in the cellar, Elisabeth said.

Fritzl denied this.

"I am not a man who would molest children," he said. "I only had sex with her later, much later."

But Elisabeth asserts that it is true, and there is circumstantial evidence to support her accusations.

Elisabeth's father required her to be home half an hour after school finished, and she was terrified of being late. Friends who accompanied her would disappear when her father showed up. She was not allowed out in the evening or to invite friends to the house.

As Elisabeth grew toward womanhood Fritzl grew increasingly possessive. He flew into a rage if she wore makeup, attempted to dress fashionably, or mentioned boys. As a result, she became sullen and withdrawn. She was easily pretty enough to have a boyfriend, but she kept to herself.

Elisabeth was just twelve in 1978, when Fritzl applied for planning permission to turn his basement into a nuclear shelter. This was not uncommon in Austria at the time. Fritzl worked on building the shelter single-handedly over the next six years, turning the bunker into an unbreachable fortress. However, in due course, he would need help to install the steel and concrete door, which weighed nearly a third of a ton.

In 1983, building inspectors came to look over the alterations and gave their seal of approval. Elisabeth was then fifteen. The following year, she ran away from home to escape her father's predations. She found work as a waitress at a motorway truck stop and lived in a hostel. But Fritzl found out where she was and brought her back.

When she was seventeen, she tried again. She and a friend fled to Linz, then on to Vienna. But Fritzl tracked her down again and, with the assistance of the police, brought her home.

When Elisabeth was eighteen, she planned to run away again. At that age, she could not be forced to return home again. She even had a bag packed. So when she disappeared no one was surprised. Her friends were happy for her, thinking she had escaped at last. To the respectable older generation in Amstetten, she seemed like an ungrateful child who had now gone completely off the rails, while Fritzl pretended to be the concerned father.

"Ever since she entered puberty Elisabeth stopped doing what she was told. She just did not follow any of my rules any more," he said. "She would go out all night in local bars, and come back stinking of alcohol and smoke. I tried to rescue her from the swamp, and I organized her a trainee job as a waitress."

He also complained that she was "promiscuous." Nothing could have been further from the truth.

"I admit I have always valued decency and good behavior," he said. "I grew up in the Nazi era, and strictness and discipline were very important then."

Fritzl didn't touch Elisabeth during the first few weeks after she returned from Vienna, but then it started all over again. She entered a training program as a waitress at a highway rest stop at Strengberg on the autobahn that ran from Linz to Vienna. She and other girls in the program slept in a dormitory below the kitchen and Strengberg was little more than ten miles from Amstetten, so Fritzl could keep an eye on her.

Later she was sent to a catering college, where she lived on campus. While the sexes were strictly segregated there, she met an eighteen-year-old trainee chef named Andreas Kruzik, who described her as a "pretty, but serious and withdrawn girl." He managed to talk to her and tried to make her laugh. They went for long walks in the woods together and, soon, fell in love. They even talked of running away together and getting married. However, when it came to sex, Elisabeth would always hold back at the last moment.

Elisabeth finally decided that she wanted to go through with it, but before they had a chance, Fritzl turned up to take her home. Andreas feared that Elisabeth's father may have heard of their marriage plans. Before she left, she made him promise to keep their love a secret. This sounded reasonable enough. He knew that her father was a martinet.

The couple could not even say good-bye properly as her father barred her from talking to boys. They promised to write. Andreas kept his promise, but Elisabeth never replied to any of his letters. He was heartbroken at the time. It was not until twenty-four years later that he discovered why she had not written.

While Elisabeth was at college, she had been writing to another male friend. She had told him of a plan she had to move in with her sister and her boyfriend. She mentioned Andreas and was unhappy that she would be living far away from him. Nevertheless, she was determined to move and would send him her new address when she could. This other friend did not hear from her again either. Within days, she would begin her long incarceration.

Once the door was in place, the dungeon Fritzl had been planning for six long years was complete. Now Elisabeth was his alone, to do with as he pleased. At first he beat her to get his way. He was a big man, and she soon realized that there was no point in fighting her father. Then the beatings lessened, but there was no slackening in his demand for sex. Elisabeth was kept on the leash for the first nine months. She lost count of how many times he raped her during that time. There was no alternative. She had to endure the unendurable.

For four years, her father kept her in complete isolation. And he was unrepentant. "Why should I be sorry?" he said. "I took good care of her. I saved her falling into the drug scene… That is why I had to arrange a place where I gave her the chance—by force—to keep away from the bad influences of the outside world."

There is no indication that she ever took drugs or was even interested in doing so.

The day after Elisabeth disappeared, Rosemarie Fritzl went to the police and reported her daughter as missing. Soon after, Fritzl gave police a letter he had forced Elisabeth to write. It was dated September 21, 1984, and was postmarked Braunau am Inn, Hitler's birthplace. In the letter, Elisabeth said she had had enough of living at home and was staying with a friend. She warned her parents not to look for her, otherwise she would leave the country.

There were other loose ends to tie up. Fritzl told Elisabeth's boss at the Rosenberger restaurant in Strenberg that she had run away from home and would not be coming back to work.

As days turned into weeks, Fritzl ordered Elisabeth to write other letters to her mother. She was to pretend that she had run away to join a religious sect and asked the police not to look for her. These letters must have been agonizing to write. With each one, she was digging herself a deeper grave, further reducing the chance that anyone would come looking for her. No one questioned the validity of the letters. No one asked who or what sect she had joined, or asked whether such organizations operated in Austria—they don't. Sects that isolate members from their family and friends are practically unknown outside Japan and the English-speaking world, where their strange antics often generate massive publicity. Once Elisabeth turned nineteen, her disappearance was no longer a police concern. The police then stopped searching for her, and the authorities forgot that Elisabeth Fritzl had ever existed.

Rosemarie was browbeaten. Other members of the family dared not question Fritzl. To acquaintances, he made a show of being a concerned parent and said that Interpol was still looking for her, while Andreas Kruzik nursed his broken heart and concluded that he had been unceremoniously dumped.

Fritzl himself was surprised that he had gotten away with it and was terrified that he was going to be arrested. He kept meaning to release Elisabeth, he said, but as everyone would then discover what a vile monster he was, he kept putting off the day.

As her weeks below ground stretched into months, Fritzl kept up a sickening pretence of normality with his daughter. He would tell her how work on the garden above her was progressing. Fritzl would also chat about films he had seen on TV, describe trips he had made, and even keep her updated on the progress of her brothers and sisters. He did not hesitate to inform her that everyone had fallen for the lies he had told.

For her, there was no hope of rescue or release. After all, the very last place anyone would have looked for her was in her own home.

While Elisabeth maintains that Fritzl had been abusing her sexually since she was eleven, Fritzl claimed that it only began some time after he had imprisoned her. Once she was completely in his power, he said, his desire to have her grew until it became irresistible.

"We first had sex in spring 1985"—nine months after he imprisoned her, he claimed. "I could not control myself anymore. I wanted to have children with her. It was my dream to have another normal family, in the cellar, with her as a good wife and several children…At some stage, somewhere in the night, I went into the cellar. I knew that Elisabeth did not want it, what I did with her. The pressure to do the forbidden thing was just too big to withstand."

According to Fritzl, Elisabeth did not fight him. She cried quietly afterwards, he said. After that, every two or three days when he went into the cellar to bring her food and a change of clothes, he would have sex with her. He also beat her for the sadistic pleasure of it. Increasingly, he said, sex with his daughter became "an obsession."

Elisabeth had to cope with the full force of Fritzl's libido as he had stopped sleeping with Rosemarie.

"You're too fat for sex," he told his wife within the hearing of family and friends. "Fat women are below my standard."

To a friend, he said he liked thin women and boasted of having a girlfriend. No one ever guessed that he was talking about his own daughter.

After four years, Elisabeth became pregnant. She may have thought for a moment that he would have to release her so that she could have a baby with the help of an obstetrician, a midwife, or even her mother. Instead, Fritzl bought her a medical book. She must have been worried that a child produced by such a close degree of incest might be born with some genetic impairment. Fritz feigned concern.

"Elisabeth was, of course, very worried about the future," he said. "But I bought her medical books for the cellar, so that she would know when the day came what she had to do. I also arranged towels and disinfectants and nappies [diapers]."

When Elisabeth was about to give birth, Fritzl drove hundreds of miles to buy baby food, clothes, and diapers at shops where nobody would recognize him. Then he left his terrified twenty-two-year-old daughter to give birth in the cellar alone. It seems that he had lost interest in her sexually since she became pregnant. Nevertheless, in 1989, Elisabeth Fritzl gave birth to her daughter Kerstin. Both mother and child survived. At last Elisabeth would not be alone. On the other hand, the child was one more reason why her father could not let her go. Here was living, breathing proof of what he had done.

Kerstin was sickly from the time she was born. She suffered from cramps, which were eventually diagnosed as a form of epilepsy that is linked to incest.

However, after she had given birth, Elisabeth Fritzl's life did begin to improve. There were fewer beatings, though the rapes resumed. Fritzl would dress up for his visits, and he brought his daughter lingerie and sexy outfits—for his own benefit, of course. And the following year she gave birth to a son, Stefan.

All the time, Elisabeth was only a few feet from the lodgers who were living upstairs. One of them, Joseph Leitner, had known Elisabeth when she was a girl and even knew that her father had raped her. But he believed the story that she had run off to join a sect. Besides, he was afraid of her father.

Though Fritzl had banned pets, Leitner kept a dog, a husky-Labrador-sheepdog mix named Sam, who barked every time he walked passed the cellar. Fritzl warned all his tenants that the cellar was strictly off-limits. Anyone going near it would be thrown out.

Leitner now believes that Sam may have heard people moving around in the cellar below, since he would suddenly start to bark for no apparent reason. He also noticed that his electricity bill was exorbitant, even though he worked long hours and was rarely home. He got a friend from a cable TV company to check it out. They unplugged all the appliances in his room, but still the electricity meters rose very high. It now seems that Fritzl fed electricity from Leitner's one-room apartment into the cellar below. But before Leitner could make a complaint, Fritzl spotted the dog and evicted him.

Another tenant who had his suspicions was Alfred Dubanovsky, who had known Elisabeth at school and had also known of her abusive home life. He lived a few feet above her head for twelve years. Fritzl told him that the cellar was protected by a sensitive electronic security system. Dubanovsky also saw Fritzl taking food down to the cellar in a wheelbarrow at night. Leitner had seen this too, but neither of them imagined that anyone was living down there.

Fritzl would disappear into the basement at nine each morning, ostensibly to work on some electrical engineering plans. Sometimes he would also go down there after Rosemarie had gone to bed. She had been told never to disturb him while he was at work, not even to take him a cup of coffee. But neighbors would not have noticed anything suspicious. The entrance to the cellar was in the back garden, which was itself hidden by a tall hedge.

There were other clues. Fritzl once boasted to Dubanovsky: "One day my house will go down in history." And he was terrified by any mention of the police.

Another tenant noticed that food would go missing from their fridge. It seems that, when Fritzl had failed to make a shopping trip, he borrowed his lodgers' food to feed his captives.

Initially, the dungeon was just 215 square feet. There were now three people living in that confined space, and Fritzl was having sex with his daughter in front of their two children, which can only have added to her distress. In 1992, Elisabeth gave birth to a second daughter, Lisa. The baby cried a lot, possibly because she had a heart defect caused by her incestuous parentage. Fearful that someone might hear her, Fritzl decided that the child should be brought up upstairs by his cowed wife. That way Lisa could receive proper medical attention. He persuaded Elisabeth to go along with his plan. All she had to do was write another of her letters. This one said: "Dear parents, You will probably be shocked to hear from me after all these years, and with a real-life surprise, no less… I am leaving you my little daughter Lisa. Take good care of my little girl." The sect, she said, did not allow children, and she begged her parents to bring her up for her.

"I breast-fed her for about six-and-a-half months, and now she drinks her milk from the bottle," she added. "She is a good girl, and she eats everything else from the spoon… I hope that you are all healthy. I will contact you again later, and I beg you not to look for me, because I am doing well." Again she asked her parents not to make any attempt to find her.

On May 19, 1993, Lisa appeared on the Fritzls' front doorstep in a cardboard box. The letter was stuck to it. It seems that Rosemarie was skeptical, but then she received a phone call that purportedly came from her daughter. Fritzl, it seems, had also coerced his daughter into making taped messages. However this was contrived, Rosemarie bought it, and so did the authorities, apparently. Social services representatives did not even ask why a woman would entrust her child to a parent who she, herself, had run away from. Five days after Lisa's appearance on the Fritzls' doorstep, Amstetten's youth welfare office wrote: "Mr. and Mrs. Fritzl have recovered from the initial shock. The Fritzl family is taking loving care of Lisa and wishes to continue caring for her."

Fritzl even asked the police to get a handwriting expert to confirm that the letter came from Elisabeth, giving them some of his daughter's exercise books to compare it to. When the graphologist confirmed that the letter had come from their daughter and, consequently, that Lisa was their grandchild, they were allowed to adopt her. This was permitted even though Fritzl had been convicted of rape. However, in Austria, criminal records are expunged after ten years.

Even with Lisa enjoying the light and fresh air upstairs, there was still the problem of space downstairs. Kerstin and Stefan were growing and as Fritzl used no protection, it was highly likely that Elisabeth would become pregnant again. So

Fritzl decided to extend the cellar. He had Elisabeth set about digging out more than four thousand cubic feet of earth—two hundred tons of it—by hand. Over the next few years, Fritzl managed to move the equivalent of seven truckloads of earth and rubble out of his cellar without anyone noticing. At the same time, he smuggled tiles, bricks, wooden wall panels, a washing machine, a kitchen sink, beds, and pipe into the underground cellar without anybody being any the wiser. Fritzl and Elisabeth excavated a dungeon seven times the size of the nuclear bunker he had permission to construct. On top of everything else, he was violating all manner of building codes, but the authorities took no notice. And while all this was going on Elisabeth, Kerstin, and Stefan had to survive amid the dirt and confusion.

Fritzl was an electrical engineer, so he knew how to rig up the lights and power. However, he was not a plumber. Dubanovsky said that Fritzl introduced him to a man he said was a plumber who must have installed a lavatory and some primitive plumbing in the cellar while, somehow, not noticing the inhabitants. The man has never come forward or been found.

Even though the cellar could be extended and more facilities added, there would still be no more light or ventilation. Elisabeth persuaded Fritzl to install a UV light and supply vitamin D tablets to compensate partially for the lack of sunlight. But he would not extend the ventilation system, as it would risk sound escaping, and the last thing he wanted was Elisabeth summoning help.

Despite the extensive excavations, the labyrinthine complex was never more than five feet, six inches high. In some places, the ceiling was a good deal lower. Elisabeth and the children, as they grew, had to stoop. Living with such low ceilings was, by its very nature, oppressive. And now with a shower in the cellar, the atmosphere was damp.

The neighbors spotted nothing. Even Fritzl's son-in-law Juergen Helm, who lived in the house for three years, had no idea what was going on in the cellar.

Elisabeth gave birth to a third daughter, Monika, on February 26, 1994. At that point, the extension of the cellar was far from complete and there was no room for the child. Fritzl repeated the same charade he had created with Lisa, and Monika turned up on the doorstep on December 16.

However, this time to alert Rosemarie to the new arrival, a caller phoned, saying: "I just left her at your door."

This was a puzzle, as a call came through to her on a new, unlisted number. Rosemarie told the authorities that this was completely inexplicable. There was one obvious explanation, though. The call had been made by someone who knew the new number.

The letter that came with the child said: "I am really sorry that I have to turn to you again. I hope Lisa is doing well. She must have grown a bit by now. Monika is now nine-and-a-half months old. She was breast-fed for seven-and-a-half months. She now eats almost anything. But she still likes the bottle best. The hole in the teat has to be a little bigger for her."

This time the Fritzls did not adopt the child. By fostering her, they received a state benefit of $535 per month.

Monika's arrival did not go unnoticed. A local journalist took an interest. He interviewed Fritzl, who repeated the old story that his daughter had run off to join a religious group.

Two years later, Elisabeth was pregnant again, with twins. However, with no medical exam or ultrasound, she could not have known she was carrying two children. She would only have discovered this when the labor pains continued after she had delivered the first baby.

One of the children was sickly. It had difficulty breathing, and when Fritzl returned to the cellar three days later it was dead. Fritzl burned the infant's body in the furnace in the basement along with other household waste. The dead child has since been named Michael. It is not known if he would have survived if he had received medical attention.

The surviving twin, Alexander, was taken upstairs and passed off as another foundling. Again, authorities failed to investigate; instead, they handed over another foster fee.

Over the years, social services paid at least twenty-one visits to the Fritzls' home and noted that the children were doing well. Fritzl was strict, but neighbors reported that the children were happy and well-adjusted. They did well at school. The children had just one fear—that their mother might return from her madcap sect and claim them.

Fritzl was now short of money. There were two small fires in the house, each resulting in Fritzl filing an insurance claim. Despite the previous arson charges, the police performed only a cursory investigation. If one of these fires had gotten out of control, there would have been no hope for the prisoners in the basement.

As Kerstin and Stefan grew to maturity, Fritzl found himself keeping three adults in the cellar, but their living conditions made them too weak to confront him. Even if they could have overpowered or incapacitated Fritzl, there was no escape. An electronic code was needed to open the door. Anyone who touched it without using the code would be electrocuted, Fritzl said. Fritzl also told his captives that poison gas would be pumping into the cellar in the event of a rebellion.

Fritzl also claimed that there was a delayed-reaction mechanism that would open the door if he died on the outside or an accident prevented him returning, though there was no evidence of this. Meanwhile, Fritzl would leave his victims for extended periods, treating himself to long vacations in Thailand, where he indulged himself as a sex tourist.

"He was a disgusting pervert and all the ex-pats and regular vacation makers knew what he was up to," said a fellow traveler. "Rent-boys, lady-boys, he would go with anything. At one point, he was spotted by one bar regular with a sixteen-year-old."

Fritzl enjoyed the company of prostitutes closer to home too. He made regular visits to the Villa Ostende, in Linz, where he paid to have sex in the brothel's dungeon. He punched one of the girls during sex, and most of them were frightened of him.

"I was hired by him many times, and he was sick beyond imagination," said one prostitute. "He chose me because he said he liked young, plump girls who were happy to submit to him."

Other girls were shocked by Fritzl's sadistic demands and refused to have sex with him a second time.

"Ninety-five percent of the clients are entirely normal; 3 percent are slightly 'derailed,' " said the brothel's former barman. "But Fritzl belonged to the last 2 percent of extreme perverts who are surely mentally deranged... None of the girls wanted to spend time in a room with him. Two of them even strictly refused to and did without the earnings. He loved inflicting pain and wanted some of the girls to play dead and act like a corpse. He was violent and into domination."

He was also seen in S&M clubs where he would pump himself up on Viagra and other drugs.

Although Fritzl's outside interests may have given Elisabeth an occasional break from her father's rapacious sexual demands, the sexual abuse resumed whenever he returned to Ybbsstrasse. Even though Kerstin and Stefan were teenagers, Fritzl continued raping their mother in front of them. In 2003, she gave birth to her seventh child. This was Felix, and he was going to be left in the dungeon. Fritzl reasoned that, at sixty-three, Rosemarie could not cope with another child.

While the upstairs children received a normal education, Elisabeth struggled to teach the children in the dungeon as best she could. Eventually, Fritzl provided a television so that they children could get some impression of what the real world outside was like. Elisabeth tried to impose some semblance of structure on their lives, which was difficult when it was impossible to tell day from night. She made decorations and made up fairy stories and lullabies. It is plain that she was a good mother doing her best in impossible circumstances.

Fritzl claimed that he did his best for his second family in the basement. He provided a range and a freezer so that they would have fresh food while he was away in Thailand. In 2002, he bought Elisabeth a washing machine, so she did not have to wash all of their clothes by hand. They celebrated birthdays, and he smuggled a tree down to them at Christmas. But he still deprived them of light, air, and freedom. As the children grew older, the air grew so stale that they had to spend most of their time sitting down.

He bought a video player so that he could watch movies with the children while Elisabeth cooked dinner in a grotesque parody of home life. Worse, he brought videos he had shot of the children upstairs, so that the prisoners downstairs could see what they were missing. But Fritzl saw nothing wrong in this.

"It was lovely to have a family in the cellar," he said. "Elisabeth, Kerstin, Stefan, and Felix accepted me as the head of the family completely."

However, the health of his underground "family" was suffering due to the lack of daylight and the dank and fetid air.

"Elisabeth stayed strong," said Fritzl. "She caused me almost no problems. She never complained, even when her teeth slowly went rotten and fell out of her mouth one by one, and she suffered day and night with unbearable pain and could not sleep. She stayed strong for the children. But the children—I saw they were constantly getting weaker."

But he did nothing about it.

On top of ordinary colds and flu, the children suffered from respiratory problems from the poor air. Fritzl provided no medication other than store-bought medicines, aspirin, cough mixture, and the like. Without proper medical assistance, Elisabeth found she was fighting a losing battle. Both Kerstin and Felix suffered from coughing fits and strange, violent convulsions. Kerstin would scream hysterically while Felix would shake uncontrollably for hours on end. The children had never seen a doctor, and had received none of the inoculations that infants are normally given. It is a wonder that they survived at all.

The children were almost within earshot of Fritzl's seventieth birthday party at 40 Ybbsstrasse in 2005 and, the following year, the town of Amstetten honored the Fritzls on their fiftieth wedding anniversary with a celebration hosted by the mayor.

In his seventies, Fritzl found the strain of maintaining his underground family was becoming too much for him. He still found Elisabeth sexually attractive, and there have even been allegations that he also turned his attentions on Kerstin. But it was clear the situation could not go on.

Toward the close of 2007, Fritzl began preparing the endgame. The following summer, he planned to stage-manage the release of Elisabeth and her children. People would be told that she had quit the obscure sect that had held her for the past quarter century and she would return to the house that she had, in reality, never left. Her shocking physical condition— and that of her children—would be blamed on the treatment inflicted on them by the religious cult. Fritzl thought he could get away with this. After all, no one had questioned the existence of the cult before.

At Christmas, Fritzl forced Elisabeth to write another letter preparing the ground. It said that she was going to leave the sect and return home.

"If all goes well," she wrote. "I hope to be back in six months."

However, before Fritzl could put his plan into action, Kerstin fell dangerously ill. Again, he treated her with cough syrup and aspirin, but it did no good. Her convulsions grew worse. She spewed blood from her mouth and she lapsed into a coma.

Elisabeth begged her father to seek medical attention for their daughter. Eventually, Fritzl relented. Rosemarie was taking one of her periodic vacations in Italy. Once she was safely out of the way, Fritzl and Elisabeth carried the unconscious nineteen-year-old out of the cellar and up into the house above. After this one fleeting, nighttime visit to the world above ground, Elisabeth was forced to return to her dungeon. Two of her boys were still prisoners down there, and she could not leave them.

At 7 a.m. on Saturday, April 19, 2008, Josef Fritzl called an ambulance. It delivered the wan, ghostlike Kerstin Fritzl to a hospital where the staff did not know what to make of her. An hour later, Fritzl turned up in the emergency room and related his tried and tested story. His daughter had run off to join some mysterious religious sect and had dumped another of her children on his doorstep.

Again, the child had come with a note. It said: "Wednesday, I gave her aspirin and cough medicine for the condition. Thursday, the cough worsened. Friday, the coughing gets even worse. She has been biting her lip as well as her tongue. Please, please help her! Kerstin is really terrified of other people, she was never in a hospital. If there are any problems please ask my father for help, he is the only person that she knows."

It came with a postscript addressed to the stricken girl herself.

"Kerstin—please stay strong, until we see each other again! We will come back to you soon!"

On duty at Amstetten's Mostviertel State Hospital was Dr. Albert Reiter. He did not believe that a mother who had written such a letter would simply abandon her daughter as Fritzl had claimed. Nor did he think that the child's deathly pallor had anything to do with the disease she was suffering from. It was also puzzling that such a young person should have lost all their teeth. Something more sinister was afoot.

Also, strangely, Fritzl had not waited around for a diagnosis—or even for his granddaughter's condition to stabilize. He'd rushed away, adding, curiously, that they should not call the police. Dr. Reiter concluded that Josef Fritzl's story was a pack of lies. So, naturally, he called the police, who went to 40 Ybbsstrasse and interviewed Fritzl. He told them that he had heard noises outside early that morning. When he had gone to investigate, he had found Kerstin.

In the emergency ward, Dr. Reiter's patient was not getting any better. Her immune system had collapsed. She had to be put on a ventilator and a kidney-dialysis machine. Specialists called in from Vienna were of little help. Dr. Reiter felt that he did not have any chance of saving Kerstin unless he could discover something of her medical history, so appealed for her mother to come forward.

Meanwhile the police were searching for Kerstin's general practitioner to see if he or she could be of any help. They also wanted to interview the patient's mother, Elisabeth, concerning possible neglect of the girl. Fritzl then produced another letter, dated January 2008. It spoke of her two other children, who also had medical problems. They too would be returning home soon.

The letter was postmarked Kematen an der Krems, just thirty miles from Amstetten. The police descended on the town, but local doctors knew nothing of Kerstin. No one had seen anyone answering her description. Nor did they know of any sect that, according to the postmarks on the letters, had never been very far from Amstetten. Eventually, the police called Dr. Manfred Wohlfahrt at the diocesan office in St. Pölten and asked him what he knew about the sect. Dr. Wohlfahrt said that there were, to his knowledge, no odd sects working in the diocese or any of the dioceses in lower Austria. When the police showed him the letters that had ostensibly come from Elisabeth, he noted that they had been written in a very measured hand, not the sort you would use to dash off in a note to a relative or friend. Grammatically, they were very deliberately constructed and he concluded that they had been dictated.

Meanwhile government officials were combing public records for any mention of Elisabeth Fritzl, Kerstin, Stefan, or Felix. Curiously, the three children's births had not been registered, and there was no record of them having attended school. And they could not have left the country; no passports had been issued. Nor did Elisabeth have a driver's license. There were no records of her existence for the past twenty-four years.

The police then took another track. They wanted samples of DNA from Kerstin and the three other children who had turned up on the Fritzl's doorstep. If they could screen out the maternal component of the DNA, they might discover who the father was. However, Fritzl refused to give a sample.

When Kerstin's mother did not come forward after his appeal, Dr. Reiter grew desperate. He appeared on a news bulletin on ORF, Austria's public service broadcaster. Fearing that Kerstin's mother might be afraid to come forward if she thought the police were involved, he emphasized that any contact would be treated with "high discretion."

Journalists flocked to 40 Ybbsstrasse, but rather than using this opportunity to make his own appeal for Elisabeth to come forward, Fritzl grew angry. He shouted and swore, and cursed that "bloody doctor."

However, Elisabeth had seen Dr. Reiter's appeal on TV. Kerstin was dying, and she begged her father to let her go to the hospital, promising not to give him away and maintain the fiction that she had been with a religious sect—just as she had promised to do that coming summer.

On Saturday, April 26—one week after Kerstin had arrived in the hospital—Elisabeth was let out of the cellar again. Fritzl called the hospital to talk to Dr. Reiter.

"Elisabeth has returned," he said. "I am bringing her to the hospital, and she wants to see her daughter." Then he added: "We do not want any trouble. Do not call the police."

But the police were already involved. When Elisabeth and Josef Fritzl arrived at the hospital, the police pounced. They had no interest in Josef. There was no indication that he had committed any crime. But he put up a fight—to protect his daughter, the police thought at first—so he was arrested too.

At the police station, they were separated. Elisabeth Fritzl was interrogated about the criminal neglect of her daughter. The police could see immediately that there was something very odd about her. Although she was only forty-two, she had grey hair, no teeth, and a morbidly pallid complexion. She looked like a woman in her sixties who had been locked up in an institution. And plainly she was terrified.

At first she refused to answer their questions. She was, naturally, more concerned about her sick daughter. But the police were insistent. According to the letter of January 2008 that her father had shown them, she had two more children who might be in danger.

She stuck to her story. She said she had run away to join a religious sect that did not allow children. That's why she had sent three of her children to her parents. But none of that explained her appearance, or the terrible condition of her daughter.

As the questioning continued, Elisabeth grew agitated. Then she demanded repeated assurances that neither she nor her children would ever have to see her father again. After the police gave this assurance, she told them the incredible story of her twenty-four-year ordeal. They could hardly believe their ears. Herr Fritzl was a respectable family man, the backbone of the community. However, her own appearance and the shocking condition of her daughter served as material evidence that what she was saying was true.

They put Elisabeth's allegations to Fritzl. Initially, he refused to talk; then he protested that the letters he had received over the years proved that Elisabeth had been with a cult. Later, he had the audacity to say that he was disappointed that she had betrayed him so quickly.

There was one way to prove what Elisabeth was saying. The police took Fritzl back to the house and searched it. But the dungeon was so well hidden that they could not find it. However, sensing that the game was up, Fritzl led them through five rooms in the basement, including his office and a room containing the furnace where Michael's body had been burned. Along the way, there were eight locked doors. Eventually, they reached Fritzl's workshop. Behind a shelving unit in his basement workshop was a heavy steel door just three feet high with a remote-control locking device. After some convincing, Fritzl gave the police the code to open it and they squeezed through.

The police found themselves in a narrow corridor. This led to a padded room, soundproofed with rubber cladding, where Elisabeth had originally been confined and repeatedly abused. It was so well-insulated that no scream, cry, or sob could escape. Beyond that, there was a small living area. Then there was a passage little more than a foot wide that a person had to turn sideways to get down. This led to a rudimentary kitchen and bathroom. On the white-tiled walls of a tiny shower cubicle, the captives had painted a butterfly, a flower, an octopus, and a snail, in an attempt to brighten their grim surroundings.

Further on, there were two small bedrooms, each with two beds. There was a washing machine, a fridge, and freezer. Otherwise the furnishings were sparse. The police found a toy elephant perched on a medicine cabinet and scraps of paper and glue used to entertain the children. The only other distraction was a small TV, which provided flickering images of the outside world. There was no natural light and little air. The whole scene was lit by electric light bulbs, which went on and off on a timer to give some sense of day and night

In the midst of this pitiful scene, the police found two ashen-faced children: eighteen-year-old Stefan and five-year-old Felix. With a ceiling that was five-feet-six inches at the highest, there was nowhere Stefan could stand upright. Felix preferred to go on all fours and had a strange, simian gait. Both boys were in poor physical condition, bent, pale, and terrified.

When they were taken out of the cellar, the two boys were overawed by daylight—something they had never seen before. They babbled between themselves in their own coded talk, but were also able to communicate in German. Felix pointed to the sky and asked a policeman, "Is God up there?"

Elisabeth Fritzl was brought to the house to ease her sons' passage into the outside world. They were then taken to a hospital for a comprehensive checkup at dusk, as they were not used to sunlight. All four of the captives were suffering from vitamin D deficiency. They were anemic and malnourished. Their immune systems were compromised, and Felix's joints and muscles had failed to develop properly.

While Kerstin remained in a medically induced coma, the family was reunited at the Amstetten Mauer Landesklinikum Psychiatric Clinic where Elisabeth and the children who had been held in the cellar were gradually introduced to sunlight. The entire family underwent therapy. Kerstin eventually joined them at the clinic, and she was expected to make a full recovery. It was reported later that Elisabeth had a falling out with her mother and, also that she fell in love with one of her guards.

After having trouble, initially, dealing with the trauma, the children from upstairs and those from downstairs bonded and went on to cope remarkably well. DNA tests confirmed that Josef Fritzl was the father of all six surviving children. He was charged with rape, incest, coercion, false imprisonment, enslavement, and negligent homicide of the infant Michael. He went to trial in St. Pölten, pleading guilty to all charges except enslavement and murder. However, he then had to sit through eleven hours of his daughter's videotaped evidence against him. She said that she had resisted him at first, but then gave way to her father's daily demands for violent sex because she knew her life—and later the lives of her children—depended on it. Not only did he rape her thousands of times, he humiliated her by forcing her to re-enact scenes from pornographic videos he brought to the cellar and made her watch.

After her testimony, Fritzl changed his plea to guilty on all charges. He was sentenced to life imprisonment and committed to an institution for the criminally insane. He must serve a minimum of fifteen years before he is eligible for parole, though it is unlikely that he will ever be released.

Chapter 3

Colleen Stan— The Girl in the Box

ON MAY 19, 1977, TWENTY-YEAR-OLD Colleen Stan decided to hitchhike from Eugene, Oregon, to attend a friend's birthday party in Westwood, California, some three hundred miles away. Although there had been a number of murders of young women hitchhikers, "thumbing a ride" was still a common way for young people to travel in the late 1970s. Caution was advised, but Colleen considered herself an experienced hitchhiker, and a good judge of whether a driver offering a ride were safe.

By mid-afternoon on May 19, she had reached Red Bluff, California, some seventy miles from her destination. Suspicious of lone male drivers, she had turned down two potential rides there. Then a 1971 two-door, cobalt-blue Dodge Colt with a man and a woman nursing a baby inside stopped. The couple said they were going to Westwood, and Colleen felt safe to get in. They were friendly enough and seemed clean-cut. A married couple, their names were Cameron and Janice Hooker. However, Colleen noticed that, while they talked, Cameron kept checking her out in the rear-view mirror.

He asked why she was going to Westwood. She said that it was a friend's birthday and she wanted to surprise her.

"She doesn't know you're coming?" said Cameron.

"No, it will be a complete surprise."

They stopped in a gas station where Colleen used the restroom. Later, she said that a voice inside her told her to climb out of the bathroom window and make a run for it. But then she reasoned that, even if Cameron was a bit weird, he would never do anything to her in front of his wife and child.

Colleen could not have been more wrong. From an early age, Cameron had been hooked on violent pornography. After he had graduated from high school, he got a job in a local lumber mill. A year later, he met fifteen-year-old Janice, who was an epileptic. She was malleable and craved attention at any cost. Cameron persuaded her to let him tie her naked to a tree, even suspended painfully by the wrists. Throughout their courtship, their sadomasochistic and bondage games continued. Eventually, they married and moved into 1140 Oak Street in Red Bluff. Their landlords, an elderly couple, lived next door. For them, the quiet Hookers seemed like the perfect tenants.

Once they were married, Janice became tired of their bondage games. She wanted to have a baby. Cameron said she could have one if she would help him find a young female slave to take her place. There would be no sex, Cameron promised. That would be reserved for his wife. The slave would be the there to be chained, beaten, and tortured. In Cameron's eyes, Colleen seemed like the perfect candidate—the first of many, he hoped.

When Colleen got back into the car, they gave her a candy bar. On the seat beside her, she noticed a strange wooden box.

It had leather hinges and leather reinforcement strips along each edge. Only later would she find out what it was for.

About a mile down the road from the gas station, the Hookers asked if she minded if they took a little detour to see some spectacular ice caves. Colleen said she was in no hurry, just as long as they reached Westwood by nightfall.

Cameron pulled off down a dirt road. Colleen grew suspicious. There were no signs to the ice caves. But the couple were locals; presumably, they knew where they were going. Then Cameron stopped the car in the middle of nowhere. Janice got out of the car with the baby. Cameron followed. They walked down to a creek to get some cool mountain water. Colleen waited in the backseat of the car with the door open.

She was not paying much attention, but then she noticed that Janice and the baby were alone by the creek. Cameron had disappeared. Suddenly, the front seat of the car was yanked forward and Cameron sprang into the backseat beside her. He was holding a large butcher's knife to Colleen's throat and told her to put her hands in the air. It seemed clear that he was going to kill her if she did not obey. Quickly, he pulled out a pair of handcuffs, and secured her arms behind her back.

"Are you going to do what I tell you?" he asked.

Colleen was too petrified to speak, but managed to nod her head. He blindfolded her, then put a harness over her head with a broad leather strap across her mouth. Another strap went under her chin, and when the contraption was fastened at the back of her head, she found could not move her jaw to scream. Deftly, he tied her ankles together. Plainly, he had practiced this well.

It then became clear what the strange box beside her on the seat was for. He put it over her head and slammed it shut. Inside it was filled with foam rubber, roughly the shape of her head. She became disoriented and breathing was difficult. Cameron lay her down on the backseat and covered her with her own sleeping bag. Pretty soon she began to overheat.

She heard the muffled sound of the door closing as Janice and the child got back into the car. The engine started and Colleen could feel the car moving as it made its way back up the dirt road. At the highway, she felt the car turn right, back toward Red Bluff.

In town, she could hear other traffic. The car made a couple of stops. People got in and out. Then they drove out of town.

Next time they stopped, the sleeping bag was pulled off her. The box on her head was removed, and she was allowed to sit up. But all the other restraints stayed in place. Although she was shaking with fear, it was a relief to be cool and she could smell food cooking. It seemed to Colleen that her captors were having a picnic.

They drove around some more. When they eventually stopped, Colleen's ankles were untied and she was led into a house. She was taken down into a basement. Cameron told her to step up. From under her blindfold, she could see that she was standing on an ice chest. Unlocking her left wrist from the handcuffs, he locked her right wrist to a pipe above her head. Then he started removing her shoes and her clothes. Colleen was sure she was going to be raped.

Cameron then put a strap around her left wrist and attached it to a wooden beam with a hook. This meant he could release the handcuff to finish removing her clothes without ever leaving both hands free. She could smell the sweat from his body and was shaking with fear. This, she sensed, was exciting him.

When she was naked with both arms restrained high above her in the shape of a Y, she asked him what he was going to do to her. He replied, "Shut up."

He ran his hands over her body, then suddenly kicked the ice chest away. Pain shot through her arms and shoulders. Looking out from under the blindfold, she saw an open magazine on a table. It showed a naked woman suspended from the ceiling, just as she was, and she began sobbing uncontrollably. She then saw Cameron and Janice take their clothes off and have sex on the table in front of her.

When Cameron noticed she was watching them, he ordered her to put her head down. But before she could comply, he leapt up, grabbed a whip, and started beating her. The pain was unbearable. This excited him and more sex ensued. When the couple had finished, Janice put her clothes on and went back upstairs. Cameron ran his hands over Colleen's naked body again. He took photographs of her, then chained her up in a box. When she complained that she could hardly breath, he threatened to cut her vocal cords. He had done it before, he said. Then he wrapped a belt or cord around her upper body. She felt something sharp between her legs. Later, she discovered that he was trying to administer an electric shock to her genitals, but he could not get the equipment to work.

She was left tied up all night, unable to move. Sometimes she sensed that he was looking at her, admiring the red welts left by the whip. Occasionally, she could feel the touch of his hands. In the morning, she was released from the box. She asked when he would let her go. Hooker said soon. She would ask the same question and get the same answer over and over again.

He got her up on the table and chained her, spread-eagle, to a rack. He replaced her head box and left her there. An hour later, he released her and took her to a chair and handed her a plastic bedpan. She had not been to the restroom for twenty-four hours. Even so, she told him that she could not go with him watching. He stepped back, though she could not see if he was still watching as the blindfold was still in place.

He fed her, but kept her blindfolded. Then her chains were replaced with leather straps. She was stood back up on the ice chest and her arms were tied above her. Then the ice chest was kicked away and she was left suspended for fifteen minutes. When she was taken down, she was chained back to the rack and the head box was replaced. She was left like that for another day, never knowing whether she was alone or he was ogling her naked body.

The next day, she was pulling at her chains, moaning and crying, when the head box was removed. This time she heard a woman's voice.

"What's wrong?" she asked.

She indicated, as best she could, that she was cold. The woman put a blanket over her. When she was unlocked again, Cameron gave her some water and two egg-salad sandwiches. She ate the first, but refused the second. She was not that hungry. This was a mistake. Cameron explained that she should be more grateful. She was suspended from the ceiling again and whipped until she passed out from the pain. When she regained consciousness, Colleen found no support under her feet and passed out again.

When Cameron eventually took her down, she ate the second sandwich. Absolute obedience, she learned, was mandatory. Then she spent another day on the rack. He taught her to be silent. There was to be no whimpering and no conversation. He would give orders; she would obey.

Some time later, Janice returned to the basement. She slipped the head box off and explained to Colleen that, though she was held there naked, she was not going to be raped. There would be no sex. But the torture would continue. Colleen was there, it seemed, to take Janice's pain for her.

Janice then asked if Colleen knew where she was.

"Yes, in Red Bluff."

And what would she do if she were released?

"Go to the police and tell them that I had been kidnapped."

The head box was replaced. Plainly, these were the wrong answers.

The abuse soon fell into a routine. Colleen would spend twenty-three hours chained to the rack, with the head box keeping her in complete isolation. Then she would be released to use the bedpan, always with Cameron watching. She would be fed and watered; she knew never to refuse anything she was given. Then two or three times a week she would be suspended from the ceiling or be subjected to some other sadistic form of punishment. Usually, Cameron would take photographs of her in the most humiliating and degrading positions. He took no chances, developing the photographs himself.

Any form of resistance or complaint was met with a vicious whipping. On one occasion she rattled the chains on the rack because she needed to go to the restroom. He came down to the basement and supplied the bedpan. But afterward she was suspended from the ceiling and thrashed with a bullwhip until she passed out. This was the punishment for making a noise.

Escape, of course, was impossible. At all times, she was kept tethered and blindfolded. At six feet four, Cameron was ten inches taller than Colleen. Janice was petite, but Colleen learned later that she carried a shotgun during her visits to the cellar, just in case. But even if Colleen were somehow freed from her shackles and made a dash for it, she had no doubt the door to the basement would be locked. And beyond that, she didn't even know if she was in a town or out in the middle of the countryside. How far could she get before he caught up with her?

All Colleen could do was spend her twenty-three hours on the rack trying to analyze Cameron's mind and moves, seeking solace in happy memories from childhood, and praying to God for his help and guidance.

After a week, Colleen heard sawing and hammering. Hooker was constructing a coffin-shaped box, which would be Colleen's new home. The rack would still be used for special tortures, but the rest of the time, she would be kept in the coffin. It had a double skin to make it even more escape-proof. Ventilation was provided by a hair dryer with the heating element turned off. She would remain in chains in the box to make her feel even more helpless, and he stopped her ears with grease to increase her sense of isolation. If anyone came into the basement, she could not have heard them. Apparently, Cameron had removed her from the rack because he feared a surprise visit from their landlords. The box was made from cheap particleboard, which was coarse on her skin and gave her splinters. Usually she was given her sleeping bag to lie on, though it was removed for special punishment.

Sometimes, she could not wait twenty-three hours to go to the bathroom and would soil herself. This would make Cameron angry. He would string her up and whip her with a variety of lashes, from a bullwhip to a cat-o'-nine-tails, taking care not to cut the skin. He did not want to risk her getting an infection.

There were other tortures. He would string her up and burn her, or administer electric shocks to vulnerable parts of her naked body. Sometimes he would suspend her from her ankles. Colleen noticed that he drew inspiration from S&M magazines, using her as a human guinea pig.

Then there was the sex. Cameron and Janice would have sex on top of the box with her in it. He also forced her to perform oral sex on him, though Colleen did not know whether Janice knew about this. After three months, Cameron brought Colleen a toothbrush and let her clean her teeth.

Colleen grew grateful for small mercies. One morning Cameron brought pancakes and syrup for her. She ate twice that day. Then she discovered it was merely a prelude to a particularly vile act of cruelty that evening.

Her periods had ceased, probably due to stress. But then, after three months, she started to menstruate again. Hooker was furious and she feared a whipping. Instead, for the first time in three months, she was taken upstairs and given a bath.

Throughout, she was gagged with duct tape and blind-folded with a baby's diaper. Her hair was filthy and tangled, so badly that it could not be unknotted. Janice took a pair of scissors and cut it off.

But no experience in the Hooker household would be complete without torture. While being bathed, Colleen was hog-tied with her hands and feet behind her back. She was then suspended from a broom handle and dunked, head first, in the water. Hooker would keep her there until she thought her lungs were exploding, then pull her out for a second before dunking her back in. The water torture lasted two hours.

Back in the basement she was tied up again, face down on the rack, and Cameron forced her to fellate him. Then she was returned to the mind-numbing torture of the darkness and isolation in the box.

After that, Colleen was allowed a bath once a month. She had to go through the water torture one more time, but for subsequent baths, she was left alone in the bathroom to wash herself—at least she thought she was alone. She was not allowed to remove the blindfold, so she could not see if she was being watched.

Naturally, while she was upstairs in the relative freedom of the bathroom, she would think about escape. The Hookers were way ahead of her. Janice warned her that any attempt to walk out of the back door would be the same as putting a shotgun to her own head and pulling the trigger. But could she, she wondered, wrap herself in a towel and crash through the window? Would she escape injury? Could she reach safety?

There were too many dire consequences if she got it wrong. After her bath, she was returned to her box.

For the first few months of her captivity, Colleen did not even know the name of her captors. But then she heard the man ask "Jan" to pass him a small whip. Colleen knew that using the name would result in another whipping. But at least she knew something about her tormentors. She had a small secret she could cherish.

Colleen also tried to figure out what was going on in the head of the woman. Why did she allow the man—her husband presumably—to do what he was doing to Colleen? Did she enjoy watching what he did to her? Sometimes, Colleen knew, the woman whipped her too. She prodded her with sharp objects and, on one occasion, bit her. But she did not seem to take the same pleasure in sadism as her spouse did.

Then life began to change for Colleen. One night, she was let out of her box. Her chains were undone and she was set to work sanding a knotty burl. She had to do this with a heavy box still strapped on her head. The task took several nights. Later, she assumed, the burl was varnished and sold. It seems she was bringing money into the house.

One night, in late November Colleen thought, she was taken to a small workshop under the stairs and ordered to take her blindfold off. For the first time in six months, she could see. Then she was set to work shelling walnuts. As a precaution, the man put handcuffs around her ankles. When her night's work was done, her ankles had swollen up and it was difficult to get the cuffs off. After that, they were dispensed with.

A new routine began. During the day, she would be kept in the box. Then the man would come and get her, feed her leftovers, and inflict some pain on her for his own amusement. Then she would be taken to the workshop where she was put to work with her blindfold off. During the night, her usual task was to shell walnuts or pecans. Then the woman taught her how to do macramé and crochet. Again, she assumed that the product of her labor was being sold. She was left alone in the workshop all night with a bedpan, which she could use whenever she needed to. One night, she even plucked up the courage to try the door. It was locked.

However, sometimes there was no work to be done and she was left in the box all day. As the basement grew colder, Colleen knew Christmas was approaching, though she could not tell which day was the actual holiday. In the normal course of events, Christmas would be followed by her birthday—this year her twenty-first—and the New Year. Colleen passed all three in her box.

Sometime later, she was in the workshop one night when the man came to visit her. For the first time since he had held a knife to her throat, she saw his face. She also saw that he was wearing a western-style belt with the name "Cameron" engraved on the back. Behind him, Colleen could see Janice. She had bandages on her knees.

Colleen was told that a man from "The Company" was upstairs. The man showed her a newspaper article about women being sold as slaves in the United States. They were given slave names and would be held as a slave for life. Those who resisted where sent to Rent-A-Dungeon in San Francisco for "remedial training."

Cameron then produced what looked like a legal document. It was dated January 25, 1978, and purported to be a contract between "Colleen Stan, hereafter known as Slave, and Michael Powers, hereafter known at Master." In it, she was to sign herself over to her slave master, body and soul. She was to do everything she was told without question. Every part of her belonged to him. She was not to wear underwear—or anything at all without his permission. Nor was she to cross her legs in his presence.

She was forced to sign. The contract was then witnessed by the woman, who signed under the name "Janet Powers."

Colleen then asked what was wrong with the woman's knees. The man explained that she had been a slave and had escaped. When she was recaptured, she was taken to Rent-A-Dungeon where she was nailed up to be tortured to death. When he saw her, he had taken pity on her, bought her, and married her, but her knees had been badly damaged during her punishment.

Hooker then described in detail about what had happened to one slave who had run away. The Company had tracked down her family and tortured her mother until she told them where her daughter was. The girl's fingers and toes were pulled off. Her arms and legs were amputated without anesthetic. Her eardrums were punctured and her eyeballs burned out with a soldering iron. Her hair was then braided and used to suspend her torso from a hook on the ceiling of her master's bedroom. Given food and water, it took her a year to die. After what Colleen had been through already, this sounded all too credible.

From now on, she was to address him as Master or Sir and his wife and Mistress or Ma'am. She must ask for permission even to go to the restroom. To speak to them, she must kneel with her arms at her sides and look at the floor.

After she signed, a slave collar with her slave name "Kay" on it was fastened around her neck. A laminated card came from The Company, showing that she had been registered. She was then allowed upstairs to wash dishes and clean up, though she was not allowed to sit on the furniture. While doing her chores, she came across a letter written by Cameron to The Company complaining about her poor performance. This helped convince her that The Company did exist. That idea coerced her into absolute obedience. She feared for her family if she tried to run away. Nor did she want to be strung up again, or nailed up and crucified.

The master wanted to keep her naked, but the mistress insisted that she wear a nightgown upstairs in front of their daughter. But Hooker developed a new routine. When he shouted, "Attention," she was to strip off her nightgown and brace herself in the doorway between the living room and dining room. Then he would whip her for minor infractions.

In February 1978, Colleen was taken upstairs. She was then tied spread-eagle on the Hookers' water bed and left blindfolded. She felt the man on one side other her; the woman was on the other. They began kissing her all over her body. The man began to rape her, but the woman jumped up and ran into the bathroom. Colleen could hear her crying and throwing up. The man followed her to the bathroom and seemed to be trying to comfort her.

After that, the woman was brusque with her. It was as if Colleen was threatening her relationship with her husband. As Colleen was older than her "mistress," she found it particularly humiliating to kneel before her.

On April 28, 1978, Colleen was left in the workshop all day and all night. She was given no food, and outside she could hear things being moved around. In the small hours of the morning, she was handcuffed and blindfolded, and taken out of the house. She was put in the front seat of a pickup with her head in the woman's lap. After a drive of about twenty minutes, she was taken out of the pickup and guided up some steps. When the blindfold and handcuffs were removed, she found herself in a mobile home. There, in the bedroom, she was put in another box, smaller than before, which fitted under the couple's water bed. This was where she would sleep from now on. She was allowed a bedpan in there, but she would have to put up with the stench until she was let out. And who could tell when that would be? Like the previous box, this one had a double skin. Her purse and other meager possessions were stored in between the inner and outer skins. Between the two skins, she also saw a picture of another girl with dark eyes. Had she been an earlier victim? Colleen knew better than to ask.

If there was no cleaning to be done or the Hooker's appetite for inflicting pain had abated, Colleen would be left in the box twenty-three hours a day. Then in the late spring, she was given some clothes—denim shorts, a tank top, and a pair of tennis shoes. Underwear was not permitted, of course. She was then allowed out of the trailer to do some digging to install the utilities. Cameron's brother Dexter turned up. According to Cameron, he and their father, Harold, were also involved in The Company. Harold lived in Arkansas, where he had a large dungeon, Cameron said. He kept twenty-six slaves there and enjoyed torturing them.

Colleen was told not to act like a slave in front of them. There was to be no kneeling to ask permission, and she was not to walk around nude. If they knew she was a slave, Cameron said, they would borrow her. And that would be the worse for her. Instead she was to pretend to be their housekeeper and babysitter.

One day, Harold arrived to find Colleen scrubbing the trailer floor naked. Janice rushed her into the bed and got her to put some clothes on. She then asked Cameron if it was not time to take "Kay" home. Cameron pretended to do so. While Janice kept his parents busy, Cameron took Colleen outside and locked her in a storage shed. Then he drove off, pretending he was taking her home. In due course, Colleen was introduced as Kay to Janice's parents, who did not spot anything was wrong.

That summer, Colleen was frequently let out to work on the garden. The Hookers always kept a close watch on her. Nevertheless, she enjoyed being out in the sunshine. But the pleasure was not to last. One day, she was ordered out of her box to find that Hooker had constructed a reinforced frame that she could be strapped to for bondage sessions.

The problem for Hooker was that his family might drop by without warning. And his daughter was getting bigger. So he constructed a second storage shed in the garden. Colleen would be taken there, stripped naked, blindfolded, gagged, strung up, and whipped.

Janice sometimes accompanied her husband to the shed to watch the bondage sessions. Colleen was suspended by the arms. Blindfolded, she could not seen Janice and she accidentally swung toward Janice and kicked her in the stomach. Cameron was furious. He took her sleeping bag from her box, so she had to sleep on the rough particleboard. In the next torture session in the shed, he brought matches and burned her breasts.

When Janice went out, Hooker would sometimes take Colleen to the shed for a special torture session. At the end of it, he would want her to cuddle him. On one occasion, he said she could say anything she liked to him. She was taken aback. It had been more than a year since she'd had any conversation. Now he wanted to hear from his worthless slave woman. She could not think of anything to say, so she asked when he first realized that he wanted to hurt women. He said when he was five or six years old he had begun to draw pictures of women in bondage.

She asked what would he do if someone did that to his daughter. "Kill them," he said. So how did he think her father felt about what he was doing to her? That was the end of the conversation, and she was returned to her box. On a hot summer day, it was unbearably stuffy in there. For once, she was grateful that he kept her naked.

Colleen was in the box when Janice gave birth to her second daughter on the water bed above. And she was in there for another Christmas, her twenty-second birthday, and then New Year.

With another mouth to feed, Colleen's meager rations were cut. Janice got an evening job. Hooker used her absence to rape Colleen, though she had to be tied up first and he would make the sex as rough and painful as possible. Colleen did not think that Janice knew that he raped her while she was away and she was in no position to tell her. He always used a condom because he knew he could not afford to get Colleen pregnant. On other occasions, he would suspend Colleen naked from the frame while he sat and watched TV. On weekends, Janice would join him watching television while Colleen hung there in agony.

Cameron's sadism began to seek new outlets. He would drive her out to an isolated dirt road, where he forced her to run, despite her generally poor health. If she did not, he threatened to put a chain around her neck and drag her behind the car. At a lake, he would make her strip and swim ten laps. He would even do this when his children, the older now two, were in the car.

Later, Colleen would be sent out from the trailer to run around a circuit that he had already timed. If she was not back on schedule, he said he would contact The Company. The threat was enough. She enjoyed going jogging because it gave her precious minutes on her own outdoors. She did not think of escape. There was no point in running to the neighbors. She assumed they were involved with The Company. After all, they must have known that she was a slave because she had a slave collar around her neck—a new tight one that Hooker had soldered closed.

The jogging came to an end when one of the neighbors stopped her for chat. She tried to break off the conversation, but the delay prevented her getting home in the allotted time. The Hookers were furious. If she had been a moment longer, they would have called The Company.

Fear of The Company affected every part of her life. There was no escape. Colleen came to believe that they were everywhere, even in her dreams. On more than one occasion she dreamt that she had been handed on to a series of slave masters who were even more sadistic than Hooker. This made her all the more determined to be a good slave.

Colleen was set to work making macramé plant holders again, at night, chained to the back of the toilet. One night she found she did not have enough material to complete the design, so she altered the design to suit the amount of material. As punishment, she was suspended from the frame with her feet off the ground. Wires were taped to her breasts and the insides of her thighs, Cameron administered electrical shocks while he and his wife watched TV with the volume turned up to drown out her screams. When it was over, Colleen found that her flesh had been burned where the wires had been taped to her.

From her box, Colleen could hear Cameron hammering and sawing. This was never a good sign. When he let her out, Janice was not there. He told Colleen to go and have a shower. This usually meant she was going to be raped. When she came out of the shower naked, there was a T-shaped torture device he had made on the floor. He blindfolded her and strapped her arms to the crossbar of the T and her ankles to the foot. He said he was doing this, not as a punishment, but because he wanted to. Then, using a wrench, he turned a mechanism in the trunk of the T that lengthened it. He ran his hands up and down her naked body to feel the tension in her flesh. She could tell this gave him immense pleasure. He kept turning the mechanism. The pain was excruciating. It reached a point where she found she could hardly breathe and she passed out. When she came to, he forced her to beg for mercy. Then he raped her vaginally and orally. After that he began turning the mechanism again with all his might. This would have killed her if one of the straps holding her arms had not broken under the strain.

As it was, it left Colleen with a dislocated shoulder. Eventually, she knocked it back into place by hitting her arm hard against the side of box.

Later Colleen was dragged out of her box and given Cold Duck to drink. Then when she was a little tipsy she was forced to perform oral sex on Janice, who was lying naked, spread-eagle on the bed. Colleen was put back in her box. Then, while Janice and Hooker were having sex above, she found herself dry heaving.

That fall, Hooker took her out on job cutting cedar fence posts. When they reached the site where the trees were being cut, Hooker waved to a big man with a beard. He told her that he was with The Company and was particularly hard on female slaves. On the way home in the pickup, Hooker told her to remove her pants and masturbate with the handle of his whip.

The slave collar round her neck was inviting too many questions, Hooker said. So he removed it. But The Company insisted that she carry some slave identification, so he used a needle to pierce her labia and attached a gold hoop earring. This was done without any anesthetic.

Hooker got Colleen to dig a hole under one of the storage sheds. They lined it with bricks. This dungeon would be her new home. In due course, he said, he would expand it to accommodate four of five other slaves. Colleen dreaded this. As senior slave, he said, it would be her job to torture the new girls into submission.

That December, to her surprise, Colleen was asked what she wanted for Christmas. She asked for a Bible. It was not forthcoming on Christmas Day, her twenty-third birthday, or at the New Year. However, on January 11, the Bible appeared. Colleen asked the Hookers to inscribe it. Their dedication read: "A gift to Kay Powers from Cameron and Jan."

After that, when she had finished her chores, Colleen would get down on her knees, bow her head, and ask permission to read the Bible before she was put in her box. The Hookers gave their permission and Colleen was chained to the toilet where she could spend the evening reading.

That year she was given clothing—mostly second-hand—and even some underwear. Then Cameron took her panhandling in Reno. His story was that he had a bet with another member of The Company that she could make more money than his slave. Later, he took her panhandling in a mall in Red Bluff. A policeman told her to move on. She said nothing and ran back to Hooker, terrified that her encounter with the police might come to the attention of The Company.

Janice took a day job. As Cameron also worked during the day, this meant Colleen was left alone with the children most of the time. She had become a trusted slave. She was moved out of her box and was allowed to sleep in the back bathroom where the chain padlocked around her neck was made long enough for her to stand up. This was of little help when, early one morning, one of the Hookers' daughters asked her to get her some cereal. Colleen suggested that she ask her mommy and daddy. Hooker told Colleen to lock the bathroom door from the inside in the future.

With the Hookers out at work, Colleen had to cook for the whole family. But everything she did was criticized, and she was frequently beaten. She was also allowed to eat with the family—or, at least, on the floor beside the table, unless one of the Hookers' parents came to dinner.

Being unsupervised in the trailer alone during the day meant that Colleen could easily have phoned her parents. But she believed that would only succeed in putting them in danger. After all, The Company tapped the phone; she believed they ran the phone company as well as the police department.

Janice would bring home work from her job that Colleen would have to complete overnight. Colleen's reward was to sleep in her sleeping bag on the living room floor. Janice then found that her employer would not pay overtime, so Colleen had to be registered as an employee. Hooker had her social security number and date of birth from documents in her purse. All she had to do was sign the enrollment papers—using her real name, which was becoming increasingly unfamiliar to her.

By then it had been three years since Colleen had gone missing. Her name on a company's records alerted no one. Plainly everyone had given up looking for her. When the check came, Colleen was forced to endorse it over to Hooker, who put the money straight into his bank account.

Hooker was always devising new ways to terrorize Colleen. He told her that two men from The Company were coming to test her loyalty. They would want to see her tortured. When they did not appear, Janice said they were busy and had canceled, but they would come another day, so she had better prepare herself for a pretty vicious torture session.

On another occasion, Hooker took her out into the forest and left her there naked all night. It was cold. In the morning she heard hunters in the area and was terrified what they might do to her if they found her nude, so she hid as best she could. Eventually, Hooker returned and drove her back to the trailer.

Hooker enjoyed his power over her so much that he told her to start a diary and write down all the things he had done to her since she had first been captured. Though it had not been his intention, this eventually proved to be vital evidence against him at his trial.

Colleen learned to flatter Hooker, even telling him that she loved him. Sometimes she even wrote him love letters. As a result, the torture was less frequent and less severe. That summer she was allowed out into the garden again. She was even allowed to talk to the neighbors, providing the conversation was confined to gardening. Any hint that she had talked about anything else would result in a beating, or she would be returned to the box. Sometimes she was returned to the box anyway, with no reason given. And sometimes, when she was under the bed, Colleen could hear Hooker beating his wife.

On one occasion, Hooker told Colleen to take the children outside so he could whip Janice. Afterward, the girls wanted to know why mommy was crying. To deflect her husband's wrath,

Janice constantly carped about the tiniest thing Colleen did wrong so that Cameron would beat her instead.

Other curious things happened. One day Colleen was given new clothes and Janice put makeup on her. The two women then went to a bar, where they met two guys and went back to their apartment. Janice disappeared into a back room with one of them. The other one kissed Colleen a few times. He talked; she listened, not daring to tell him anything about her plight. Then Janice emerged and they went home. Colleen supposed that Janice was allowed to have a little fun as a quid pro quo for Hooker indulging himself sexually with his slave.

Colleen accompanied Janice on another date. This time she danced with another guy while Janice entertained her man friend. Another time, Colleen was given a swimsuit and was taken waterskiing with Cameron's family. There were other family outings. They went skiing. Then on a shopping trip to Chico, she was allowed to phone her father's home in Riverside, California.

They used a pay phone in a gas station. Hooker stood next to Colleen with his finger posed. If she said anything wrong he would cut her off, Hooker warned. The phone was answered by Colleen's sister Bonnie, who asked where she had been. Colleen said that she had been staying with friends. They chatted amiably. After about five minutes, Hooker indicated that Colleen should terminate the conversation, so she said good-bye and put the phone down.

Later she was allowed to write home. Hooker vetted the letters and got her to rewrite them if they contained anything he did not like. They were posted from Chico with no return address. Then Colleen asked if she could visit her family, but Hooker said that The Company would not allow it.

More calls home were allowed that fall. Colleen did not understand why he permitted this. Her family was happy to hear from her, but with Hooker standing next to her there was no way she could explain her predicament. Despite all her new freedoms, there was still no hope of escape.

One day a kindly neighbor saw Colleen crying and asked what the matter was. Colleen could not tell her. The neighbor said that people at the local church would help. Even there Colleen feared she would not dare unburden herself, but for a quiet moment she and her neighbor prayed together.

After two years' work, the dungeon under the storage shed was complete. Colleen was taken there. There was a trapdoor in the floor of the shed. Then she had to descend a ladder. The dungeon was deep, making the ceiling high enough for her to be hung up. Down there was her sleeping bag, her Bible, a portable radio, and a chair.

Once Colleen was in the dungeon, Hooker hauled up the ladder. She had been told that, if she was found there, she was to say that she used the cellar for quiet contemplation. She was to say, without irony, that in the cellar she could be nearer to God. The trapdoor was then closed. She stood on the chair and tried to shift it, but it appeared Hooker had put something heavy on it and it would not budge.

After a couple of nights, it began raining. When Hooker came to visit in the morning, Colleen was knee-deep in water. They tried bailing, but it did not work. A pump was no help either. So she was returned to the box.

At Christmas, Colleen was allowed to send home a blanket she had made. It was for a baby that had been born to the family since she had been gone. She was also allowed to phone home from the trailer. Hooker said that The Company would be monitoring the call. Her father asked her for the number. Colleen made an excuse and said she would give it to him another time. She also received a Christmas present from the Hookers—a new sleeping bag.

In February 1981, Colleen was unchained from the back toilet and allowed to sleep full time on the floor in the living room. But Hooker began to grow tired of Janice's constant criticism of Colleen. This situation grew worse when Janice found Colleen's diary, which enumerated her rapes. In it, Colleen had also talked flatteringly of her "love" for Hooker. Things reached a breaking point when the Hookers' older daughter inadvertently called Colleen "Mom." Hooker took Colleen out to the forest, tied her between two trees, and whipped her.

One day in March, Colleen was made to kneel with her head bowed before her master. He had news to tell her. The Company had decided to let her visit her family. He had to put up a $30,000 surety. But she had better not try anything. The phones would be tapped; the house bugged. If anything went amiss, the house would be swamped by security. People would get hurt. But first, as a test, The Company wanted her hung up and whipped.

This was not going to be done in any of the ordinary places, but at a small farm his father had in Oregon. The whole family drove up there. While Janice, the children, and the family dog waited outside, Hooker took Colleen into barn, told her to strip, and strung her up from a rafter. Suddenly, they heard the dog bark. Someone was coming. Hooker quickly let Colleen down, but she was still naked when his father walked in. It was dark in the barn, and Colleen was not sure that the old man could see her. Later, Hooker's older daughter asked Colleen why her wrists were so red.

On the day Hooker was supposed to take Colleen to the bus station for her trip home, everyone bid her farewell. The two girls kissed her good-bye, and the kindly neighbor gave her $10 she could ill afford. But Colleen was not going anywhere, not that day. Hooker drove around for an hour, then told Colleen to lie down in the car. He then returned and locked her in the shed. That night, he smuggled her back into the trailer, got her to strip, and put her back in the box.

Over the next few days, Colleen was hung up repeatedly and savagely beaten. Then came one final test The Company wanted her put through. She was to put a shotgun in her mouth and pull the trigger. Colleen did this without hesitation. The hammer came down on an empty chamber. She had passed the test.

On March 20, 1981, Hooker set off up Interstate 5 with Colleen in the car. As they neared Sacramento, he said he wanted to check in with The Company's headquarters there. She was left in the car for a quarter of an hour while he disappeared into an anonymous building. When he returned, he said that The Company were too busy to see her, but he had been given all the appropriate paperwork to allow her a home visit. The company's secretary had wished her luck. As they continued their journey, Hooker instructed her on what to say to her family and, once again, went through the security arrangements The Company had set up.

At Riverside, Hooker dropped Colleen outside her grandmother's house. She paid a quick visit and they arranged to go to church together the next day. Then Hooker drove Colleen over to her father's place. He dropped her there and drove away. Her stepmother and sisters were there. Her mother, who lived nearby, turned up a little later.

They asked her where she had been for the past four years and why she had not stayed in touch. But they did not put too much pressure on her; they were afraid that they might push her away forever. It was clear that they assumed that she had joined some weird cult. The police had given up looking for her long ago. To them, she was a simple runaway. Colleen had been twenty when she went missing. Because she was an adult, there was little the authorities could do. In her heart, Colleen wanted to tell her family the truth, but she was too afraid of The Company.

Colleen sat up much of the night with her sister Bonnie, catching up on family news. The following day, they went to church with their grandmother. In her prayers, Colleen even remembered Hooker and The Company for allowing her to visit her family. After a family lunch, the phone rang at her father's house. Colleen answered it. It was Hooker. He said he would be there in ten minutes.

When he arrived, he introduced himself as Mike and said that he was Colleen's fiancé. When they asked for his phone number, he said he was in the midst of moving at the time and would give them the number when the new line was installed.

Bonnie was worried. Colleen seemed strange around "Mike." She had always been so affectionate with former lovers. But when Colleen's stepmother produced a camera, Colleen knew she had to play the part and put her arms around Hooker.

When they left, Colleen managed to persuade Hooker to stop at her mother's house so that she could say good-bye. On the way back to Red Bluff, she told Hooker how grateful she was.

They arrived home the following morning. The trailer was empty. Janice and the kids were staying with her family. Colleen was then raped and returned to the box. It was the beginning of a long incarceration.

For the next three years, Colleen was allowed out of the box only after the children had gone to bed. She could empty her bedpan, drink a glass of water, eat some leftovers, and was then returned to the box—though sometimes she was not let out at all. She only ate on average four or five times a week. Her weight decreased dramatically and, kept constantly in the dark, her hair began to fall out.

That summer, the Hooker family went away for three days. Colleen was left in the box with a quart of water and a pack of cookies. While they were away, the temperature in Red Bluff soared over 120°F. It got so hot that she feared she might die if she didn't get out of there. She kicked at the end of the box and something gave way. But then she stopped, fearing the consequences if she were caught. When the family returned, Colleen was too weak even to stand. Hooker fixed the box and said nothing.

Whenever Janice and the children were out, Colleen was taken out of the box to be tortured, beaten, and raped. Hooker thought up more horrors for her. With her lower legs tied to the back of her thighs, she was handcuffed and sat on the commode with a rubber gas mask over her head. The eyes of the gas mask were taped over. Only one tiny air hole was left open. Hooker would put his finger over this until she was on the verge of suffocating. Then when he tired of this game, he left her bound up while he went for something to eat. When he released her after two hours, she had lost all feeling in her legs.

Janice went into the hospital for four days in April 1982. This allowed Hooker to indulge the full range of torture and abuse. After being kept in the box for so long, the lack of light had made Colleen's bones brittle and, when she was tied up in the frame, part of her big toe came away. Hooker was furious that she had bled on the carpet.

In October 1983, she was transferred back to the dungeon under the shed. This was a relief after being confined in the box. She was given some clothes and there was an infrared lamp down there to keep her warm. There, she could read the Bible and she tuned the radio in to a Christian radio station.

The Hookers' children had been warned not to go near the shed, but when their niece turned up, she peeped inside. Hooker feared that Colleen had been discovered, so after just a week in the hole, it was back in the box for Colleen.

Later that year, Hooker stopped raping Colleen and a new relationship developed between her and Janice, who was also taking an interest in the Bible. Janice kept getting Colleen out of the box so they could study the good book together. Hooker encouraged this.

On her twenty-seventh birthday, Colleen was given a birthday cake. This was the first acknowledgement of her birthday since she'd become a captive. She asked to be allowed to work. Hooker thought it would be a good idea for her to bring some money into the household again. First, though, after three years, she had to be reintroduced to the family. She was given clothes to wear and a story to tell. The girls were glad to see her back.

She was allowed to sleep in the bathroom again, with a chain around her neck. In front of others, she was to stop calling the Hookers "master" and "mistress." Instead, she was to call them Cameron and Jan. But as a good slave, she still called them "sir" and "ma'am," fearful of returning to the box.

On May 21, 1984, Janice drove Colleen to Red Bluff to look for a job. Eventually they found her a position as a housekeeper at a motel that was only a few hundred yards from where she had been picked up when hitchhiking seven years before. It was also just a short distance from the Red Bluff Police Department, and the Highway Patrol used the Denny's restaurant next door. But Colleen believed that turning to them would mean risking the wrath of The Company, torture, and death.

Now that she was working, Colleen was allowed to sleep on the floor in the living room again. She was permitted to visit the home of another housekeeper from the hotel after work, and the Hookers let her take on overtime, working at the front desk.

Colleen went on family outings and grew close to Janice. They went to church together. On one occasion they talked to the pastor about the troubles they had at home—leaving out any references to sexual slavery and torture. After that, the pastor even visited them at the trailer.

It was then more than a year since Hooker had last raped Colleen. Now he put the pressure on. God wanted her to have sex with him. When Janice agreed, Colleen gave in.

Hooker talked of making Colleen his second wife. One day, he said, they would move to Lake Tahoe where she would have his baby and he would have more slaves. Hooker's relationship with Colleen began to unsettle Janice once more. She decided to put an end to it. One day, Janice turned up at the motel and told Colleen that Hooker was not a member of The Company. Colleen could hardly believe her ears. She broke down. For seven years, she had been a prisoner of his lies. Perhaps fearing that Colleen would go to the police, Janice still maintained that The Company existed and that Colleen should fear it. It was just that Cameron was not part of it.

Colleen never understood why Janice had suddenly decided to tell her the truth. Was she worried that Hooker was about to kill both of them? Or, now that Hooker was having sex with Colleen again, was she tired of sharing her husband?

The two women decided to escape. Colleen quit her job and they went to visit the pastor. Janice told him that her abusive husband was having an affair with Colleen, while Colleen said that Hooker had made her his sex slave and that her real name was Colleen Stan. However, the girls were still at home and it was too late to make their escape that day. They had to go home and pretend that everything was normal, then make their escape in the morning. Janice was so used to being the dutiful wife that she was afraid that she would spill the beans and Hooker would end up murdering them both. Colleen suggested that she pretend to be ill and say she did not want to make him ill too, so she should sleep in the living room with Colleen. It worked.

In the morning, after Hooker had gone to work, they packed their things and went to Janice's parents' house. Colleen then phoned her father, who wired her the bus fare home. Hooker turned up that night. Colleen stayed with the girls in a back bedroom while Janice talked to him outside. Eventually, he drove away. Then Janice told the whole story to her parents who, like the pastor, could not really take it in.

The following morning, Janice drove Colleen to the bus station. She begged her not to go to the police, saying that they should give Cameron a chance to change.

Before she got on the bus, Colleen called the trailer. Hooker answered. She told him that she was about to get on the bus and go home, and there was nothing he could do about it. She heard him cry.

Arriving in Riverside the next day, she told her family of her kidnapping and her years of captivity, though she spared them the painful details of the rape, the torture, and the box for fear of hurting them. She learned that her family had made every effort to find her, even visiting Red Bluff. But she had simply vanished into thin air.

Colleen called Janice to tell her that she had arrived home safely. Over the next few months, they exchanged calls. Colleen wanted to know if Cameron had really changed or whether he was coming down Interstate 5 to get her.

Hooker called too, on one occasion, just to ask her how to make a tuna sandwich. For the first time in his life, there was no one to look after him. Colleen even felt a little sorry for him.

This soon passed when her cousin Linda, a firebrand, phoned Hooker and told him what she thought of him.

Three months after Colleen returned home, she got a call from Janice. She'd gone to the police and told them everything. After Colleen had left, Janice had returned to Hooker. He had gone into counseling with the pastor and had burned most of his bondage gear, his collection of pornography, and the pictures he had taken of Colleen being tortured. But Janice began to suspect that Cameron had not really changed his ways. She left again and, fearing for the safety of the children, gave the pastor her permission to call the police. Janice was given immunity from prosecution for her testimony against her husband. He was arrested.

Soon after, Colleen got a call from the Red Bluff Police Department. They visited her in Riverside, interviewing her for three hours and taking pictures of her scars.

The police found that Colleen's story matched what Janice had told them—except in one detail that Colleen couldn't have known about. More than a year before Colleen had been kidnapped, the Hookers had picked up another girl named Marie Elizabeth "Marliz" Spannhake. But when Hooker got her down into the basement, she would not stop screaming, so he got a kitchen knife and cut her vocal cords—exactly as he had threatened to do to Colleen.

They could not stop the bleeding, or take Marliz to the hospital. Hooker then tried to kill her with a pellet gun. When that only wounded her further, he finished her off with his bare hands, choking her to death. Without a trace of remorse, Hooker buried Marliz in a shallow grave. Marliz was the girl whose picture Colleen had seen in the box under the Hookers' water bed.

The police could not find Marliz's body, so they did not charge Hooker with murder. Instead, he was charged with the kidnapping of Colleen and seven counts of rape. Apparently, the other tortures he had inflicted on her and keeping her in a box were not against the law in California at the time. However, other felony charges followed. There were three counts of false imprisonment, two counts of abduction to live in an illicit relationship, one forced oral copulation, one sodomy, and one penetration with a foreign object—the whip handle.

Hooker's friends and family could scarcely believe the charges. Meanwhile, Colleen's home was besieged by the media, who were calling her "The Sex Slave" and "The Girl in the Box." She moved out to live with a new boyfriend, though her father smuggled her into the house so that they could enjoy Thanksgiving together as a family.

Colleen was eager to return to normal life and she got a job in a store. But there was still the trial to go through. First she had to undergo a thorough medical examination. It was important for the prosecution to get a detailed record of the electrical burns on her body, the scarring from straps and whips, the damage to her shoulder from stretching, her inexpertly pierced labia, and her general poor state of health from years of malnutrition and confinement. Every mark on her body backed up her story.

When Colleen turned up to court, the district attorney thought she was dressed far too sexy to pass for a victim and bought her a whole new outfit—a white dress and flat shoes.

Hooker pleaded not guilty. However, after Colleen had testified at a preliminary hearing, the case went to trial.

Due to a shortage of funds in California—and the fact that this was not a murder case—the DA was forced to plea bargain. Colleen's advocates began a political campaign to prevent this. When it appeared that Hooker might serve less time in captivity that Colleen had, the state granted additional funds and the plea bargain was dropped.

At the Superior Court of California, the defense argued that the statute of limitations had run out on the 1977 kidnapping and that she was free to leave at any time after early 1978, so she was a "willing participant" in what had gone on from them on. The prosecution countered that the kidnapping had been continuous up until she left in 1984.

The box and many of the instruments Hooker had used to torture her were brought into court. Nevertheless, conviction was not a forgone conclusion. The defense would argue that these instruments were used in a consensual relationship between two adults and, consequently, no laws had been broken.

Janice was the first witness to take the stand. She outlined her bizarre relationship with Cameron and detailed his aberrant sexual interests. Her husband had dyslexia, she said, and she had to read him articles on brainwashing techniques that he had then employed on Colleen.

She explained the pact they had made: she could have a baby, if he could have a slave girl. After Cameron first suspended Colleen by the arms in the basement, Janice claimed she was terrified that he might do her some permanent damage. After a few weeks, Janice said she asked Cameron to let Colleen go. He refused. She admitted that she was the one who found the slave contract in one of Cameron's magazines and typed it out to make it look official. Colleen had signed it unwillingly, she said.

Janice told the court about The Company. She had been suffering from arthritis and, at the time the slave contract had been signed, she'd recently had an operation on her knees. Cameron had promised not to have sex with his slave girl. To test him, she had given him her permission to see if he would really go ahead with it. But when he had actually started raping Colleen, Janice had run from the room. However, she admitted whipping Colleen while her husband watched and fueling his fantasies by reading S&M magazines to him.

Colleen was sometimes confined in the box, Janice admitted, because Janice felt jealous. But Janice said Hooker's abuse of Colleen had not brought her the respite from pain that she had hoped for. He continued to torture Janice in the same fashion as Colleen. She was only spared the electric shocks and the box.

Janice said that Cameron had read passages from the Bible to her, showing that both his wife and his slave owed him absolute obedience. Despite everything, she said she still loved him. He had been a good provider. Without him, she would not have been able to afford to take care of her children. However, she was frightened that, if what he did became public, she might go to prison and lose her daughters.

Then when Cameron wanted to make Colleen his co-wife, Janice explained, and sleep with them alternately—and even have a baby with Colleen—it all became too much and Janice decided to confide in the pastor. He told her that they must send Colleen home. Hooker would never have agreed to this, so Janice contrived to get rid of Colleen by telling her that Cameron was not a member of The Company. The pastor then told her to forgive her husband. She tried to do that, but she began to fear that he might harm their children, so she gave the pastor her permission to call the police.

Janice maintained that, like Colleen, she was one of Cameron's victims, not his accomplice. Even though he had Colleen as his slave, he had continued to torture her.

Then it was Colleen's turn. She found it intimidating to testify in the courtroom just a few feet from Hooker. She was also afraid that he might get off and come after her. The defense maintained that, after the initial abduction, the relationship had been consensual. She had told Cameron that she loved him and had written him love letters. She had even been photographed with her arms around him. Colleen insisted that she had done all these things so that he would not hurt her. During her first six months of captivity alone, she had been hung up naked ninety or a hundred times and whipped savagely. It took her three and a half days in court to detail the barbarity that he had inflicted on her.

The Hookers' neighbors testified that they thought that something odd was going on in their trailer. They thought it strange that, while the woman they knew as "Kay" worked in the garden, she did not have a suntan. Even the Hookers' two daughters—now nine and seven—were called to testify. The most damning evidence was pictures of both Janice and Colleen being hung up, and a photographic negative of Colleen's slave contract that had been found among Hooker's papers.

Cameron Hooker took the stand in his own defense. He said that he had long been fascinated with bondage, discipline, sadism, and masochism. Between consenting adults, these things were legal and, he believed, normal. Janice shared his interests and let him practice such things on her.

Many people kept slaves, he said, and many other people willingly became slaves. He had a fantasy about practicing bondage on a girl who could not say "no." Having his own slave girl was part of the pact that he struck with Janice when she had a baby. They considered putting a classified advertisement in a paper, asking for some girl who would consent to bondage, but did not have the money.

He said that on the day they first saw Colleen, he and his wife were on their way to the mountains to practice bondage outdoors. When they gave Colleen a lift, she appeared to be spaced out on illegal drugs and the idea of kidnapping her came to him. He admitted to the initial kidnapping, but as the statute of limitations had run out, he could not be charged with that.

In the basement, he said he hung her up for just five minutes. Then, after he and his wife had had sex, he lost interest in bondage. He only put Colleen in a crate with a box over her head, not as torture, but to keep her quiet.

The next day, he felt bad, but he did not know what to do, so he tied her to the rack. After three days, they decided to let her get dressed and to take her where she wanted to go. But when Janice asked Colleen what she would do if they let her go, she said that she would go to the police. When Hooker went to talk to her, he said that she appeared to be suffering from withdrawal symptoms and asked for pills from her purse. Colleen maintained that they were contraceptive pills, as she feared she was going to be raped.

The withdrawal symptoms subsided, he said. He still wanted to let her go, but he was afraid that she would go to the police, so he built a double-skinned box to keep her in as they could not afford to soundproof the basement. She was allowed out of the box each night and they talked. There was no bondage or sex, he said.

After three months, he said Colleen asked him about bondage. On the first occasion she had started to cry after being hung up for just five minutes. Janice, he said, could stand twenty minutes. Colleen wanted to try again, he maintained. She managed fifteen minutes without crying.

He admitted the other things that they had done to her—dunking her in the bath, cutting off her hair, forcing her to work—but put a different light on them. She liked doing macramé and Janice taught her to crochet. Colleen kept asking why they were not having sex, he said, but he had promised Janice that he would not. They talked and Colleen, he said, displayed affection for him.

Janice found the slave contract and said that the story about the all-powerful Company might allow them to let her go. Colleen believed the story and was terrified. But then, once the contract was signed, Janice began to treat Colleen like a slave.

During her second pregnancy, Janice wasn't interested in sex. To turn her on, he tied Colleen, with her consent, spread-eagle on the bed. He was kissing Janice while touching Colleen. Then he started having sex with Colleen, but Janice could not handle it. So Colleen was returned to the basement, apparently disappointed that the sex was over so soon, according to Hooker.

They then decided to release Colleen by pretending that they were buying her freedom from The Company. She was told that she could go anywhere, but The Company would punish her if she went to the police. But first they wanted her to help them move into their mobile home.

Colleen was very helpful during the move. She slept in the box, or the bathroom, but did not need to be restrained. She had turned herself into a slave voluntarily and did not try to escape. She helped Hooker dig trenches to run the utilities to the trailer and worked with him cutting fence posts. When he tied her to a tree, they spent time talking and kissing. However, he did tell her that when they released her, she must never talk about The Company, or The Company would make her someone else's slave. He said he never threatened her family.

Hooker maintained that he treated Colleen well, but Janice treated her like a slave and that depressed her. When he offered to take her back to her family, she said she did not want to go back to taking drugs. Her family was abusive. She said she wanted to stay where were she was. She needed the stability of having Hooker's loving family around her.

According to Hooker, Colleen was happy to stay as a slave, but Janice wanted her to go because she feared he and Colleen were falling in love. She wanted Colleen punished. When he hung Colleen up, he went to look for more straps and came back to find Janice giving Colleen electric shocks.

After that, he and Colleen began indulging in sex and a little light bondage, then some heavy bondage. Although she cried when Janice told her off, Colleen didn't cry when he put her on the stretcher. She could take more pain than he could dish out, he said. They dug the dungeon under the shed because the children were getting older and they could not continue their bondage sessions in the trailer. Again, Colleen cooperated in its construction. The whips, he said, were used as toys. They were never meant to hurt anyone. But during one of these sessions, Colleen kicked Janice in the stomach. It was Janice who went to get the matches and burned Colleen's breasts, he said.

When Janice went out to work, he and Colleen had sex. It was her idea, he said. She talked about getting married and having a baby. When Janice went with other men, he was not bothered because he was in love with Colleen.

They took her out shopping and waterskiing, and bought her a Bible. He was a poor reader, so he got her to read out passages to him.

Colleen had wanted to go gambling, so he took her to Reno where she panhandled to get a stake. She also panhandled in Red Bluff to get the fare to visit her family. He took her to his father's farm to have another backdrop for their bondage.

At Colleen's home, he had introduced himself as "Mike" because he did not want more troublesome in-laws tracking them down. Colleen had returned to Red Bluff with him because she loved him. She said so. And she went back in the box to save his marriage. Otherwise, Janice would have left him.

When he got things sorted out in his marriage, Colleen came out of the box again. She and Janice grew friendly. Colleen then wanted to go back to work. He took most of her wages because she wanted to contribute to the household finances. The bondage and sex began again. Colleen and Janice also began having lesbian sex together. The idea of Colleen becoming a co-wife came from the Bible, where Abraham took the slave girl Hagar as his second wife after Sarah, his first wife, proved barren.

Then Colleen discovered that The Company was not real. She phoned to say that she was going back to her family so that she would not come between him and Janice. She was doing it for the sake of their two daughters. He told her he loved her.

When she got home, Colleen called him to say that she still loved him, he said. Janice had returned to him and they resumed bondage. Colleen bombarded him with letters and phone calls. He did not write back.

He maintained they had the perfect love triangle with each of them loving the other two. But in the end, the two women ganged up on him and had him arrested, so that the two of them could get back together.

According to Hooker, both Janice and Colleen participated willingly in bondage. After the initial kidnapping, he never held her against her will and he never raped her. She loved him. Her letters proved that. She could have left at any time. People saw her out jogging, and she went out on dates with other men. It was only when he found himself the odd one out in a love triangle that they tried to get rid of him by sending him to prison.

Hooker's family and friends testified that they had seen "Kay" on numerous occasions. She was their housekeeper and babysitter, but seemed very much part of the family. The defense even called a psychiatrist who had testified in the trial of Patty Hearst to counter the prosecution's assertion that Colleen had been brainwashed. He said that, although she had been coerced during the first six months of her captivity, after that, the coercion stopped. From then on, she participated willingly.

The prosecution then dropped the charges of false imprisonment and abduction to an illicit relationship. The jury took two and a half days to find Hooker guilty on all the other counts, except one final rape where the jury was divided. It seems that, after seven years of brutal mistreatment, Colleen might have tacitly accepted her tormentor's advances.

The day after the verdict, Colleen got a phone call at home. It was Hooker calling from jail. After that, he was not allowed to make unsupervised calls.

Hooker was sentenced to 104 years. The judge said: "I consider the defendant the most dangerous psychopath I have ever dealt with, in that he is the opposite of what he seems. He will be a danger to women as long as he is alive."

Given time served, time off for good behavior, and other sentence reductions, Hooker will be eligible for parole in 2022 when he will be sixty-nine. However, by that time, the authorities might have been able to put together a case against him for the murder of Marliz Spannhake.

Chapter 4

Gary Heidnik and the Basement Baby Farm

JOSEFINA RIVERA HAD BEEN ON THE STREETS for much of her twenty-five years. Of mixed African-American and Puerto Rican descent, she had been educated in a Catholic school. But she had dropped out as a teenager and turned to prostitution. The children she bore had been taken away by the welfare authorities and put up for adoption. Life on the streets of Philadelphia had made her tough—tough enough to survive an ordeal that killed at least two others.

Josefina used the professional name "Nicole" when she approached johns in the street. And there were plenty of them. She was a good-looking woman with fine features inherited from her Hispanic father

On the night of November 25, 1986, Josefina was working the corner of Girard and Third in Philly's run-down north side. She had argued with her boyfriend, Vincent Nelson, that night and walked out on him. Clad in skin-tight jeans and sneakers, she was cold and business was slow. The following day would be Thanksgiving. It was already eleven o'clock, but she did not want to go home without turning a least one trick. She needed the money for a hot turkey dinner.

She had about given up hope when a brand new white and gray Cadillac Coupe de Ville pulled up. The trick was a stranger, but she was glad to see him. She was freezing her butt off on the street that night. She named her price. He offered $20. She took it. Then she would quit for the night.

The john's name was Gary Heidnik. He took her to a nearby McDonald's where he had a coffee. He bought her nothing, but while he drank his coffee, she examined him closely. He wore a Rolex watch and expensive jewelry. These clashed oddly with the cheap, fringed cowboy jacket he wore. He was not especially clean either, and his blue eyes were as cold as marble. They sent a shiver down her spine, she said later.

Heidnik suggested that they go to North Marshall Street, which was known, at that time, as "OK Corral" because of a recent shoot-out between drug dealers. He had a house there.

When Heidnik parked his new Cadillac in the garage, Josefina was surprised to see that Heidnik had several other automobiles, including a 1971 Rolls Royce. He also had an unusual door-locking system, which, he explained, he had devised himself. Only he could work it, he said.

Inside the house, Heidnik asked if she wanted to watch a pornographic video to put her in the mood. She said she was a professional—she did not need to be in the mood. She looked at her watch and said she had to be getting home. Anger flashed across his face. To calm him, she said that she had three children at home. She needed to be quick as she had to relieve the babysitter.

They went upstairs. The stairway, she noted, was papered with $1 and $5 bills. In the bedroom, there was a water bed. Heidnik flung a grubby $20 at her, stripped off his clothes, and jumped onto the bed. She stripped too, and the sex act was over in a few minutes. Relieved, Josefina reached for her blue jeans, to get dressed and go home.

Suddenly, Heidnik grabbed her by the throat. Josefina had been a prostitute long enough to know not to risk antagonizing a violent client. Half-strangled, she gasped her surrender. Heidnik handcuffed her and dragged her naked from the room. On the way, he grabbed back his $20.

He pulled Josefina down the stairs to the cellar and chained her to a pipe. The room was cold and damp. The walls and floor were filthy, the light was dim, and there were tiny windows high above the floor.

In the middle of the floor, a pit had been dug. Josefina feared that it would be her grave. She began to scream. Heidnik slapped her and threw her down on a filthy mattress. He lay down, rested his head on her naked lap, and slept like a baby.

The next day, she found that her chain was long enough to allow her to reach one of the basement's boarded up windows. It was at about head height, but she managed to pry the boards off and squeeze her way out. Out in the garden, she began to yell, but the neighbors were used to screaming, loud music, and even the sound of gunshots coming from Heidnik's house, day and night. They took no notice. Heidnik heard her, too, and came running. He dragged her back into the basement by her chains. He slung her in the pit, covered it with boards and heavy sacks, and turned the radio up full blast.

It seems that Gary Heidnik wanted to have babies and he would do anything to get them. He was born in 1943. His parents separated when he was seventeen months old. His father accused his mother, a Creole, of being a drinker and wild woman. His mother accused his father of gross neglect of his marital duties.

Gary and his older brother, Terry, stayed with their mother until they were school age; then they moved in with his father, who had remarried. Gary's father was a strict disciplinarian. When Gary wet the bed, his father would show the soiled sheets to their neighbors. Sometimes he would even dangle Gary feet-first from an upstairs window as punishment.

Gary Heidnik's reaction to this mistreatment was to embrace the American dream. He joined the Boy Scouts and told friends that he was going to become a millionaire. He had an IQ of around 130—not far from genius level. But, in his early teens, he fell out of a tree and landed on his head, and suffered permanent brain damage. Later, Gary tried to kill his brother.

After a number of suicide attempts, Gary was committed to a mental hospital. When he was discharged, he went to a military academy but he was still suffering from psychiatric problems. He made at least three more suicide attempts. He flunked out of the academy, but life was so intolerable back with his father that he enlisted in the army. In his army papers, he described himself as "colored" like his mother. She had gone on to marry twice more and had become an alcoholic by the time she committed suicide in 1971. After joining the army, he never spoke to his father again.

In the army, Gary learned he could make money without working for it. He became a loan shark, making more than his army pay in extortionate interest rates. But then he lost everything when he was suddenly posted to Germany before he could call in his debts. Still in the army, Heidnik began to exhibit strange psychiatric symptoms. He was discharged with a 100 percent disability pension of $2,000 a month. He never had a permanent job again.

From childhood, Heidnik had followed the stock market reports. For him, it was a splendid mathematical puzzle. He quickly turned his army pension into vast sums of money. But, apart from his collection of cars, he did not flaunt his wealth. He bought pornographic magazines and books featuring black women. He preferred to live around African-Americans. It gave him access to black prostitutes. He was addicted to them. He liked to buy them fancy wigs and flamboyant clothes. Best of all, he liked mentally challenged girls who had no defense against his intellect. And he wanted to have children by them.

One of his girlfriends, an illiterate black girl called Anjeanette Davidson, had an IQ of just 49. When he got her pregnant, he refused to let her see a doctor, saying that he would take care of her himself. But he beat and starved her. Rescued by her sister, she was rushed to the hospital. She was so emaciated that she had to give birth by Cesarean section. She was unable to look after the child, which was put into foster care.

Heidnik also tried to shoot a man who rented a room in his house. The bullet grazed the tenant's cheek, but the charges were inexplicably dropped. When he moved away, the owners of his old place found stacks of pornographic magazines and a pit he had dug in the basement. They had no idea why the pit had been dug.

Though otherwise not a religious man, Heidnik started a church called the United Church of the Ministers of God. It performed a double function. It gave his enterprises tax-free status, allowing him to keep more of the money he made on the stock market. Its funds grew from $1,500 to $545,000 in twelve years. And under the guise of doing good works, the church gave him seemingly innocent access to mentally challenged black girls.

Heidnik thought having his own church also gave him a direct line to God, and God said that he must make babies.

The run-down neighborhood Heidnik lived in was a good cover for his activities. It was full of drug dealers and prostitutes, and the police were so stretched, they took no notice of his strange antics. One neighbor filed a complaint about his activities, but they gave an incorrect spelling of his name and the police did not follow up.

Heidnik already had a criminal record. In 1978, he had been charged with kidnapping, rape, false imprisonment, and involuntary deviant sexual intercourse. He had taken his girl-friend Anjeanette to visit her sister Alberta, who had an IQ of just 30 and had been an inmate of the state mental hospital for twenty years. Heidnik suggested that thirty-five-year-old Alberta go on an outing with them. She was found, days later, locked in a garbage bin in Heidnik's basement. Alberta was deemed unfit to testify, but Heidnik was sentenced to three to seven years for the lesser charges of abduction and assault.

Heidnik spent most of his sentence in state mental institutions. Periods of hospitalization continued after he was released, but no one kept an eye on him when he was on the street. Even when Anjeanette Davidson disappeared, no one suspected Heidnik, though he was later thought to be responsible for her murder.

In 1985, he married Betty Disto, a Filipina whom he contacted through a marriage agency. But when she arrived in the U.S., she found a black woman sleeping in Heidnik's bed. The woman was a lodger, he explained. A week after their wedding, Betty found him making love to three black women in exotic positions in their bedroom. This was an American custom, her new husband said.

Other women were brought to the house, and his bride was forced to watch him have sex with them. He also beat her, refused her food, and forced her to have anal intercourse. She left after just three months, charging him with indecent assault, rape, and other felonies. When she did not turn up in court, the charges were dropped. She was pregnant and only dared tell Heidnik by postcard. He refused to support the child, claiming that he did not have a job. The family court investigated. But with Betty gone, he still did not have the children he craved.

Three days after re-capturing Josefina, Heidnik went out looking for twenty-five-year-old Sandra Lindsay, a good-looking black girl and a former lover he had known for four years. Like his other lovers, she was classified as mentally handicapped and he had a grudge against her. He had made her pregnant and he had offered $1,000 if she would let him keep the child, but she had gotten an abortion.

Heidnik found Sandra and brought her back to the house. She, too, was stripped naked and chained up in the basement. Josefina was hauled from the pit and introduced to her. Heidnik then spelled out his plans for a baby farm. Soon there would be more naked black women chained up in the basement and Heidnik would move between them like a butterfly pollinating beautiful flowers. He then forced the two women to perform various sexual acts with him. The rest of the night, he spent digging out what he called the "punishment pit," making it deeper and wider.

The following morning, there was hammering at Heidnik's door. It was Sandra's sister Teresa and two cousins. Heidnik did not answer the door and, eventually, they went away. Sandra's mother believed that Heidnik was holding her daughter and went to the police. They scarcely bothered to look into it. Sandra was just another black whore who had gone missing. Heidnik forced Sandra to write a postcard to her mother, telling her not to worry, that she would call. Then he took it to New York where he posted it. Later he sent a Christmas card, enclosing a $5 bill.

As good as his word, Heidnik captured other sex slaves. He planned to have ten in all. He told Josefina and Sandra that they were all going to give him babies that would grow up in "one big happy family." He got to work on this project immediately, demanding sex from his captives. They were in no position to refuse. The routine was always the same. First they would have to stimulate him orally. But he had no desire to ejaculate in their mouths. Once he was ready, he would put his penis in their vaginas.

On December 22, 1986, he picked up nineteen-year-old Lisa Thomas. She was not a prostitute, but she let him give her a ride to her friend's house where she had left her gloves. He then took her for a meal at TGI Friday's and asked her to go with him to Atlantic City the following day. When she said she had nothing to wear, he gave her $50 and took her to Sears, where she bought two pairs of jeans and two tops. She went back to his house to try them on. There, he gave her a drink and she passed out. When she came to, she found herself naked on his water bed. They had sex, but when she tried to leave, he began choking her. Then he handcuffed her and dragged her down to the basement. She was sure that he was going to kill her. Once in the cellar, he lifted some boards covering a hole in the floor and out clambered two other naked black girls, Josefina and Sandra.

After they had been introduced, Heidnik brought his captives some peanut butter and jelly sandwiches. But before the starving girls could eat, they had to go through a humiliating routine. First they had to kiss his ass, then lick his balls, and suck his penis. After that he would have sex with them. Then they could eat.

He did not confine his sexual activities to the basement. He had a regular arrangement with a girl named Jewel. She came to his house for sex once a week. There would usually be another girl there. Gary liked to have sex with Jewel while biting on the other girl's breast; then he would have sex with the other girl while biting on Jewel's breast. Jewel was happy to accommodate him but had one caveat. He had to have sex with her first. She did not want him to put his penis inside her after it had been in the other girl.

On New Year's Day 1987, he picked up and imprisoned twenty-three-year-old prostitute Deborah Dudley. He imposed discipline by putting one of the girls in charge while he was away. When he returned, he would ask who had committed any misdemeanors, then hand out the appropriate punishment.

On January 18, he picked up eighteen-year-old prostitute Jacqueline Askins. Again, after sex, he dragged her down to the basement where he chained her up with the others, then beat her buttocks with a plastic rod to ensure future compliance.

The following day was Josefina's birthday. He let her pick a meal from the menu of a local Chinese restaurant. He also brought champagne for the girls. He did not drink himself; it was not one of his vices. However, he believed there was reason to celebrate. He thought both Josefina and Sandra were pregnant, though this proved not to be the case.

All the girls were shackled and chained, and Heidnik forced them to have sex with him every day. He would penetrate them one after the other, until he climaxed or grew tired. For entertainment, he would force them to have sex with one another. Being half-starved, they did not get pregnant. This made Heidnik angry and he beat the girls.

He found Sandra the most troublesome. He tied her wrists to an overhead beam and left her dangling there for a week, force-feeding her. Eventually, weakened, she choked on a piece of bread and died. He cut her down and kicked her dead body, then he left it lying on the floor while he fed the other girls ice cream.

When they had finished, he put Sandra's body over his shoulder and carried her upstairs. Later, they smelled cooking flesh. The odor was so strong that neighbors complained. A young policeman knocked on the door and peered through the kitchen window. There was a pot on the stove, but the cop could not see what was in it. The crowd in the street told him to break in, but Heidnik opened the door a few inches and explained that he had just burned his dinner.

Deborah fought back against Heidnik. She would not easily submit to his sexual demands. As a punishment, he unchained her and took her upstairs. When she returned to the basement, she was dazed and silent. Josefina asked what had happened. Deborah said that she had seen Sandra's head boiling in a pot. Her ribs were in a roasting pan, and her other body parts were being prepared for the freezer. The meat was fed to his captives. The bones were given to his dogs. Heidnik told Deborah that if she did not submit to his will, she would end up that way too. Later he added dog food to their meals of minced body parts.

Occasionally, one of the girls would be taken from the basement and washed in the tub. Then she would have to perform a sexual act with Heidnik before he would return her to her shackles.

In the meantime, Heidnik went about his regular business. He stayed in touch with his broker and kept up with his stock transactions, and all the time he had the girls in his basement. He visited car showrooms and went to court over his maintenance payments. He even went out on dates with his latest girlfriend, a black nurse.

When he was out, he would put the girls in the pit and cover it over with planks, which he weighed down with heavy sacks. They found it hard to breathe in there and would scream. This gave him another excuse to beat them. To hide their screams from neighbors, he would play religious music loudly day and night.

Despite what she had seen, Deborah remained defiant, and Heidnik devised a new punishment for her. He pushed Deborah, Jacqueline, and Lisa into the pit and got Josefina to pour water over them. Then he touched their bodies or their chains with live electric wires. Deborah was electrocuted and killed.

Heidnik decided not to dismember Deborah. Instead he forced Josefina to sign a letter saying that she had killed Deborah, then he unchained her. Together, they drove out into the wilds of New Jersey, where they dumped Deborah's body.

Josefina had seen Heidnik kill two other girls by then. There was only one way to get out of the basement alive, she realized. She would have to get him to trust her completely. Her plan was to maneuver herself into the position of his confidante.

To flatter his ego, she began to flirt with him. This bothered the other girls. They thought she was conspiring with their sadistic jailer. But Josefina was smarter than they were— and she, a common prostitute, was smarter than Heidnik with his IQ of 130.

First, she consented to join in his regular sexual encounters with Jewel. Soon Heidnik began to take her out to McDonald's and buy her wigs. But he never let her out of his sight. He warned her that if the police ever caught up with him, he would plead insanity and she would get life for murdering

Deborah because of the confession she had signed. He also said that if she tried to escape, he would kill the other two girls.

With two of his harem now dead, Heidnik took Josefina to look for new candidates. On March 23, they saw twenty-four-year-old Agnes Adams, whom Josefina knew from a strip club where they had both worked. Heidnik knew her too, but not by name. In the sex trade, she went by the name "Vicky." He had picked her up before; the first time had been in January. He'd offered to pay her $35 for oral sex, but when he got her back to his house, someone had parked across his driveway, so he gave her $10 and took her back downtown.

Then in February, he had taken her back to his house. This time he parked and they went inside. She gave him oral sex. He paid her the $35. Then he let her leave, locking the door behind her. So when he picked her up with Josefina in the car, Agnes had no reason to be wary. Back at his house, she went upstairs and had sex with him. Afterward, Heidnik choked her, handcuffed her, and dragged her down to the basement.

As Josefina was seemingly free to come and go, the other girls grew suspicious of her. They plotted to attack Heidnik with the broken glass and lengths of pipe that littered the floor of the basement. But when Heidnik discovered the plan and beat them viciously, they assumed Josefina had betrayed them.

Heidnik became paranoid about the women listening to him moving around the house. He tried to drown out the sounds of his movements with more loud music. But later, he took more drastic action. He tied the girls to a beam and punctured their eardrums with a screwdriver. Only Josefina was spared. The other girls then resented her more, but Josefina did not care. She had a plan.

Although her children had, in reality, been adopted long ago, Josefina had said that she had three children at home when she had first come to Heidnik's house, as an excuse to get the sex over with. On March 24, 1987, four months after she had first been taken captive by Heidnik, she persuaded him to let her go home and visit these phantom children. In exchange, Josefina promised to return with a new woman for Heidnik's harem.

Heidnik drove her downtown and dropped her off near her home. He was confident that she would return. If she did not, it did not matter much. In his eyes, she was a simple-minded black whore. If she went to the police, no one would listen to her wild accusations.

When he dropped her off, they agreed to meet at Girard and Sixth Street, around midnight. Again she promised that she would come with a fresh woman for him.

As Heidnik drove off, Josefina was seized with fear and panic. She ran back to the apartment where she used to live with her boyfriend, Vincent Nelson. The night before Thanksgiving, when she had gone out to pick up her deadly trick, they'd had a terrible fight. She had been missing for four months now. What must Vincent be thinking? It did not matter. There was nowhere else to go.

She beat on his door. When he opened it and saw her, he was angry. Where the hell had she been? She began babbling.

"She came in," he said, "and as we were walking up the steps, she was rambling on, you know, talking real fast about this guy having three girls chained up in the basement of this house and she was held hostage for four months... She said that he was beating them, raping them, had them eating dead people, just like he was a cold-blooded nut. Dogs in the yard were eating people's bones. I just thought she was crazy. I really didn't believe her, and I still don't believe this shit."

None of what she said made any sense to him, but he took her in. Her sheer terror impressed him. Plainly, she needed help.

After a couple of hours, he realized that, whatever she was talking about, this Heidnik guy was responsible for giving her a hard time. He promised to sort him out. At midnight, he went with her down to Girard and Sixth. But on the way he began to get cold feet. What if some of the things Josefina had said about chains, torture, and murder were true; this freak could be dangerous.

Just one block short of the gas station, Vincent stopped at a pay phone and called the police. He put Josefina on the line. The desk sergeant found her story hard to believe, but he said that he would send out a patrol car anyway.

The car picked them up at the phone booth. Vincent ran through Josefina's story of girls chained in the basement, being raped, being fed dead bodies. He said that he himself did not believe it. Nor did the cops. But they took her to the precinct. It was only when she showed them the scars and bruises on her body, and the shackle marks around her ankles, that they began to concede that there might be something to her story.

A patrol car was sent over to the gas station at Girard and Sixth. There was a white and gray Cadillac waiting there, just as Josefina had said there would be. The officers pulled their guns as they approached. Heidnik was not alarmed when the police ordered him out of the car at gunpoint. He asked whether they were arresting him for not paying his child support. But why the guns? They handcuffed him and took him in for questioning.

Meanwhile, another squad was sent to North Marshall Street. They banged on the door. No one answered. They had no search warrant, so they just had to sit there and wait until someone got one.

More than four hours later, the warrant came. The police crowbarred open the metal door. In the front room, they found a huge collection of pornographic videotapes and erotic books, all containing pictures of naked black women.

In the basement, they found two naked black women huddled under a blanket. They screamed as the police came in, but they were shackled and chained, and could not run away.

Once the police had calmed them, the women pointed to large sacks in the middle of the floor. The police had heard Josefina's stories and feared that the sacks could contain a dismembered body. The girls quickly indicated that they should move the sacks. Under them were boards. When the police lifted them, they found a shallow pit with another naked black girl squatting in it. She had her arms handcuffed behind her and was chained and shackled.

All three were starving and filthy. An ambulance was called to tend to them and take them to the hospital. Then an officer looked in the fridge. He found a human rib.

Heidnik was charged with indecent exposure, simple assault, aggravated assault, issuing terrorist threats, reckless endangerment, unlawful restraint, false imprisonment, criminal solicitation, indecent assault, rape, involuntary deviant sexual intercourse, murder, and the possession and abuse of a corpse. He cheerfully admitted to several other murders.

Within hours of his arrest, Heidnik was attacked by another prisoner. This would be the first of a number of attacks in jail.

Heidnik also tried to commit suicide but was caught before he could go through with it.

In court, his defense made what it could of the antagonism between the surviving victims. The other three girls still did not trust Josefina, who they thought had sided with Heidnik against them. And in her three-hour testimony, Josefina was almost sympathetic to Heidnik because "the city was always taking his babies away." The same thing had happened to her.

Jacqueline was so small that Heidnik had used handcuffs to shackle her ankles. Much was made of the fact that she was given extra long chains on her manacles. Was she not the one who was given special favors?

"He did that so I could open my legs for sex," she said. And she sobbed while she described the beatings and the deviant group sex that the girls had been forced into.

She and the other surviving victims expressed their distrust of Josefina and her motives. But this squabbling made little difference to the jury. They dismissed any attempt to show that Heidnik was insane after his financial advisor from Merrill Lynch was called to testify. Heidnik, said the broker said, was "an astute investor who knew exactly what he was doing." The figures spoke for themselves.

Heidnik was found guilty of the first-degree murders of Sandra Lindsay and Deborah Dudley. He was also found guilty on six counts of kidnapping, five counts of rape, four counts of aggravated assault, and one count of involuntary deviant sexual intercourse—all the charges except for involuntary deviate sexual intercourse with Josefina Rivera. The jury gave no explanation for their acquittal on that count.

Heidnik was given two death sentences. The victims were awarded $34,000 each. Mrs. Heidnik—aka Betty Disto—and her son received $30,000 from Heidnik's estate.

When Heidnik's father heard that his son was a sexual deviant and murderer, he was sympathetic to the victims. "I hope he gets the chair," he said. "I'll even pull the switch."

Throughout the whole ordeal Josefina Rivera had been extraordinarily resourceful. After it was over, she was stoic. She said later, "It's something that happened. I won't forget it. But I don't dwell on it."

Heidnik tried to kill himself again in January 1999 with an overdose of the drug Thorazine, which he had been prescribed. He was executed by lethal injection on July 6, 1999; he was the last person to be executed by the state of Pennsylvania.

Chapter 5

Elizabeth Smart— The Knifepoint Disciple

ON THE EVENING OF JUNE 4, 2002, Ed and Lois Smart had attended an award ceremony at their fourteen-year-old daughter Elizabeth's school in Salt Lake City, Utah. They returned to their home in the affluent neighborhood of Federal Heights, where they lived with their six children. Ed locked up the house that night, but he did not switch on the alarm.

"We never set the alarm at night when we were all home," he said later. If the children got up during the night, they would set it off.

The family said their prayers together. Then Ed and Lois kissed the children good-night.

"I just remember her coming over and giving me a big hug and a kiss and saying good-night, and the two girls [Elizabeth and her nine-year-old sister Mary Katherine] going off into their room, and that was the last time I saw her," said Ed.

In the early hours of the morning, Mary Katherine awoke to find Elizabeth was no longer in the queen-size bed they shared. She was up and there was someone else in the room. It was a man, but he was not their father or one of their four brothers.

"He placed his hand on my chest," Elizabeth later said in court, "and then put the knife up to my neck."

The intruder came around to Mary Katherine's side of the bed and tapped her on the shoulder. Sensing danger, the little girl pretended to be asleep. She heard Elizabeth stub her toe in the dark and say: "Ouch."

"He told me to get up quietly, and if I didn't, then he would kill me and my family," said Elizabeth. "He was whispering, but it was still loud enough it could wake someone. He was dressed in sweats, sweatshirt, stocking cap, tennis shoes."

Elizabeth then asked: "Why are you doing this?"

The reply was indistinct, but Mary Katherine thought he said, "For ransom."

The nine-year-old opened her eyes enough to see the man. It was dark and she wasn't able to see much detail. However, she remembered that he had black hair on the back of his hands and was wearing a light-colored hat. Mary Katherine thought he was carrying a gun.

When she thought they had gone, Mary Katherine got out of bed to go and tell her parents what had happened. In the hallway, she saw Elizabeth and her captor. Fearing that if he saw her, he would take her too, Mary Katherine returned to bed and pretended to be asleep again.

Eventually, she got up, wrapped herself in a blanket, ran into the master bedroom, and shook her father.

"She's gone," she said. "Elizabeth is gone."

It was 3:58 a.m.

Ed got up and went to look for Elizabeth. She sometimes slept elsewhere in the house if Mary Katherine had been kicking in her sleep. But Mary Katherine was insistent. A man had come with a gun and taken her sister away.

At 4:01, Ed called the police, begging them to hurry. Lois had discovered an open window where the screen had been slashed with a knife. It became clear that the terrible tale Mary Katherine was telling was no bad dream. By the time the police arrived twelve minutes later, Ed had alerted the neighbors. He told them to check their kids. Family and friends rallied around, forming ad hoc search parties.

Elizabeth was not the type to sneak out with a boyfriend. Indeed, she was angelic—she played the harp and was a featured soloist at a concert for the Paralympics at the 2000 Winter Olympics at Salt Lake City.

Somehow, the kidnapper had managed to leave without stepping on the creaky floorboard that Ed always heard when the kids moved around at night. The intruder had taken Elizabeth out through the kitchen door, leaving the cut in the screen as the only clue to his crime.

No one on the quiet cul-de-sac where the Smarts lived had heard any suspicious traffic that night. A neighbor's security videotape showed no activity before the police arrived. It looked as though the kidnapper had taken Elizabeth on foot up through the backyard toward the mountains beyond. However, police dogs could only follow her scent for a few yards beyond the house.

As the searchers spread out, they asked early morning joggers and dog walkers if they had seen anyone answering Elizabeth's description. No one had. There was no sign of her. Some had intended to search the old lime kilns established by

Brigham Young's Mormon pioneers back in the nineteenth century, but the police asked them not to. Later, the police took a dog team there, but found nothing.

To preserve any evidence of a trail, the police also asked Elizabeth's friends and family not to search the mountains beyond. All the family could do was support each other and organize fliers and a reward. The police offered $10,000; private donations raised that to $250,000. A hundred policemen joined the search, and helicopters scoured the surrounding area.

The Smarts' house was sealed as a crime scene at 6:54 a.m. By 7:30 a.m., local TV and radio stations were broadcasting missing person bulletins. Ed Smart broadcast his own appeal, asking the kidnapper directly: "Please let her go."

The Smart family were Mormons, and members of their church rallied around them.

The police examined the Smarts' home computer in case Elizabeth had met a sexual predator in an Internet chat room. In recent months, Ed had been renovating the family's $1 million home in preparation for sale. The police compiled a list of contractors, workmen, and real estate brokers who had been at the house, so they could be interviewed. One of them was Brian David Mitchell, but it would be months before he became a suspect.

Mitchell was a Mormon, who at one time had been second counselor to the bishop in a Salt Lake City ward, but he and his wife, Wanda Barzee, had been excommunicated from the Church of Jesus Christ of the Latter-Day Saints because of their "activity promoting bizarre teachings and lifestyle far afield from the principles and doctrines of the Church." Mitchell had written a bizarre manifesto outlining his beliefs called "The Book of Immanuel David Isaiah." It said that Mitchell was a "ministering angel" who was sent to Earth to correct the Mormon church and restore its fundamental values, such as polygamous marriages.

Although the Mormons had officially ceased to practice polygamy in 1890, Mitchell believed it was wrong to have done so. He was determined to have multiple wives, if not by consent then by force. In section four of the manifesto, dated February 17, 2002, he wrote: "And thou shalt take into thy heart and home seven times seven sisters, to love and care for…and thou art the jubilee of them all, first and last, for all are given unto them, for thou art a Queen, Oh Hephzibah!" Apparently, Hephzibah was Barzee, who was to accept and care for Mitchell's forty-nine additional wives, while remaining his lead wife.

On the night of the kidnapping, Mitchell took Elizabeth on a four-mile hike up to Dry Creek Canyon, where he had built a hidden shelter for his new wife. It was a twenty-foot ditch with a lean-to over it. Barzee was waiting at the campsite and tried to force Elizabeth to bathe.

"She eventually just proceeded to wash my feet and told me to change out of my pajamas into a robe type of garment," Smart recalled. "And when I refused, she said if I didn't, she would have Brian Mitchell come rip my pajamas off. I put the robe on… He came and performed a ceremony, which was to marry me to him. After that, he proceeded to rape me."

She was kept tethered to a tree by a cable and raped as many as four times a day. It was plain that he wanted her for sex, though he often talked about religion.

"He used religion to get what he wanted," Elizabeth said.

He forced her to consume drugs and alcohol, and showed her pornography, which was intended to lower her resistance. On one occasion, he forced her to drink so much that she threw up, so he made her lay face down in her own vomit all night.

As his bride, he renamed her Augustine and starved her when she was not compliant. Once, to fight off his sex attacks, she bit him.

"He said if I did that, he would never have sex with me again and I would be the most miserable woman in the world," she said. "He said that, but it didn't stop him."

While Elizabeth was being held at the camp, the police were following other leads. A milkman who delivered to the Smarts' cul-de-sac each morning said he'd seen a green car cruising past their house at 7 a.m. on June 3. The car drove passed him, then doubled back. Fearing that he was going to be robbed, the milkman wrote down the license plate number and called the police. The driver had been wearing a light-colored hat.

On Sunday, June 9, a vigil was held for Elizabeth in Liberty Park. A police officer noticed a green Saturn in the parking lot with the license plate number 266HJH. This was not an exact match to the number that the milkman had written down, but it was close. The police staked out the car, but when the driver returned, he leaped into the car and drove away before they could stop him.

Later that day, a small boy found some license plates abandoned near his home. They carried the number 266HJH. A fingerprint on them came from Bret Michael Edmunds, a twenty-six-year-old man who was wanted for assaulting a police officer. But Edmunds was six foot two; Mary Katherine had said the intruder was the same height as her sixteen-year-old brother Charles, who was five foot eight. However, Edmunds had done some work for people in the neighborhood and the search was on.

Ten days after the police started looking for him, Edmunds checked into a hospital in Martinsburg, West Virginia, with a damaged liver caused by a drug overdose. He had given a false name, but the name and phone number he used as an emergency contact belonged to one of his relatives in Utah. Edmunds was in a bad way. One of the hospital workers called the emergency number, and the relative, knowing the police were looking for him, called them.

Federal marshals found the green Saturn in the parking lot of the hospital. By the time investigators turned up from Utah, Edmunds was barely coherent. But it soon became clear that he knew nothing about Elizabeth Smart's kidnapping and there was nothing in his car to link him to her abduction.

Another early suspect was Richard Albert Ricci. He was on the list of people who had worked on the Smarts' home. In the spring of 2001, he had done some painting and work around the yard. Outgoing and talkative, he got on well with his employers. However, when the police checked him out, they found he had a long criminal record. A former heroin addict, he had stolen to support his drug habit. In 1983, he had shot a policeman in Salt Lake City after robbing a pharmacy, and he was a four-time parole violator.

Later, Ricci had abused alcohol and prescription drugs. He also had a strange compulsion to sneak into children's rooms and steal worthless items that they might easily have assumed they had simply misplaced. He was closer to the height of the man Mary Katherine had described. Investigators discovered that he worked for a local nursery and the day of the abduction happened to have been his day off. Ricci apparently knew that he would be a person of interest in the case. He told a neighbor that the police would be coming to see him because he had once worked at the Smarts'.

Ricci declined legal representation, and he and his wife allowed the police to search their house without a warrant. Inside, the authorities found a light-colored hat and a machete. In the garden, they found trinkets stolen from the Smarts' home. Although there was no direct evidence to connect him to the kidnapping, Ricci was held on a parole violation charge.

Eventually, Ricci was brought to court on burglary charges. While Ed and Lois had found it hard to believe that Ricci was responsible for the kidnapping, they came to believe that he knew something about it; perhaps he was even in league with the perpetrator. They attended court in the hope that he might give them some sort of sign, but he avoided eye contact with them.

That evening, Ricci collapsed in his cell. He was rushed to the hospital, where it was discovered he had a brain hemorrhage and he fell into a coma. Doctors tried to operate, but he died. Any information he did have about the kidnapping was then lost.

As the police could not rule out the possibility that the kidnapper was one of the Smarts' extended family, all the male relatives were asked to take a polygraph test that lasted up to eight hours. This, again, led nowhere.

Then Mary Katherine remembered something. Suddenly, four months after the abduction, she recalled that the man who had taken her sister was a homeless drifter who had done a day-and-a-half's work on the house the year before. The man had called himself "Emmanuel." However, the police still considered Ricci their man. When they searched the police database for the alias "Emmanuel," nothing had come up. They did not realize the name "Emmanuel" was on the system—Brian David Mitchell had recently been arrested for shoplifting.

The Smarts contacted John Walsh, the host of *America's Most Wanted*, who had already devoted some airtime to Elizabeth's kidnapping. He broadcast an update on the case. Then Walsh was asked about Elizabeth Smart on *Larry King Live*, and he mentioned Emmanuel.

By chance, Ed Smart bumped into sketch artist Dalene Nielsen and persuaded her to produce a new artist's impression of Emmanuel. This was then shown on *America's Most Wanted*, along with a description of the kidnapper. Derrick Thompson was watching the show and recognized the culprit. He called his brother Mark, who confirmed his suspicions. The man was their stepfather; Derrick and Mark were Wanda Barzee's sons.

Brian David Mitchell was born on October 18, 1953, in Salt Lake City. He was the third of six children born to Mormon parents Shirl and Irene Mitchell. Shirl, a social worker, and Irene, a schoolteacher, were vegetarians and raised their children on a regular diet of whole wheat bread and steamed vegetables. The family was described by neighbors as being odd but decent.

Brian was a normal kid, joining the cub scouts and playing Little League. Irene was a caring mother, but Shirl had some distinctly odd ideas when it came to raising children. He tried to teach his son about sex by showing him explicit pictures from a medical journal. Other sexually explicit material was available around the house. Shirl also liked to test his son's initiative by dropping him in unfamiliar areas of town to see whether he could find his way home. Constantly being put to the test, Brian became aggressive and withdrawn.

At sixteen, Brian exposed himself to a child and was sent to juvenile hall. After he returned home, he was constantly fighting with his mother, so his parents sent him to live with his grandmother. Not long after the move, Brian Mitchell dropped out of school and began using alcohol and drugs regularly.

Mitchell was nineteen when he married sixteen-year-old Karen, after she discovered she was pregnant. They had two children together—a son named Travis and a daughter named Angela. When they broke up, Mitchell was granted custody of the children due to Karen's alleged infidelities and drug abuse. She remarried and petitioned for her kids to be returned to her. Rather than give them up, Mitchell fled to New Hampshire. After a period as a fugitive, he decided to accept the court's decision and returned the children to their mother.

In 1980 Mitchell's life changed after his brother returned from a religious mission and the two began to talk. Brian stopped using drugs and alcohol, and returned to the Church of Jesus Christ of the Latter-Day Saints. The following year, he married his second wife, Debbie, who had three daughters from a previous marriage. They had two children together. According to Debbie, Mitchell, who had at first been gentle, became controlling and abusive, dictating what she could wear and eat. His interest in Satan disturbed her, though Mitchell claimed he was simply learning about the enemy. But it was Mitchell who filed for divorce in 1984, claiming Debbie was violent and cruel to his children, turning them against him.

After they separated, Debbie reported her concerns that Mitchell may have sexually abused their three-year-old son. While it was not possible to prove that Mitchell abused the boy, the court recommended that his future visits be supervised. Then Debbie's daughter accused Mitchell of sexually abusing her over a period of four years. Debbie reported this to the church, but LDS leaders advised her to drop it.

Debbie also saw the episode of *America's Most Wanted* and recognized Emmanuel as the man she had once been married to. She called the police and told them about Mitchell, including the sexual abuse of her daughter. She said that while she believed that Mitchell could have kidnapped Elizabeth, she felt he would not have killed her.

The day Mitchell divorced Debbie, he married forty-year-old divorcee Wanda Barzee. She had left her six children with her ex-husband, but when she remarried, some of them moved in with the newlyweds. They found Mitchell's behavior increasingly strange and threatening.

Mitchell worked as a die-cutter. But at home, he often flew into a rage, particularly at Barzee. His religious views became increasingly eccentric. He claimed to speak to angels. The children began to move away. By the 1990s, Mitchell had begun calling himself "Emmanuel." He grew a long beard and regaled people with his prophetic visions.

Barzee called herself "God Adorneth" and the two of them were seen tramping the streets of Salt Lake City dressed in long robes. The residents of Salt Lake City referred to them as "Joseph and Mary." They lived by panhandling. Occasionally, Mitchell took a job to make ends meet, even shaving off his beard and cutting his hair if necessary. The Smarts regularly offered odd jobs to people down on their luck and, in November 2001, Lois Smart gave Mitchell a few hours' work around the house. It was then that he met Elizabeth.

Elizabeth Smart lived in Mitchell's makeshift camp from June 5 to August 8. "Joseph and Mary" were now seen with another follower in tow. Both Barzee and Elizabeth covered their faces with veils so no one would see that this new hobo in a grubby white robe was the sweet blonde-haired kidnap victim whose picture graced posters across the state. Besides, there was no reason to imagine that this new follower was a kidnap victim. The three of them could be seen gorging themselves on the salad at all-you-can-eat buffets in cheap fast-food restaurants. Elizabeth would go alone to replenish her plate and return to the table without any visible coercion.

By the time Mary Katherine had realized that Emmanuel was the one who had kidnapped her sister, Mitchell, Barzee, and Elizabeth had left Utah and moved to Lakeside, California. Fifteen miles inland from San Diego, Lakeside had a large population of transients, so the three travelers fit in easily. However, Mitchell drew attention to himself by preaching in the shopping district and the police had to ask him to move on.

Mitchell now had two wives, but he wanted more. He spotted the twelve-year-old daughter of an official named Virl Kemp at a local Mormon church. So he tied back his hair, dressed in jeans and a plaid shirt, and went along to Sunday service. Mitchell introduced himself as Peter and asked questions about the church. Kemp invited him home for dinner, but it soon became clear that Mitchell knew more about the church than he let on. He was, of course, merely casing the house. Later, he returned to break in and kidnap Kemp's daughter. Fortunately, the house was secure and Mitchell could not gain entry.

By the time the crucial edition of *America's Most Wanted* aired on February 15, 2003, Mitchell was already in custody. A resident of Lakeside had reported seeing a man in long johns breaking into a preschool at Lakeside Presbyterian Church. The police arrived and found Mitchell asleep on the floor. He gave a false name and date of birth. However, he was identified by his fingerprints. He had already skipped a court appearance for shoplifting in Utah, but that was a misdemeanor and did not show up on the computer. That he was being sought in the Elizabeth Smart kidnapping case had not made the system yet. Nevertheless, he was held over the Presidents' Day weekend.

When Mitchell did not return to their camp in the woods, Barzee grew frantic. Leaving Elizabeth behind, she went to an altar that Mitchell set up called Golgotha to pray for his safe return. Elizabeth was left on her own, but again she made no attempt to escape.

In court, Mitchell—who insisted his name was Michael Jenson—explained that he had broken into the preschool because he was drunk. He was fined $250 and given three years' probation.

Two weeks later, when *America's Most Wanted* aired another update on the Elizabeth Smart kidnapping, the program showed photographs of Mitchell that had been provided by Barzee's sons. A viewer in Lakeside called in to report having seen a man answering to Mitchell's description, traveling with two women who wore veils over their faces.

In the Lakeside Library, the librarians saw the three of them wearing the dirtiest street clothes they had ever seen. They had no idea that the man, woman, and girl were the robed people who had been seen around town for the past four months. The girl was wearing a T-shirt, jeans, and a pair of oversized sunglasses. The older woman had hold of her wrist, while the man studied a map that a librarian had found for him.

The library manager, Dusty Harrington, said, "We just thought they were a homeless family, and my first thought was, 'Why isn't that kid in school?'"

It seems that Mitchell was studying the map because he intended to go back to Utah. On March 4, the threesome were seen by rock climbers near Escondido, twenty miles north of Lakeside. Mitchell again introduced himself as Peter and said he was on his way to Las Vegas with his wife and daughter. They were wearing robes and veils.

A week later, near the I-45, North Las Vegas police officers talked to three robed hitchhikers who were heading for Utah. They gave their names as Peter and Juliette Marshall, and their daughter Augustine. The transients had no identification, but the police had no reason to detain them.

The following day, when Ryan Johnson picked them up from a Springville McDonald's, they were dressed as they had been in the Lakeside Library, though Elizabeth now wore a gray wig. In the rear-view mirror, her eyes seemed to want to say something, Johnson said. But no words came from her mouth until she got out. The door handle came away in her hand and she said: "I'm sorry." Nothing more.

Mitchell had said that they were going to Salt Lake City. So Johnson dropped them at the bus stop on the road to Provo and gave Mitchell all the quarters he had in his ashtray, about $5 worth. When he got to work, he thought he ought to call the police and report the strange family he had seen. In his haste, he dialed the wrong number. When there was no reply, he gave up.

At a bus stop outside Utah Valley State College, less than forty miles from Salt Lake City, Mitchell got involved in a heated argument with a recently returned LDS missionary who wanted to know why blonde hair was poking out from under his daughter's gray wig. Mitchell stormed off, but returned to get on the bus to Salt Lake City.

The three alighted in the suburb of Sandy around noon on March 12. They used the restrooms in a Walmart, then began walking toward the Salt Lake Temple, which was no more than twenty miles from Elizabeth's home. Carrying tarps and packs, they attracted attention. Almost simultaneously two couples in passing cars recognized Mitchell as the man they had seen on *America's Most Wanted*. They dialed 911.

Within two minutes of the call from her dispatcher, Officer Karen Jones pulled up beside the three in a patrol car. She got out and asked who they were. Mitchell repeated the regular story that they were Peter and Juliette Marshall and Elizabeth was their daughter Augustine. When asked for identification, Mitchell said they had none, and no possessions, as they were the messengers of God. Jones then addressed Elizabeth directly. She confirmed that the girl was the couple's daughter, Augustine Ann Marshall.

A second patrol car arrived. Officer Troy Rasmussen got out. The first thing he said was, "That looks like Elizabeth Smart." Jones agreed.

Jones returned to her car and ran the names she had been given through the dispatcher. There were no matches. She came back to Mitchell and said: "You people don't exist."

Mitchell explained that there was no record of them because they traveled around a lot and had given all their worldly goods away. He was asking them if they accepted the Lord Jesus Christ as their savior when a third cop arrived. He recognized Elizabeth and Mitchell. He had watched *America's Most Wanted*. Nevertheless, Elizabeth stuck to her story.

More police officers turned up. Elizabeth was taken aside. She was asked again for her name. She said, "Augustine Marshall."

One of the detectives had been on the team investigating Smart's disappearance. He said that there was one way to find out if she was Elizabeth Smart. He phoned Ed Smart and asked him to come to Sandy Police Station. Now beginning to panic, Elizabeth blurted out: "You think I'm that girl who ran away, but I'm not."

The police then assured her that they had never stopped looking for her. Her parents would be anxious to see her and she was not in any trouble. They were there to protect her. But still she was afraid. For the past nine months and one week she had been repeatedly raped and abused. Mitchell and Barzee had made her sleep in the cold, starved her, stolen her privacy, dressed her in strange clothes, and covered her face. And all the time they had told her that she was evil, her family was evil, everything around her was evil, and they had used the scriptures to terrorize her.

An officer arrived with a missing person's flier, showing Elizabeth's picture. There was no mistaking her. Tears welled up in her eyes.

"Are you Elizabeth?" she was asked.

"If thou sayeth," was her whispered reply.

The police took this as a yes, handcuffed all three, and put them in separate police cars for the short drive to the Sandy Police Station. Elizabeth's father was already on his way.

When he arrived at the police station, Ed Smart recognized his daughter immediately, despite the radical change in her appearance. They hugged.

"Is it really you?" he asked.

"Yes, Dad," she replied.

That night, she returned to the same queen-size bed she had been taken from months before.

Brian Mitchell and Wanda Barzee were indicted by a Utah grand jury, but were found not mentally competent to stand trial. They were to be held until they were deemed fit. Barzee refused to take medication; a bill was passed through the Utah state legislature to allow forcible administration in such cases.

In October 2009, Barzee was found competent to stand trial and, on November 17, was sentenced to fifteen years in prison for her role in the kidnapping.

Hearings about Mitchell's mental competence continued. Those who examined him began to reach the conclusion that he was faking psychiatric illness and that he was a psychopath who could manipulate people into thinking he was incompetent. Finally on March 1, 2010, he was found fit to stand trial.

Nevertheless, at the federal trial on kidnapping charges that began on November 8, 2010, the defense argued that Mitchell was insane at the time he committed the offense. But his two stepdaughters testified that he had abused them before he called himself Emmanuel and claimed to be a prophet. On May 25, 2011, Mitchell was sentenced to life imprisonment.

Chapter 6

Sabine Dardenne, Laetitia Delhez, and the Belgian Pedophile Ring

BELGIAN SCHOOLGIRL SABINE DARDENNE was twelve years old when she was kidnapped on her way to school in Tournai. Her father saw her off that day. He watched her ride her brand new bicycle, a green Dunlop Viking, as far as the nearby motorway underpass. There, she gave a little wave and rode out of sight. The journey to school took between ten minutes and a quarter of an hour. Usually Sabine met her friend Davina along the way, and sometimes Davina's little brother would ride along with them.

But on May 28, 1996, there was no sign of Davina or her brother. It was possible that their mother had taken them to school in the car. Or Davina might have decided not to wait and to ride on ahead. Or she could have been simply running late. In any case, Sabine decided to head on alone that day.

She was riding past the high wall of the local football stadium when she heard the sound of a vehicle coming up behind her, so she pulled to the side. She was fifty yards beyond Davina's house, passing a house with a high hedge, when a rusty old camper van pulled up beside her. The side door slid open. A man leaned out, plucked Sabine from her bike, and threw her in the back. It was all over in a split second. Apparently, her kidnappers had been planning the snatch for weeks.

Sabine tried to fight her abductor off, but she was just four foot nine and weighed only sixty-eight pounds. She was small for her age, more like a ten-year-old than twelve, she said later. He was a full-grown man. He shoved some pills in her mouth and wrapped her up in a blanket. He told her to shut up and nothing would happen to her. But Sabine was a fighter. She had no intention of shutting up. Who were her attackers? She wanted to know. What were they doing? What about her bike? Didn't they realize that she was going to be late for school?

The van stopped. They collected her bike and the bag with her swimming things, which she had dropped, and threw them into the van. She seized the opportunity to spit out some pills, but she had already swallowed some of them and was beginning to feel drowsy.

Though the man in the back of the van threatened her, she kept on yelling. But as the van took off again, she began to cry. She was scared out of her wits.

From the floor in the back of the van, she could not see where they were going. From the sound of the wheels, she guessed they were heading down the motorway. She decided to pretend to be asleep, then try and overhear what they were saying. The guy in the back of the van who had grabbed her was clearly in charge. He had a mustache, greasy hair, and "horrible" eyes. The driver, whom he ordered around, was just "a loser," according to Sabine.

Her captors were Flemish speakers from the north part of the country. She did not recognize an accent and could not tell exactly where they were from.

When the van stopped, they put her in a trunk. It was so small they had to bend her double. After a couple of minutes, the trunk was opened again and she found herself in a room with the man with the mustache. The blinds were drawn. In the corner was a cot and some toys. There was a microwave oven and a frying pan, and cupboards and shelves filled with all manner of things. On the back wall, there was a half-completed fireplace. The floor was littered with bricks and cement. In the middle of this mess was a table and chairs. Sabine noticed a telephone on top of a fridge, but it was too high for her to reach. Next to it was a staircase. Another door had planks nailed across it. She never discovered what went on in the room beyond.

Her kidnapper took her upstairs. He told her to undress and get into one of the bunk beds. Once she was naked, he put a chain around her neck. It was just long enough for her to reach a chamber pot. He left her there overnight.

The following day, he returned and told her that he had saved her life. His boss had wanted to kill her. Instead, he had persuaded him to demand a ransom from her parents for her safe return. The day after that, he brought in the driver, who repeated this story. Apparently, the boss wanted to get revenge on Sabine's father, who had been in the police force. The boss was now asking for either $1 million or $3 million francs for her return. Sabine figured that, by borrowing from everyone they knew, her parents might be able to raise $1 million. But even if they sold their house and everything else, $3 million was out of the question. It was clear that if the kidnappers did not get the money, they intended to kill her.

In the meantime, they took Polaroid pictures of her naked in her chains. In another bedroom, there was a double bed. The man with the mustache took her in there and sexually abused her. She could not stop crying, which annoyed him. He seemed to think that she should have enjoyed it. She said that he did not beat her or rape her, but the things he did to her were so disgusting that she did not want to think about it.

She complained about being naked all the time. Eventually, he gave her back her underwear, and then, some time later, her jeans, which she could wear when she went downstairs to eat. But regularly, she was taken up for more photo sessions and "other things," which she called his "circus."

Then she was told that her parents had refused to pay the ransom. The police would not come up with the money either. She was in grave danger.

The monster who had kidnapped her and done disgusting things to her now cast himself in the role of her savior. He said he had kidnapped her because his boss had ordered him to. As no money had been forthcoming, his boss again wanted to kill her. The house, he said, was the headquarters of the boss's gang. The boss might come at any time. However, there was a secret hidey-hole where he could keep her safe.

He took her downstairs. Behind the shelving, there was a large concrete door. With the shelving in place, it was completely invisible. Her captor was really proud of his handy work. Behind the door were stairs that led down to the cellar, which was full of junk. To one side, there was a metal grate. Beyond it was a bed made from wooden slats with a filthy mattress on it that was falling apart.

The cellar was only three feet wide and nine feet long, and was lit by two light bulbs. It was dirty and was so dank that Sabine feared that she might suffocate down there, until he showed her the ventilation system he had made out of the fan from an old computer.

At the bottom of the bed, there was just enough room to put her school bag and a chamber pot. To one side was a bench and a table. On the other side there was a plank that served as a shelf, which she put her crayons and glasses on. High up, there was another shelf. On it was an old TV set connected to a Sega game console. The walls had been freshly painted bright yellow. Sabine got the impression that her captor had made this hellhole just for her.

Once she was installed in the cellar, he brought her some bread, milk, and jerry cans full of water. These were emergency provisions, he said, in case he could not come to feed her for any reason. Sabine comforted herself with the idea that she was not going to be hidden down their forever. Her parents would work something out. She was also sure that the whole of Belgium was looking for her. In the meantime, she had her French homework to do, textbooks to read, paper and pens so she could write, and a video game to play.

Indeed, the whole of Belgium was looking for her. Police helicopters were roaming the skies above the area where she had been taken. Posters with her picture and description were plastered on walls across the country and abroad.

Other avenues were also explored. Had she perhaps run away because her parents were angry with her for failing her math exam? At one point, her father even came under suspicion. As hope faded, Sabine's name joined a list of other missing girls—eight-year-old Julie Lejeune and Melissa Russo who had disappeared in June 1995, and seventeen-year-old An Marchal and nineteen-year-old Eefje Lambrecks, who had gone missing together on August 23, 1995. Soon another name would be added to the list—Laetitia Delhez, aged fourteen and a half, who was to go missing on August 9, 1996.

At one point, Sabine asked her captor what his name was. He said she could call him Alain or Marc, whichever she chose. She said that she would prefer it if he remained anonymous. The truth was his name was Marc Dutroux and he was a dangerous pedophile. Born in Ixelles, Belgium, on November 6, 1956, Dutroux was the oldest of five children. His parents, both teachers, emigrated to the Belgian Congo, but returned to Belgium when Dutroux was four. When they separated in 1971, Dutroux stayed with his mother. He married at the age of nineteen and fathered two children. The marriage ended in divorce in 1983; by then he was having an affair with Michelle Martin. In 1986, Dutroux and Martin were arrested for the abduction and rape of five young girls. Dutroux was sentenced to thirteen years, and Martin got five. They married while in prison in 1989 and would eventually have three children together, as Dutroux was released for good behavior after just three years.

Dutroux was an electrician by trade, but in the mid-1990s he was unemployed and living on welfare in the city of Charleroi, known at the time for its high unemployment. He supplemented his income with mugging people, dealing drugs, and stealing cars that were smuggled into eastern Europe and sold in Slovakia, Poland, and Hungary. But his most lucrative sideline was in the sex trade. He made and sold pornography, and sold young girls into prostitution across Europe. By 1996, he owned seven houses in Belgium. Most of them stood vacant and were the perfect hiding places for the girls he kidnapped who were then used in pornographic videos or sold as prostitutes.

The police knew of his activities. In 1993, an informant reported that Dutroux had offered him between $3,000 and $5,000 to kidnap young girls. In 1995, the same man told the police that Dutroux was building a dungeon where he intended to keep girls whom he would later sell into prostitution. That year, Dutroux's own mother wrote to prosecutors telling them that her son had been keeping young girls in one of his empty houses. But no one did anything about it.

Sabine was the latest in a line of girls that had passed through Dutroux's hands. While he held her captive in his cellar, Dutroux worked on Sabine psychologically. He told her that her parents would not pay the ransom. They did not care. Then he told her that they probably thought she was dead and had packed all her things up in cardboard boxes. The police had given up looking, he said. His boss, if he found her, would kill her. Sabine, Dutroux said, only had him to depend on—if she wanted to live.

Sabine had to obey strict rules. She was not to cry out or make any other noise. Otherwise, his boss, who was often in the house, would come and kill her. She should occupy herself with her schoolbooks and the Sega game. When he came to get her to take her upstairs to get something to eat or do "other things," he would say, "It's me" before he opened the door. If anyone else came, she should lie perfectly still and keep absolutely quiet.

Not only was Sabine terrified that the mysterious boss would come and kill her, she was also afraid that Dutroux would grow tired of her and dispose of her himself. So she had to do anything he wanted, just to stay alive. If that was not bad enough, Dutroux would describe the tortures that his boss used on those he intended to kill.

Her life became a circle of hell. When she was let out of the cellar, she would be taken upstairs to be given something to eat. Dutroux would have prepared this himself, and it was usually inedible. Then she would be taken to the bedroom where she would have to do whatever he wanted, no matter how disgusting it was to her. After that, she was returned into the cellar. She did not know which was worse: suffocating in the cellar or being forced to watch fuzzy pornographic films on a satellite channel while he did terrible things to her.

Even the ordinary things in life became almost unendurable. When she asked if she could bathe, he decided that he must wash her himself. They would take a bath together. To remain even passably clean, she had to undergo this hideous ordeal. He would scrub her so hard that she would come out of the bathroom covered in red sores.

Naturally, she kept an eye out for ways to escape. While she was upstairs eating, she noticed that he sometimes left a key in the lock, but he always kept himself between her and the front door. If she had reached the door, it would not have made any difference, he realized. She did not know where she was, and he would have grabbed her as soon as she got outside.

Occasionally, the doorbell would ring. He would go out for a second or two, then return, saying that it was one of the gang. Stories about the gang and his boss began to bore her.

Sabine also kept up a psychological battle against Dutroux. As well as asking when she could go home and see her parents again, she asked him for the things she needed for everyday life—better food, a pillow for her bed, clean clothes, paper to draw on, a toothbrush. This made him angry. She could tell that he did not use a toothbrush himself. It also annoyed him when she refused to drink curdled milk or eat moldy bread. It was as if it was her fault they had gone bad. In the end, though, she had to take what she was given—she would be forced to eat rancid hamburger while he feasted on steak.

She asked to be allowed to call her parents, only to be told that the line had to be kept open in case they called to agree to the ransom demand. It did not make sense, as he had already said they had refused to pay. Then he told her that the phone on top of the fridge was the hotline to the boss. If she tried to use it, she would get through to the boss, and she knew where that would lead. The boss, he said, was richer and more powerful than the prime minister

To hold herself together, Sabine began to think of Dutroux as an idiot who was prey to a thousand tricks. It was her job to run rings round him. She badgered him until he bought her a clock radio. At least she could hear some music, though she could not tune in to a news channel and remained cut off from the outside world. The numbers on the clock also provided her with a diversion. She would associate each number with something from her everyday life—her father's age, her mother's birthday, the address of her grandmother's house. Next she began working on him to get her a new mattress. The one she had was falling apart, and there were insects inside it. Some of them flew around. Sabine was afraid of insects, but she did not like squashing them. Her body was covered with bites. Eventually, he sprayed the cellar with insecticide.

As there was no one else to talk to in the cellar, she began talking to herself. This helped keep her spirits up. She kept up her schoolwork, especially math. When she failed her math exam, it was a great disappointment to her parents. In idle moments, she thought about her dog, Sam, and her goldfish, Tifi.

She used an exercise book as a diary to record the terrible things that she had to undergo. She also wrote a letter to her parents, describing her situation. Dutroux said that a friend of his would take it to her mother. In response, he said, her mother told her to eat properly, wash, and enjoy the sex. As they could not afford to pay the ransom, she was going to have to stay there, so she should make the best of it and be Dutroux's new girlfriend. Sabine could not really believe that her mother had said any of those things, but there was no way for her to know whether or not the letter had been delivered. So she wrote to her parents again saying that she accepted her prison, despite the squalor and abuse. She also that they must have done something really bad for her to be punished this way. But how was she to enjoy the revolting things he did not her? It did not make sense.

On June 21, Dutroux announced that he was going on a "mission." This was good news, as she would be spared doing "other things." On the other hand, she would have to stay locked in the cellar. She could not stand the dark, so she left the light on all the time. And he left her with extra provisions— canned tomatoes and meatballs (she should drink the juice), moldy bread, and cookies.

When Dutroux returned, he began a new routine. Instead of leaving her in the cellar at night, he chained her to his bed and forced her to sleep next to him. But she did not dare go to sleep for fear he would start doing things to her while she was unconscious. Although she was not strong enough to fight him off, putting up some sort of fight helped her self-esteem. She spent the nights staring at the ceiling, thinking of ways that she could kill him or at least drive him over the edge.

To annoy him, she whined about everything: not being able to call her parents, her chain not being long enough, not having a *TV Guide*. Other times, she would curse, call him an asshole or a shit, or tell him what he was doing to her was not normal. It made no difference. He merely dismissed her complaints and "sniveling." Eventually, she realized that he liked to see her cry, so she resolved to give that up. This was difficult. As a late developer, her twelve-year molars were just coming in, and she suffered from a constant toothache. She had to keep quiet about this, however. The first time she had mentioned it, he offered to pull them out himself.

From a sideways peek at the mail, she discovered his name and the address of the house where she was being held. She was in Marcinelle, a suburb of Charteroi, fifty miles from her home in Tournai. She also noticed that one of the old magazines he lent her had a cell number on it, and she asked him if he had ever been to prison. He admitted that he had, for a long time. But he boasted that the law now meant nothing to him. He could do what he liked. He was clever enough to cover his tracks and, this time, the cops did not have a hope in hell of catching him.

As one of her small acts of rebellion, she began to look through the junk in the cellar that she had been told not to touch. In an old shoe box, she found pictures of a naked girl. It was her.

Although she hated having him around, things were even worse when he went away. She suffered from claustrophobia in the cellar. It was always either too hot or too cold. Down there, she could not wash, clean her teeth, or empty her chamber pot. He would go away for as long as six days at a time, and it was impossible to get away from the stench.

It was ingrained in her to keep perfectly quiet while he was away. But once the power went off and the ventilation fan stopped. She feared that she was going to suffocate and started screaming as loudly as she could. It made no difference. No one came. Eventually, the electricity came back on again.

However, screaming out loud had stirred up her will to fight. She braced herself against the wall and pushed at the concrete door. To her surprise, she managed to move the door, at first by just an inch. After taking a breath and a sip of water, she pushed again. This time there was a crash and the mechanism jammed. Now she could not open the door any farther; nor could she close it. She feared that, when Dutroux saw what she had done, he would kill her. She knew he had a gun. He had shown it to her. But when he came back, he merely cursed her for being so stupid. The boss could have come and seen the entrance to the hidey-hole. He would have come in and gotten her, then tortured her and killed her. Dutroux's eyes bulged with anger as he said this. But to Sabine's surprise, he did not hit her. He fixed the door, and she never tried to shift it again.

As well as being his sex slave, Sabine was also expected to be Dutroux's servant. She had to get him his coffee, though she was not allowed any herself. While she had to clean the house, she was not allowed to clean the filthy cellar where she lived. There was no washing machine in the house, so her clothes grew filthy. When she got the chance, she would wash out her panties in the bathroom.

She wrote more letters detailing the terrible things that she had to endure at Dutroux's hands. They were never sent, of course.

As time went on, the sexual abuse got worse. Dutroux finally raped Sabine and showed no sympathy for the physical suffering he put her through, let alone the mental anguish. In her letters to her mother, Sabine pleaded with her to let her come home. Whatever she had done to deserve this punishment, she said, she would not do it again. From now on, she promised, she would be the perfect child.

The rape had left her hemorrhaging badly and in terrible pain. She was afraid that she was going to die from loss of blood, alone in her underground prison, and began to wish that he would finish her off with a bullet in the head. She put all her hope in her letters, while knowing in her heart of hearts that they were not being delivered.

She produced one letter in the form of a questionnaire with the answers "yes" or "no" to be circled. It was returned duly filled in. Dutroux made some attempt to reply, though the handwriting was clearly his, not her mother's. In the answers to more general questions, he even made simple grammatical errors that her mother would never have made.

As her captivity dragged on, Sabine became consumed with despair. She had finished reading all her books and was fed up with the Sega. There was no one to talk to. She could hardly have a conversation with Dutroux, whose stock replies were "shut up" and "stop sniveling." It was summertime and she wanted to go out in the sunshine. He shoved two chairs together and told her she should sunbathe—naked, of course—right there in the front room.

She kept bugging him to let her see her friends. This had unintended and tragic consequences. One day, as he was leaving, he said he was going to bring her a friend. Two days later, he announced that her friend was there. She would see her later. Sabine could hardly believe her ears.

First, she had to endure another "sunbathing" session. Then she was taken upstairs where she found another girl naked and chained to the bunk as she had been when she first arrived. The new girl asked Sabine how long she had been there. Sabine replied seventy-seven days.

Sabine was now in mental turmoil. She had asked Dutroux for a friend, and he had brought her one. He was now going to put this girl through what she had been through and she felt that, partly, it was her fault. On the other hand, there would be someone to talk to. Dutroux even promised to clear out the cellar so there would be more room and said he would get plumbing for a bathtub.

The new girl was fourteen-year-old Laetitia Delhez. Dutroux tried to get her to walk around naked, but she kept putting her clothes back on and he gave up. Soon she joined Sabine down in the cellar. She brought important news. She had seen Sabine's picture on posters that had been pasted up all over the country. Her parents were going crazy trying to find her. Sabine could hardly believe this. Why hadn't they paid the ransom? It suddenly became clear to Sabine that everything Dutroux had told her was a lie.

Laetitia had been snatched in Bertrix on the French border. She had been walking home from the swimming pool when an old van pulled up alongside her. Dutroux had grabbed her and bundled her though the side door in the same way Sabine had been taken. From Laetitia's description, it seemed that the driver was the same man Sabine had seen.

She had also been force-fed pills. As Sabine explained what life was like in the cellar, Laetitia kept dozing off due to the effects of the drugs. With the two of them in the cellar, the air became more fetid than ever. It even came as a relief when Dutroux came to take Laetitia upstairs, though Sabine knew what he was going to do with her.

Laetitia was two years older than Sabine. She had already had her first period, so Dutroux forced her to take contraceptive pills—though they were past their expiration date. After the first time Laetitia was raped and abused, Dutroux suddenly stopped coming to get her. A couple of days passed and they figured that he must be on a "mission," though he had not provided them with extra provisions first.

In fact, on August 13, 1996, Dutroux, his wife, and the driver Michel Lelièvre had been arrested. There had been a witness to the abduction of Laetitia Delhez who noted down part of the license plate number, which matched the one on a van registered to Dutroux. The house was searched by an officer of the child protection squad, but he found nothing. He later was later criticized for this, but Sabine said that he could hardly be blamed as the secret dungeon in the cellar was masterfully concealed.

Two days later, Laetitia and Sabine heard a noise upstairs. They feared that the boss and his gang had come to kill them. They hid themselves under the blanket. Then they heard footsteps and men's voices. Things were being removed from the shelves upstairs, and they could hear bricks being chipped from the walls. The two girls were terrified.

Then they heard Dutroux's voice saying, "It's me," as usual. But there were other men with him. Fearing the worst, Sabine said that she was not coming out. Laetitia then recognized one of the men who had come into the cellar. He was a policeman from Bertrix. Sabine was still hesitant. She turned to Dutroux and asked if she could leave. She even asked whether she could take the colored pencils he had bought for her with her. He said she could. As they left, both Sabine and Laetitia gave Dutroux a kiss on the cheek.

Sabine then flung herself onto the nearest policemen and did not want to let him go. Laetitia did the same with the policeman from Bertrix. Then after eighty days in the cellar, Sabine was taken out into the sunshine and fresh air. It was only at the police station that Sabine discovered they had given up any hope of finding her alive. It was Laetitia the police were looking for when they visited Dutroux's house.

The two girls' parents arrived to take them home. When Sabine arrived back in Tournai, she saw a huge banner saying, "WELCOME." The streets were full of neighbors, all there to welcome her home, along with a throng of journalists covering the story.

Sabine then learned that thousands of people had been out looking for her. They had dredged the river and scoured the countryside. The ongoing search had been coordinated by the center that had originally been set up to look for eight-year-old Julie Lejeune and Melissa Russo, then An Marchal and Eefje Lambrecks.

Delighted to be back in her own home, Sabine had conflicting feelings. Her parents had not packed her things away the way Dutroux had told her. On the other hand, there were new things around the house that they had bought while she was in her dungeon. Life had gone on without her. She was still sad because of the terrible things that had happened to her, but everyone in the streets was celebrating. The newspapers the next day were full of Sabine and Laetitia's release. It was only when she read them that Sabine realized the extent of the efforts that had been made to find her. She felt ashamed that she had doubted her parents.

Two days later, the bodies of Julie Lejeune and Melissa Russo were found buried in the garden of a house Dutroux owned in Sars-La-Buissiere. After being raped repeatedly, the two girls had starved to death when Dutroux was sent to prison for car theft from December 6, 1995, till March 20, 1996. Sabine realized how close both she and Laetitia had come to the same fate. Dutroux refused to admit responsibility for the deaths of Julie and Melissa, saying that he had left his accomplice Bern Weinstein instructions to feed them. He also said that Weinstein had also kidnapped the two girls, admittedly on a commission from Dutroux. However, Dutroux did admit that, annoyed at Weinstein's failure to feed the two girls, he had given him barbiturates and buried him alive alongside Julie and Melissa in Sars-La-Buissiere. In due course, his body was found.

Sabine was interviewed again by the police. She was determined to tell every tiny detail of what had happened to her so that Dutroux would be held to account. During her interviews, she discovered that, after Dutroux and his accomplices were arrested, the driver Michel Lelièvre had admitted being a party to the kidnapping of Laetitia Delhez. The police told Dutroux about Lelièvre's confession and made it clear that they were going to lock him up and throw away the key unless he began to cooperate. That was when Dutroux admitted he was holding two girls. The police were surprised. At the time, they were only looking for Laetitia. However, Dutroux said that he had Sabine as well and took the police to them.

It was difficult for Sabine to readjust to everyday life. She wanted everything to go back to how it had been before. That was impossible. Her parents were, understandably, overprotective. The neighbors got together and bought her a new bike, but her parents would not let her ride it to school.

Being back in school was good, though. Kids her own age seemed to understand better what she was going through. Her classmates did not ask a single question. They wanted to give

Sabine a party, but when she said she saw no cause for celebration, they instead gave her a "missing" poster, signed by the entire class.

When Dutroux's house was searched, the police found over three hundred pornographic videos featuring children. Six thousand hair samples taken from the dungeon were analyzed to determine whether or not Dutroux had kept other victims there. Meanwhile, Lelièvre admitted kidnapping An Marchal and Eefje Lambrecks, who had been on a camping trip to the Belgian port of Ostend. Their bodies were found under a shed next to another of Dutroux's houses, which had been occupied by Bernard Weinstein. At one time there had been four girls at that house in Marcinelle—Julie and Melissa in the dungeon and An and Eefje chained up upstairs. Eefje had made several escape attempts. Once, she managed to get out onto the roof, but Dutroux had caught her. Eventually, he found them so troublesome, he drugged them and buried them alive.

During the investigation, businessman Jean-Michel Nihoul was also arrested. He had organized an orgy at a Belgian chateau that was attended by police officers, several government officials, and a former European commissioner. His mistress Marleen De Cockere was charged with criminal conspiracy concerning Dutroux's activities. Seven other people were arrested in connection with the pedophile ring, and nine police officers in Charleroi were detained for questioning over possible negligence in the investigation.

There was a massive outcry about the whole affair in Belgium. The public demanded that parole conditions for convicted pedophiles be tightened. There was also a call for the reinstatement of the death penalty, which had been outlawed in Belgium just months before Sabine and Laetitia were found.

Community outrage boiled over when Jean-Marc Connerotte, the investigating judge in the case, was dismissed for having attended a fund-raising dinner to help the search for missing children. The Belgian Supreme Court decided that this might taint his objectivity in the Dutroux case. As a result, 300,000 people took to the streets of Brussels, dressed in white as a symbol of innocence. This was the largest demonstration in Belgium since World War II. Some believed that the government was involved in a cover-up, and strikes broke out across the country in protest. The prime minister promised to speed up reforms to the judicial system, and even the king of Belgium had to speak out on the Dutroux case.

A parliamentary committee investigating the matter published a report saying that were it not for failures in the investigation of the pedophile ring, the four murdered girls could have been saved. The committee called for a complete reorganization of the Belgian police force.

Meanwhile the police had made another mistake. Dutroux was allowed to travel to Neufchateau to consult files he would use in his forthcoming trial. While there, he knocked out one of his police guards, and then knocked another to the ground and took his gun. Then he stole a car and made a break for it with half of local law enforcement on his tail. Sabine heard helicopters circling above her school. Another pupil asked her if she was frightened when they heard that Dutroux had escaped. But Sabine was sanguine. She figured that Dutroux would have to be an idiot to come within a million miles of her.

As a precaution, police officers were sent to patrol the school corridors, and bodyguards were sent to her home, but by the time she got home after school Dutroux had already been captured. Taking refuge in the woods, he had given himself up to a forest warden. However, his escape forced the resignation of the state police chief, the minister of justice, and the minister of the interior.

After his escape attempt, Dutroux went on trial for assault and theft, and was sentenced to five years. But his trial in connection with Sabine and the other girls was delayed when a magazine in Luxembourg printed the names of fifty alleged pedophiles said to have come from the files of the Dutroux investigation.

Dutroux managed to stall things further by claiming that the Belgian state was violating his human rights. He went to court to demand that he be released from solitary confinement, undergo fewer body searches, and be allowed to sleep uninterrupted. This outraged the Belgian people again, considering what he had put his victims through. The state argued that Dutroux was given special treatment for his own protection.

Then an unauthorized interview was released by a Belgian TV channel. In it, Dutroux was heard admitting that he kept Julie, Melissa, An, and Eefje—in effect admitting his guilt. The authenticity and admissibility of this evidence then had to be examined. These issues meant that his trial for the substantive charges of murder and kidnapping was postponed repeatedly. It was more than seven years before the case came to court.

The trial eventually began on March 1, 2004. There were four defendants: Dutroux, his now ex-wife Michelle Martin,

Lelièvre, and Nihoul. By this time Dutroux was maintaining that he was merely a pawn in a pedophile ring masterminded by Nihoul. Dutroux claimed the girls he kidnapped were to be sold by Nihoul, who provided them to pedophiles. To muddy the waters further, Dutroux claimed that two police officers helped in the kidnapping of An Marchal and Eefje Lambrecks.

The investigating judge, Jacques Langlois, then alleged that it was Martin who had left Julie and Melissa to starve, not Weinstein. She had been afraid they would attack her if she went down into the cellar to feed them, although she claimed she had no idea how or why they had died.

Jean-Marc Connerotte then testified that Dutroux had constructed the dungeon and its ventilation system so well that it would have been difficult to detect the girls' presence even with sniffing dogs. He also testified that his investigation had been hampered by people in government. Contracts had been taken out against investigating magistrates. He needed armed guards and bulletproof vehicles to protect him from powerful individuals who did not want the truth to come out. And he blamed incompetence of the police in Charleroi for the deaths of Julie Lejeune and Melissa Russo.

The failure of the Belgian authorities was demonstrated again when a key to Dutroux's handcuffs was found in his cell, apparently having been smuggled in inside a bag of salt. Those running the prison were then accused of trying to organize his escape.

The final showdown came on April 19, 2004, when Sabine Dardenne, now aged twenty, took the stand. She told of the ordeal he had subjected her to, both physically and mentally, for eighty days. She rejected out of hand the apology he had given in court. When she met his stare, he was forced to lower his eyes.

On the second day of her testimony, Dutroux accused her of asking him to kidnap another victim so that she could have a friend. He also claimed that he had protected her from the pedophile ring.

"So, if I understand you, I should be thankful?" she countered.

Sabine's letters home were also submitted into evidence. One had been found under Dutroux's mattress. Although it had been addressed to Sabine's mother, Sabine had never let her read it, figuring that it would only increase her mother's suffering to know what her daughter had been through. Sabine had been grateful that the letter had been left there unopened, so Dutroux had not enjoyed any perverse pleasure from reading it.

The person who opened it was the investigating judge, and it provided important evidence in the prosecution of Dutroux and his accomplices. Sabine was glad that the letter was seen by the jury, even though parts of it were read aloud in court. It was important for people to know the depths of evil Dutroux was capable of.

Laetitia Delhez also testified. Then the two of them accompanied the court on a visit to the house and the dungeon where they had been held.

Back in the courtroom, Dutroux admitted to the kidnapping and rape charges, expressing his "sincere regret." But he denied committing murder, blaming Martin, Lelièvre, and Nihoul.

At the end of the three-month trial, the task for the jury was not an easy one. The eight women and four men were sent to a fortified army barracks in Arlon, where the judge asked them to evaluate 243 questions. They had to review around 400,000 pages of evidence, including the testimony of more than five hundred witnesses. It took three days for them to return with a verdict.

Dutroux was found guilty of kidnapping and raping all six girls, and murdering An Marchel, Eefje Lambrecks, and Bernard Weinstein. Lelièvre was found guilty of kidnapping, but acquitted of murder. Martin was convicted of kidnapping and rape. The jury could not agree on a verdict in Nihoul's case and were sent back to reevaluate the 243 questions. The evidence showed that he was involved in supplying prostitutes, but the court accepted that he had nothing to do with pedophilia. He was eventually acquitted of involvement in the abductions of the girls, but was convicted of human trafficking and drugs charges.

On June 22, 2004, Dutroux was sentenced to life and put at "the government's disposition." That means, if he was, by some oversight, paroled again in the future, the government could return him to prison. Lelièvre got twenty-five years; Martin got thirty; and Nihoul, five. But the question left unanswered was: Was there really a vast network of pedophiles at work in Belgium as Dutroux claimed?

Sabine Dardenne has said that she has never completely overcome the guilt she felt over Laetitia, who she believes was abducted because she asked for a friend. But her request was the innocent plea of a twelve-year-old; Laetitia does not blame her. Indeed, if Laetitia had not been kidnapped, Sabine would probably not have survived and Dutroux would have been free to abduct and abuse other girls.

Chapter 7

Natascha Kampusch—
The Girl in the Cellar

BORN IN VIENNA ON FEBRUARY 17, 1988, Natascha Kampusch was raised by her mother, whose second marriage broke up soon after Natascha was born. The girl did not lose touch with her father and she had a relatively stable childhood, though she was a persistent bed wetter. Looking back, she recalled a general atmosphere of disquiet. She heard stories of child pornography rings and serial killers at large in Austria and neighboring Germany.

"To my recollection, hardly a month went by during my primary school years that the media didn't report yet another abducted, raped, or murdered girl," she said.

At school, teachers warned their pupils about the dangers. They were shown films in which girls were molested by their older brothers or boys were abused by their fathers. The world was not safe and people were not to be trusted. Both at school and at home, the message was clear—never accept sweets from a stranger, never get into a car with a stranger.

In her book *3,096 Days*, Natascha Kampusch listed thirteen incidents that she heard about where young girls were molested or killed in those years. She watched the news reports and even heard a psychologist advise victims not to resist their attackers and risk being killed. Natascha comforted herself that she was not the fragile blonde that child molesters seemed to prefer.

When she was ten, she spent the weekend with her father in a vacation house he had bought just over the border in Hungary. He brought Natascha home to her mother's apartment late and allowed her to cross the dark courtyard in front of her home on her own. Once inside the apartment, Natascha found that her mother had gone to the movies, so the child went to wait in a neighbor's apartment. When her mother came to get her, she was furious and said that Natascha was not to see her father again. This upset the girl. Fed up with her parents' arguments, Natascha couldn't wait to turn eighteen, so she could be self-reliant and move out. She already relished her independence, having recently persuaded her mother to allow her to walk to school on her own. Not that she wasn't afraid, but she wanted to prove to herself and her mother that she was no longer a little child.

On her first day of going to school on her own, her courage deserted her and she began to cry. Nevertheless, she continued on her way. In a quiet back street, she saw a slim young man standing by a white delivery van. Immediately, the hairs stood up on the back of her neck. All the rapes and murders she had seen on TV came flooding back. As she neared him, he looked her straight in the eye and her fear vanished. His blue eyes were strangely empty, as if he needed protection. But it was Natascha that needed to be protected. As she walked past him, he grabbed her by the waist and threw her into the van.

Later, she could not remember whether she had screamed. All she could remember was one of those silent screams you have in dreams where you open your mouth and nothing comes out. She cannot remember fighting back either. But she must have. The following day, she had a black eye and thought that she must have been stunned by a blow. She also remembered thinking that this could not really be happening to her.

Her captor was Wolfgang Priklopil, a thirty-six-year-old communications technician who still lived with his mother. He ordered her to sit down on the floor in the back of the van and not move. Otherwise, he said, she would be in for a nasty surprise.

Natascha thought at first that she was being kidnapped for ransom and wondered who was going to pay it. Neither of her parents had money. Then she thought that it would be a good idea to strike up a conversation with her abductor. She decided to use the *du* form of address, one used with family and friends, and the first thing she asked him was his shoe size. She remembered that on *Aktenzeichen XY ungelöst*, a German-language TV program similar to *America's Most Wanted*, the importance of an exact description of the criminal was always stressed. Priklopil told her to shut up.

By that point, Natascha was convinced that she was going to die and felt she had nothing to lose, so she asked him whether he was going to molest her. He said he would never do that; she was too young. But then he said he was going to take her out to the forest where he was going to hand her over to the other men who wanted her. Then he would never see her again. This was much scarier. She concluded that she had fallen into the hands of a pedophile ring who were going to do unspeakable things to her and she fell silent.

Priklopil repeatedly tried to make calls from his cell phone, but got no reply. They came to a halt in a pine forest outside Vienna, where he tried to make another call. Then he cursed. The men he expected to meet were not there and would not be coming.

She wondered whether he had locked the door, but she knew that she could not run very fast. If she tried to escape, he would catch her and might kill her.

After a while, he drove back toward the Gänserndorf where her grandmother lived and where, until recently, her mother had a shop. Natascha asked him where they were going. He said Strasshof, a small town nearby. Eventually, they came to a halt in a garage. Priklopil wrapped Natascha in a blanket and carried her into the adjoining house. She asked him to let her go to the toilet. He stopped and ushered her into a guest bathroom.

On the way, she took the opportunity to peer into another room. It seemed to be well-appointed. This made sense. The criminals' houses she had seen on the TV were large and expensive.

The lock on the bathroom door was insubstantial and afforded no protection, so she could not stay in the bathroom. When she emerged, he wrapped her in the blanket again and carried her downstairs, where he lay her on the floor and left her. When he returned, he screwed a light bulb into a fixture in the wall. She could now see a pallet bed, fixed to a wall by hooks, a stainless steel sink, and a toilet without a lid. The small room had walls covered with oak paneling. It reminded her of a sauna, the sort of place a pedophile would lure young victims to molest them, she thought. In fact, this small dungeon had been built as an air-raid shelter by Priklopil's father and grandfather during the Cold War.

Natascha remained remarkably composed. She begged him to release her, saying she would say nothing. If he did not keep her overnight, she said, nothing would happen to him. She would say that she had run away. She appealed to both his sympathy and his reason. It did no good. He began making up the bed, and it became clear that he was going to keep her overnight. But the panic she had felt earlier had subsided. There was nothing to be done but to accept the situation and make herself at home.

He asked her whether there was anything she needed. She reeled off a list—a toothbrush, toothpaste, cup, hair bush. He then explained that he was going to have to go to Vienna to get a mattress from his apartment and he left her locked in the cellar.

She thought of the lessons she was missing at school, and her parents. But she would not let herself cry. After all, the ordeal would be over the next day she told herself. Her parents would remember how much they missed her and loved her, and they would be nicer to her in the future. And her school friends would think she was a hero. But first she was going to have to escape by overpowering her captor or killing him.

Priklopil returned with the mattress and all the things she had asked for. He also brought some of her favorite chocolate cookies. He then searched her school bag in case, he said, there was a radio transmitter hidden in there. He said that she was trying to trick him by playing innocent. She was cleverer than she made out. Natascha found this confusing. One minute he was doing everything to make her feel comfortable; the next he was treating her as an enemy.

Whenever he left her, she felt that the small room was closing in on her. So when he returned, she asked him to read a bedtime story and give her a kiss good-night. She wanted to make everything seem as normal as possible. He did what she asked, but when he left, the illusion was shattered.

When he returned the next morning she listened carefully while he unlocked the door. It took some time, so she figured that it was not going to be easy to escape. She then bombarded him with questions. Why was he keeping her there? What was he going to do with her? How long did he intend to keep her? Then she tried to threaten him. The police were looking for her, she said. If he did not let her go, he would go to jail. He was unresponsive, though he said he would let her go soon.

Left alone again, she studied her cell and found that not a single chink of light entered the room from outside. Nor was there any sound except for the fan that ventilated the cellar that kept whirring twenty-four hours a day. She tried hammering a water bottle against the wall. No one came. The light was on twenty-four hours a day too. This was unbearable but, she figured, it was better than the total darkness that came when he unscrewed the bulb.

She began pacing her cell. It was six paces long and four paces wide—eight-foot-ten by seven-foot-ten. It was also about seven feet ten inches high and contained some four hundred cubic feet of musty air. Soon, she was in total despair.

When Natascha did not come home from school, her mother called the police. They searched the area with dogs and helicopters, but the search yielded no clues and was called off after three days. Posters of the missing girl were put up in schools, and reports of sightings flooded in. Only one pointed in the right direction. A twelve-year-old girl said she had seen Natascha being pulled into a white van. The police did not take her seriously. One man even demanded a ransom of $1 million Austrian shillings; he was the first of many con artists.

Natascha was anguished over what she knew her mother was going through. She tried to think of ways she could communicate to tell her that she was still alive. It was impossible. Every moment she thought that someone might burst in and rescue her. Then hope faded as she realized that Priklopil had been planning her imprisonment for some time.

Indeed, that was the case. Although the cell itself had been built some time earlier, Priklopil had recently sought advice on soundproofing from his colleague Ernst Holzapfel. However, what puzzled Natascha was that Priklopil did not act like a man whose wish to kidnap a child had suddenly been fulfilled, but rather, like a distant relative who had suddenly had a child thrust upon him.

In some ways, he was quite a caring individual. He made her open her mouth to check that she had cleaned her teeth properly and cut her finger nails for her. Chewing gum was banned in case she choked on it. Oranges were peeled and fed to her segment by segment. But Natascha objected to being treated like a small child. On the other hand, he did bring her the foodstuffs she requested. Eventually, he brought her a hot plate and a small electric oven, along with canned food, so she could cook for herself.

Natascha heard that to avoid being raped by Russian soldiers at the end of World War II, Austrian woman stuck thin slices of lemon peel to their skin to make it look like they had some terrible disease. She tried this and begged Priklopil to take her to the doctor. He was not fooled and pulled the lemon rind off. As a punishment, he turned the light off.

She found the loneliness of being in the cellar unbearable, so would do anything to keep him in there with her. They played games together—Nine Men's Morris, Chinese checkers, Parcheesi. Priklopil then brought her a computer— a Commodore 64—with games on it. However, he muttered darkly about other men who would come and photograph her and do "other things" to her. This made it difficult for her to sleep at night. She did not want to be caught unawares. What would they do to her? Would they do it to her there? Or would they take her elsewhere?

He gave her fresh clothing and burned the shoes her mother had given her for her birthday. The sweaters he gave her were left over from his military conscription. They kept her warm, but she always liked to wear at least one item of clothing of her own. It was cold in the cellar, so he brought her an electric heater. He also gave her a chaise longue and returned her school things to her, after burning the school bag.

She tried to get him to send a letter to her parents. They had to know that she was alive, she said. It was loaded with clues as to where she might be. He refused, but she persisted and he finally give in—or said he did. The following day, he appeared with an injured finger. The letter had been grabbed out of his hand. The people that had ordered him to kidnap her would not allow him to send it.

He let her record a message for her mother that he promised to play over the phone for her on her birthday. In the end, he did not do that. Instead he changed his story. He now told Natascha that she had been kidnapped for ransom but her parents would not pay up. They did not love her and did not want her back.

Natascha did not really believe this and set about collecting any evidence she could concerning her kidnapping. She asked her kidnapper his age. He even told her his name, then thought better of it and gave the name of his best friend instead.

She wanted to know why he had singled her out. Once he said that he had seen her school picture. Usually he maintained that she had come to him like a stray cat. You were allowed to keep strays, he said. Only toward the end of her captivity did he say that he wanted her as a slave.

Natascha Kampusch said that she learned to adapt herself to her kidnapper in a way she would not have been able to do as an adult. She is proud that she could do this. As a child, she was still used to being told what to do. This, she believed, saved her life.

After a few weeks, Priklopil brought a table and chairs down into the cellar so that they could eat together. Natascha encouraged this. Anything was preferable to hours of loneliness.

The plumbing was primitive, but Priklopil would bring warm water down so that Natascha could bathe. She would have to undress and he would wash her down. She was a little embarrassed at being naked in front of him, but she said he was neither tender nor salacious. Rather he washed her as if she was a car or a household appliance.

After a month, in the absence of any other lead, the police began to take more seriously the story given by the twelve-year-old girl who had seen Natascha being bundled into a white van, and announced that they would be checking up on the seven hundred owners of white vans in the vicinity. When they came to interview Priklopil, he said that he had been at home the whole day on the day that Natascha had gone missing. He could produce no witness to this; nevertheless, the police accepted his story and they left without examining the car or searching the house. Priklopil was so confident that they would not find his secret cellar that he invited the police to look. They declined the offer and apologized for inconveniencing him.

Two days later, an anonymous witness reported that a white van of the type the police were seeking was seen parked outside Heinestrasse 60 in Strasshof, Priklopil's home. The owner, the caller said, was a "loner" who lived there with his elderly mother. He was also thought to have a sexual penchant for children. The caller gave a good description of Priklopil.

In Vienna, other witnesses said that, on the morning Natascha went missing, they had seen a white van with Gänserndorf license plates in the area. Strasshof was in the Gänserndorf administrative district. Even this lead did not spur the police into action.

While the police investigation was going nowhere, Priklopil told Natascha again that his hopes of getting a ransom from her had been dashed. Her parents had said that they did not want her back. But he could not let her go because she had seen his face, so she would have to stay with him forever. She began to reconcile herself to the situation. One of the first books Natascha read while being held captive in the cellar was *Alice's Adventures in Wonderland*. There were disturbing parallels. She too was underground in a world that did not make any sense.

She tried to turn the prison he had made into her own space and asked for a clock and a calendar. This, she figured, would help her retain some connection with what was happening in the world outside. It was no good relying on him to tell her what day it was. He could be lying. He also switched the light on and off when he felt like it. Without a clock, she could not tell whether this corresponded to day and night. She asked specifically for a clock with a loud tick like one her grandmother had. The regular ticking of a clock, she thought, would be a comfort.

She also asked for cleaning products, so she could keep the place spick-and-span. She particularly liked those scented with lavender, so she could imagine being outdoors. To overcome her feeling of powerlessness, she began drawing. That way she could indulge her own fantasies, rather than merely be a victim of Priklopil's.

After a while, he brought her a television set with a video player and cassettes of programs he had recorded. Some of these were news programs, but he edited out reports concerning her disappearance in an attempt to maintain the fiction that no one was looking for her. Later he brought her a radio, but had fixed it so that it only received Czech stations. That meant she could listen to music, but she could not understand what anyone was saying. He brought her a Walkman, but only provided a few cassettes so she had to listen to the same songs over and over. It was only after two years, when he figured that any search for her was over, that he bought her a regular radio so she could listen to Austrian stations.

The radio and TV were a comfort, but the thing that worked best to fill the long hours of loneliness was reading. Priklopil brought her children's classics, comic books, and crime novels. As she became dependent on books and tapes, he could restrict them when he wanted to punish her for minor infractions, such as using too much air freshener or singing. Otherwise, he could restrict his visits. Normally he would come to the cellar once in the morning and again in the evening. But he also might arrive on a Thursday with an armful of ready meals, then disappear until Sunday evening. He put the lights on a timer. But Natascha had to live with the fact that, if there were fire, a burst pipe, if she had choked on a sausage skin or something happened to him so he could not return with food, she would die there underground, all alone.

Eventually, she got him to install an intercom. If she wanted something, she would press a button and a light would go on upstairs. Not that this necessarily brought him running—especially on weekends when his mother visited, as she found out later. Later he added a speaker system. He used it to order her around. He would tell her when to brush her teeth, turn the TV off, read her book, do her math assignment, eat her food— sometimes specifying how much or how little she should eat. However, Natascha soon discovered that one of the buttons cut out his voice. Once he realized that she was not listening, it would take him up to an hour to open all the doors to get to her, so she could have, for that period, a little peace. However, he replaced the intercom with a new two-way system that she could not turn off, allowing him to eavesdrop on her twenty-four hours a day. It was so loud when he talked, it was torture. And, if she could not convince him that she was doing exactly what she was told, he would come and take away her prized possessions. She even began to fear that he had installed hidden cameras to watch her every move, perhaps even infrared ones so that he could watch her in the dark. Just in case there were peepholes hidden behind, she filled every crack in the wood paneling with toothpaste.

While studies show that people in solitary confinement deteriorate mentally very quickly, Natascha managed to hold on to her faculties. On the first Mother's Day, she made her mother a present using just paper and crayons, because scissors and glue were not allowed. Despite what Priklopil said, Natascha knew her parents still loved her.

As time passed, his demands became more stringent. She was not to speak unless spoken to. She was not to look him in the face. She was to do exactly what she was told. Even her demeanor was to be totally submissive. He also told her that she was to be grateful that he had "saved her"—she could not manage this. The only thing she found she could be grateful for was that he had neither raped nor killed her. He then ordered her to address him as "master." She refused. He continued to insist but found he could not make her and, eventually, he dropped the matter.

She then realized that, though he had absolute power over her, he was in fact a weak man and she told him that she forgave him as "everyone makes mistakes sometimes." He appeared contrite; he said he would give her anything she wanted, except her freedom. She said what she wanted most of all was a hug. He plainly had problems with physical closeness and it took her a little time to train him to hold her not too loosely and not too tight.

After six months' captivity, Natascha grew depressed. Her classmates would be moving up a grade; she was being left behind. The only thing she thought could alleviate her dark mood was to have a scented bath like the ones her mother used to prepare for her. She pestered him about it and, eventually, he gave in. This meant he would have to take her upstairs. He warned her that if she screamed, he would have to kill her. All the doors and windows, he said, were secured with explosive devices. If she opened one, she would blow herself up.

Finally, he opened the door and let her out of the cell. Beyond the first wood door, there was a massive second door made out of concrete. She discovered later that it sealed hermetically. If the ventilation system had failed, she would have suffocated. Beyond the door was a passageway twenty-seven inches high and nineteen inches wide. They had to crawl through this. It brought them out in a maintenance pit in the garage. The entrance to the tunnel had been hidden behind a dresser and a safe, which he moved aside. The pit was covered with floorboards that had a trapdoor cut in them. It was clear to Natascha that, even if the police had searched the house, they would never have found her in her cell.

He indicated that she should stay silent and he repeated his threats as they went up the stairs into the house. But though she was free of the cell, Natascha realized that she was still a prisoner. There was no way she could overpower him and escape.

Priklopil ran her a bubble bath. He stayed while she undressed. She protested but, by then, she was used to him seeing her naked. After she had a long soak, he toweled her dry and returned her to her cell.

That fall, Priklopil painted her cell. Natascha was allowed to pick the color. For days afterward, she felt nauseous from the fumes. Bookcases, cupboards, and a bunk bed were brought in and assembled. During the redecorating, he grew angry and threw a heavy drill at her. Fortunately she saw it coming and ducked. The problem with the new furniture he had brought was that it took up most of the floor space and the cell became unbearably claustrophobic.

At Christmas, he cluttered the place further with a plastic tree. He also bought her everything she asked for, including a small educational computer, a pad of drawing paper, and a box of watercolors. She had oil paints as well, but no turpentine, perhaps because he was afraid of the harmful fumes in the confined space of the cell. She then delighted in painting pictures of her parents, which she had to hide from Priklopil.

On New Year's Eve, she was left in her cell in complete darkness. Priklopil always saw the New Year in with his only friend, Ernst Holzapfel. They set off large and expensive fireworks. Years later, she was allowed upstairs to watch them and, when she was sixteen, she was even allowed out into the garden.

In the new year, she was allowed upstairs to take a shower every two weeks. Sometimes he would let her stay upstairs to eat and watch TV. Every moment spent outside the cell was precious, though she found it impossible to relax around her captor. The petty rules he surrounded her with were beginning to have their effect. Her power to resist began to wane, though it never disappeared completely.

The presents kept coming. The most important item was her Horse-Riding Barbie, and Natascha made new outfits for her. He encouraged her to sew and knit, and do other handicrafts. She seized the chance to make presents for her family, but did not tell him that's what they were. Whenever she mentioned her parents, he flew into a rage. He was her family now, he said. He had rescued her and she belonged to him. This would make her cry. He would lock her in her cell and turn off the lights until she was "good" again.

Natascha began to think that Priklopil wanted to create his own perfect world where he was the most important inhabitant. To do that, he had to deny her any other social interaction. Priklopil's self-esteem was so low that he even denied her a mirror to see her own face. He tried to erase her identity and make her his own creation, but she somehow still found the energy to fight back. In her struggle against Priklopil, she found a strange sort of freedom. She was no longer a confused child in the feud between her mother and her father. And, since her abduction, she had stopped wetting the bed.

In the fall of 1999, Priklopil decided that Natascha should change her name. She did not mind, as she had never really liked the name Natascha anyway. Priklopil suggested that, from then on, he call her Maria and she agreed. It was her middle name anyway and both her grandmothers had been called Maria, so Maria it was.

That December, on a cold, moonlit night he took her out briefly into the garden. Again, she was warned that any attempt to scream or escape would be met with death. He also implied that he would also kill anyone who came to her rescue.

One morning, early in the year 2000, she awoke to find that she was having her first period. When Priklopil came to the cellar, she asked him to go and buy the sanitary towels she had seen advertised on the TV. This presented Priklopil with a new problem, in his own mind at least. He was convinced that, sooner or later, the police would turn up. Whenever she had been upstairs, he meticulously wiped anything she had touched to get rid of the fingerprints. Now that she had her periods, she was forced to sit on piles of newspapers. The tiniest spot of blood left on the furniture might render telltale DNA. Later, as his paranoia grew, he forced her to wear a plastic bag over her hair. Every stray hair he found around the house, he burned. Eventually, he shaved her head.

Now that she was on the verge of womanhood, the relationship between the two of them had changed. He no longer ordered her around like a child. Instead, he gave her what he considered to be womanly chores to do around the house. Even though she was upstairs, nobody could see her. The blinds were kept permanently down. The garden was full of shrubbery, screening the house from the neighbors. It was on a quiet backstreet. She rarely heard a car drive by or anyone outside. The only noise was from the nearby main railroad line to Vienna, so she was just as isolated as ever.

Now that she was upstairs, he could watch her all the time and she had to do exactly what she was told at all times. She had to ask permission to sit down or stand up, and he would tell her which way to look. While she cleaned, he would stand behind her giving orders. Everything had to be spotless. He would even accompany her to the toilet. She was never alone for a moment. When her chores were done, she was returned to her dungeon for the night.

Upstairs, she noticed that Priklopil had a copy of *Mein Kampf* on his shelves. He said he thought Hitler had been right to gas the Jews and that he, himself, was a follower of Austria's far-right Freedom Party. He was delighted when the Twin Towers were attacked on 9/11, saying that New York was the center of a Jewish conspiracy for world dominance.

Although Natascha was still only twelve, Priklopil got her to help with strenuous renovation work, dividing the house into apartments. He frequently lost his temper and beat her. He apologized afterwards, but that did not stop him from doing it again. At fifteen, she began to hit back, but still she was no match for him physically and she was frequently injured.

Priklopil weighed her regularly and cut her rations, saying it was to prevent her growing fat. She then found herself constantly hungry and suffered stomach cramps at night. She realized that the regimen was not designed to keep her slim and attractive, but rather weak and submissive.

She was now bald and emaciated, and he made her work almost naked, figuring she would be less likely to run out into the street if she had no clothes on. The only relief came on the weekends, when he would lock her downstairs with books, videos, and a ration of food, leaving her there for three days.

Often she would eat all the food on the Friday night so that at least once a week she would have a full belly.

Gradually, Natascha began to learn a little more about her tormentor. His father had died a few years earlier when Priklopil was twenty-four. She was locked in the cellar over the weekends because his mother came to cook and clean, and he didn't want her to see Natascha. It seems that, after he had moved back into the family house in Strasshof, she had taken over his apartment in Vienna. Priklopil's mother left recipes that Natascha had to follow to the letter, though no matter what she did, he said it was never as good as his mother's.

Shortly before the abduction, Priklopil had lost his job at the electronics firm Siemens. He was registered as unemployed, but when sent for job interviews he deliberately acted stupidly so he would not get a job. Meanwhile, he and Ernst Holzapfel earned money renovating apartments. Priklopil had no other friends, let alone a girlfriend. The only women in his life were his mother—and Natascha.

Though Priklopil was clearly crazy, Natascha had grown close to him. She began addressing him as Wolfgang or even Wolfi. As she had refused to call him "master," he had upped the ante and insisted that she call him "My Lord" and kneel in front of him. Her refusal now resulted in a beating.

When she was fourteen, she spent the night above ground. He locked her in his bedroom with him and tied her hands to his so that she could not move away from him in the night. Later, he used plastic handcuffs to keep her tethered to him. Natascha has refused to talk about what went on in the bedroom in hope of preserving her privacy. She has said that she was subjected to minor sexual assaults as part of her daily humiliation, but what occurred in the bedroom was not about sex. Others have their doubts; some feared Natascha had been abused when *Stern* magazine discovered that Priklopil was well known on the S&M scene in Vienna.

In the summer, Priklopil let Natascha go out in the garden to sunbathe. And once, while he was looking after a next-door neighbor's house while they were away, he took her for a swim in their pool. She was grateful, but it would not happen again. A dark period began. There were regular beatings. He starved her and kept her in the cellar, tormenting her by chanting, "Obey! Obey! Obey!" into the intercom and keeping her in the dark for long periods for minor infractions to his increasingly rigid code.

Natascha watched with fascination as the trial of Marc Dutroux began on the television. Sabine Dardenne's cell had been even smaller than her own. Now she was confronting her tormentor in court. Then Natascha heard on the radio about the publication of a new book about missing persons. Her case had been included, and everyone had concluded that she was dead. No one was ever coming to rescue her. They had given up looking for her long ago. She decided to commit suicide.

In fact, she had tried several times before. Once she had tried to strangle herself. On another occasion, she had slit her wrists. This time she waited until Priklopil locked her in the cell for the night. Then she put paper and toilet rolls on the hot plate and turned it on. She waited for the place to fill with smoke, believing that she could suffocate herself this way. But when she began to cough uncontrollably, she panicked and doused the smoldering paper with water. In the morning, he smelled the smoke and saw the burned paper, and he beat her black and blue for trying to escape. One day, while they were working, Natascha asked if Priklopil would open a window. He refused, saying that she wanted to scream and run away. She promised that she would stay with him forever and never run away. Nevertheless, he dragged her to the front door, opened it and told her to go.

"Just see how far you get, the way you look," he said.

She was wearing hardly anything. Her bruises were showing. Her ribs were sticking out. Her hair was only a short stubble. She lost her nerve.

On another occasion, he threw her outside naked. Again, she could not find the courage to run away. She knew that he could run faster than she could, and he threatened to kill her, and any neighbor she ran to. She felt she could not be responsible for that. He told her that her parents were in jail. She could not go home. There would be no one to take her in. She begged to be let back into the house. All she could hope was that someone might witness one of these scenes and wonder what was going on.

To break her spirit further, he took the doors off the toilets, so she would not be out of sight for a minute. Then he changed tack. He let her hair grow back and bleached it blonde in an effort to make her into what he thought of as a "perfect woman."

Priklopil became so confident that she would not run away that he decided to take her out. If anyone thought they recognized her, she was to pretend she did not know what they were talking about. If questioned further, she was to say that she was Priklopil's niece. Then they got in his van and drove slowly down Heinestrasse. It was the first time she had been out in seven years.

In a small wooded area outside Strasshof, she was allowed to get out of the van, briefly. Everything felt unreal. Soon after, they went out to a drugstore where she would be allowed to buy something for herself. Before they went in, she was warned not to say a word or everyone in the shop would die. At the checkout, the cashier spoke to her. She could hardly believe that she was exchanging words with someone other than her kidnapper. When they got home, there were more beatings to endure, but she promised herself that next time they went out she would find the strength to ask someone for help.

One morning, Priklopil gave her a T-shirt and jeans. He said that they were going to a home improvement store. Priklopil took the road toward Vienna, past where Natascha's grandmother had lived. The good times she had spent with her grandma seemed a lifetime away. Tears filled her eyes as they passed the turnoff to the apartment where she had lived. Her mother would be having her morning coffee, she surmised, surely thinking her daughter was dead. Natascha's sister's apartment was also nearby. Priklopil noticed that she was upset and ordered her to keep her eyes on the floor.

The DIY store's parking lot was full. Natascha was ordered to wait in the van until she was told to get out. Then she was to walk into the store in front of Priklopil and not make a sound. Inside he directed her down the aisles with a slight pressure on her shoulder.

Natascha looked for someone she could turn to for help, but everyone seemed self-absorbed and unfriendly. She began to feel that, if she asked anyone for help, Priklopil would simply brush it off, saying that there was something wrong with her or that it was a practical joke. He would not have to kill anyone to cover up his crime because no one would take her seriously.

Then a sales assistant asked: "Can I help you?"

"No thanks," said Priklopil. "We're fine."

Once again, she had missed her opportunity to break free.

That night, she lay awake for a long time. She realized that she could not involve anyone else in her escape from captivity. She had to do it all herself. Somehow she would have to find the strength.

Natascha had been keeping a secret diary that included a record of her beatings. Now she used it to build up her resolve. She wrote a list of instructions to herself. She was not to react to his abuse and the things he did to undermine her self-confidence. No matter what he said or did, she must not react in any way. She told herself that she must be stronger. But most of all, she must "never, never give up." When she plunged into despair, she read the list of instructions out loud.

She realized that, at first, she had spent all her effort trying to get out of the cellar; then she had strived to get out of the house. She had achieved both of those goals. What she had to do now was escape his controlling influence. And she had a secret weapon—Priklopil himself. When they went out, she noticed that he was in a state of near panic. She could feel him shaking. The man was conflicted. He was torn between wanting to live a seemingly normal life with her and the fear that she would destroy everything by trying to escape. It was a conflict that she could exploit.

The next time they went out, they were stopped at a police checkpoint. While Priklopil handed over his papers, Natascha weighed the options. This was a perfect opportunity to escape, but again her thoughts turned to the safety of others. If she jumped out of the car and sought help from the police, Priklopil might take off and crash into the oncoming traffic. She stayed her hand. The police officer said his papers were in order and handed them back. Another opportunity had been lost.

As Natascha approached her eighteenth birthday, Priklopil talked about taking her on a ski trip. She had always wanted to learn to ski. He was a practiced skier and took her to buy some ski pants. She stood in the changing room while he handed her pair after pair. At last she could see herself in a mirror. She was pale and emaciated with thin hair. Seeing herself was torture. She was so pitifully thin that even extra-small pants were too large. Eventually, they had to get ski pants from a children's store. In the end, she was relieved to get back in the car. She found it distressing to be around people. The brightly colored clothes stirred memories of what it was like to have a normal life.

Priklopil then began to blame Natascha for the reckless expense of taking her skiing. He made her figure out how far the ski resort was, so she would know how much the gas would cost to take her there and back. Despite all the money he was spending on her, he said, she would probably spoil everything by acting up.

"You are nothing without me," he screamed, banging his fist on the table. "Nothing."

Natascha did not react. One of the instructions she had written in her secret diary read: "Don't answer back when he says that you can't live without him."

Besides, the trip was not for her. Priklopil had often gone skiing, leaving her locked in the cellar. He was taking her so that he could indulge the fantasy that he was going with a willing partner who would admire his prowess on the slopes.

She played on this. On their way to the car, she said she had changed her mind and wanted to stay home. He had a crowbar in his hand and brought it down on her thigh, splitting the skin. Despite her injury, they set off.

At the ski rental shop where they stopped to get Natascha some boots, Priklopil became extremely nervous. Natascha would have to talk to the assistant, who would ask how the boots fit. Again, he threatened to kill everyone in the shop if she attempted to give him away.

After getting the boots, he decided that they could not take the ski lift. Again, it would have given her a chance to talk to people. They would have to drive up to the slopes.

Her first attempts at skiing met with some success. Suddenly, she felt proud of herself, a feeling she had not had in a long time. Priklopil, of course, criticized and swore at her each time she did something wrong. Nevertheless, the experience boosted her confidence. To see the vast skies and the mountainous panorama filled her with exhilaration.

Then she had to go to the toilet. Priklopil had no choice but to let her go. However, he directed her to a restroom away from the restaurant area where there would be fewer people and stood outside the door. When Natascha went in, there was no one else inside. She delayed, hoping that someone else would come in. Then the door opened. She thought it might be Priklopil coming to get her because she had been too long. However, it was a woman. For the first time in eight years, Natascha found herself alone with someone other than her kidnapper.

Natascha plucked up all her courage and approached the stranger. But when she opened her mouth nothing seemed to come out. She spoke but the woman took no notice. It was like a bad dream. The woman turned, smiled at Natascha, and left. Later, she learned that the woman was Dutch and did not understand German. But at the time, it fed into Natascha's worst nightmare. Perhaps she was invisible. It reminded her that she must not try and seek help, but depend on herself to make her escape.

For her eighteenth birthday, Natascha was allowed to bake a cake. But the nearest she came to having a party was to watch videos of Turkish and Serbian wedding celebrations that Priklopil had. He bought her a second cake in the shape of a "1" and an "8." Despite her continued captivity, this was a special day for Natascha. Even before she had been kidnapped, she had dreamt of being eighteen so she could leave home and be free.

The sight of the "18" cake made her redouble her resolve to escape. She was no longer a child. Despite what he said, she did not need anyone to look after her anymore. Back in her dungeon, she began to revive the ambitions she had had as a little girl—to become an actress, write a book, make music, be free.

The conditions of her captivity grew slightly better after her eighteenth birthday. She was allowed out to help with the gardening. The neighbors had seen her. Twice they had shouted greetings over the fence. Priklopil had told them that she was "temporary help." As a reward for her work, he had bought her an orange dress that made her feel almost normal.

After the conversion work in the house was finished, work started on a new apartment Priklopil had bought in Vienna.

Again, Natascha was to be an unpaid laborer. She hoped that the new location would present new opportunities to escape, but whenever Priklopil left the apartment for a moment, he jammed the door closed or screwed boards across it, turning it into a makeshift prison. As it was, she was usually too weary from overwork and her poor diet to make a break for it.

An opportunity to escape did present itself when a neighbor came to check out the new apartment. But he was from Yugoslavia and spoke little German. Even so, while they talked in the doorway, Priklopil made sure to keep Natascha behind him. There were also fresh beatings to put up with. He demanded absolute obedience. When he said that black was white and white was black, she was forced to say so too. Nevertheless, she was convinced that her opportunity to escape would come soon.

She noted that Priklopil was becoming more delusional. He had been saying that, if he could trust her not to run away, he would take her on vacation and buy her nice things. But when she promised not to escape, he said he knew she was lying.

And it was not just a matter of Natascha's getting away from him. Over the years, he had got inside her. She feared that she might commit suicide if she escaped, finding herself unable to cope with freedom. She didn't want to go to the police either. They would lock him up, but that would only be doing to him what he had done to her. She had no desire for revenge. She only felt pity for a man who thought he could terrorize someone into loving him.

Natascha was also afraid of being presented as a victim as the girls in the Dutroux case had been. She wanted to stop being a victim once she was free of Priklopil. She even planned how she would handle the media. She may have disappeared into the cellar as a child, but she would emerge a full-grown woman.

Priklopil was in a good mood. The apartment they had been working on was going on the market. His money worries would be over for the time being, and he planned to sell the white van he had used to kidnap her eight and a half years before. While they were fixing it up, Natascha realized that her last link to the world before her abduction was about to disappear. It was as if she were condemning herself to the cellar forever, and she had to speak out.

She told Priklopil that now that she was an adult she had to move out. She said he must have known from the beginning that, sooner or later, he had to either kill her or let her go. She stiffened herself for the blow. It did not come. Instead, he said that she knew he could neither kill her nor free her. But Natascha explained that he had put them in a position where one of them had to die. She had tried to kill herself several times. It would be better, she said, if he committed suicide as there was no other way out for him. Then she said, he was not to worry. If she ran away, she would not go to the police. Instead, she would throw herself under a train. When she said this, it surprised her. But now she knew that she would run away at the next opportunity.

On the morning August 23, 2006, Natascha awoke as the light came on. Hunger drove her out of bed. There was nothing to eat in the cellar, but she brushed her teeth to take away the sour taste of an empty stomach. Normally she would have tidied up her cell. But that day she could not be bothered.

However, she put on her new orange dress and waited for her jailer to open the door.

She asked whether she could put on a pair of panties. He said this was out of the question. Indoors she had always had to work half-naked to discourage her escaping. In the garden, she had to go without underwear.

That morning, like many others these days, she went through the big concrete door. The sight of it always made her shudder. Once when he had left her alone for several of days, she had used her last ounce of to strength to break down the inner wooden doors. But there was nothing she could have done about the concrete door. It only opened from the outside. If something prevented him from coming to open it, that door meant that she would die from thirst or starvation. It was a constant terror.

That day, like so many before, she crawled out of the narrow passageway. Once upstairs, she took deep breaths, relishing the fresh air. Even though it was she who was starving, he forced her to get him two slices of bread and jam from the kitchen. She had not had dinner the night before, though he had given her a tiny piece of cake, which she was to have for her break-fast. She had wolfed it the night before in lieu of dinner and she knew that there would be nothing more for her now.

She washed the dishes and looked at the calendar. It was the 3,096th day of her captivity. They set to work writing an ad for the apartment. The details were put on the Internet. Then they went out into the garden. Around noon, he told her to vacuum the interior of the van, to get it ready to sell. While she was doing this, his cell phone rang. From what she could hear, it was someone who was interested in the apartment. Deep in conversation, Priklopil wandered away.

As soon as he was out of sight, she seized her chance. She dropped the vacuum cleaner and ran. She headed toward the railroad tracks. She had no great hope of getting away. Perhaps Priklopil would catch her and kill her. But she now felt that death was better than going back into the dungeon.

Suddenly she saw three people and begged them to call the police. They said they could not as they did not have a cell phone with them.

With tears in her eyes, she climbed over a fence into a garden. There was a woman opening the window. Natascha told her to call the police, she had been kidnapped. The woman wanted to know what Natascha was doing in her garden. Natascha again begged her to call the police, then added: "My name is Natascha Kampusch."

It was as if a spell was broken. She was no longer Priklopil's Maria. For the first time in so many years, she had said her own name.

Fearing a bloodbath, she insisted that the police should come in an unmarked car.

The woman was mistrustful and told her to wait by the hedge because she did not want Natascha on her lawn. Nevertheless, she called the police.

Much to Natascha's dismay, a police car turned up with lights flashing. Natascha expected gunfire to break out at any moment. The police told her to put her hands up.

She told them her name, her date of birth, and her address. They had their doubts. This emaciated teenager looked nothing like the plump primary school girl who had gone missing eight years before.

While they contacted headquarters, she said that she had been kidnapped by Wolfgang Priklopil and held prisoner at Heinestrasse 60. They were still only yards from Priklopil's front door and, as far as she was concerned, still in great danger.

The police put her in the car and Natascha ducked down low in the backseat, frightened that Priklopil might see her. When they reached the police station at Deutsch-Wagram, the detectives there greeted her warmly. They had checked out the details she had given and were convinced that she was the lost child they had been trying to find for so long.

They offered her some food. She refused it, knowing that since she had gone without for so long, it would give her stomach cramps. A kindly woman police officer gave Natascha her jacket to keep her warm, then sat her down while Natascha poured out her story.

Taken back to Vienna, Natascha found herself swamped by the media. Then she heard that Priklopil was on the run. She knew he would kill himself.

Her mother was waiting at police headquarters in Vienna. It was a tearful reunion. Her sisters came too, then her father. But her beloved grandmother, sadly, had died.

While she was being examined by a police psychologist, the police went to Heinsestrasse 60 and found no explosives around the windows and doors. But they did find the dungeon.

That evening, they took her to a hotel in southern Austria where she was protected under armed guard. Priklopil was still at large and might want to kill her. So Natascha found herself locked up once more. She listened to the radio to see if she could find out what had happened to her kidnapper, until the psychologist put a stop to it. The following day, she returned to Vienna. On the way, she was told that Priklopil had jumped in front of a train and was dead. At last, she was free.

She was advised to change her name and go into hiding. That was the only way she could lead a normal life, she was told. But Natascha did not want to live in the shadows. She had done that, forcibly, for too long. Two weeks after her escape, Natascha decided to give interviews to the major Austrian news media.

Natascha Kampusch went on to have her own chat show on Austrian TV. She eventually took possession of the house at Heinsestrasse that played so large a part in her life in order to prevent it from being torn down or turned into some macabre museum. She has visited it regularly, but says that if she ever sold it, she would have the cellar filled in.

Chapter 8

Katie Beers— Lost from View

ON THE WEEKEND BEFORE her tenth birthday, Katie Beers was staying with her Aunt Linda, her wheelchair-bound god-mother, in West Bay Shore, Long Island. On Wednesday, her birthday, Katie had to be back with her mother, Marilyn. The two women were embroiled in a custody battle over Katie. That Sunday, Aunt Linda was holding a pre-birthday party for her favorite niece. Katie called a family friend, forty-three-year-old building contractor Joe Esposito, and left a message on his answering machine, saying that they had saved him a piece of cake.

At 11 a.m. on Monday, Esposito returned her call. He said he had taken the afternoon off work to have fun with her. Before the party, he had delivered a Barbie Dream House, but had been unable to stay. Some neighborhood kids would assemble it while they were out.

At 1:20 p.m., Esposito arrived at Linda Inghilleri's yellow-shingled house on Ocean Avenue and came in through the side door. Katie leaped into his arms.

Esposito had been a longtime friend of both the Inghilleris and the Beers family. He was a small man—just five foot seven and slim—but they called him "Big John" to distinguish him from "Little John" Beers, Katie's sixteen-year-old half-brother. Linda thought that Esposito was gay. She trusted him with Katie, and they had been out together many times before.

Linda told them to be back by six and asked Katie to mail some letters for her. Katie grabbed her coat and purse, and the floppy hat she always wore when she went out after her hair had been shorn due to an infestation of head lice.

They took off in Esposito's black 1989 Nissan pickup and drove down to the Toys "R" Us in Bay Shore. He bought some toys, a videotape, and the Super Nintendo video game *Home Alone 2*. After a Slurpee in a 7-Eleven, they went back to Esposito's house on North Saxon and upstairs to the game room to play the video game, or so Katie thought. Instead Esposito took her into the bedroom, threw her on the bed, and kissed her. It is not clear whether he had planned to do that. It may just have been an impulse. However, he knew that he was in big trouble. Marilyn Beers had already accused him of molesting Little John, and he had been charged with a sex offense some fourteen years before. On the other hand, what happened next may have been planned for a long time.

Over the previous few years, he had dug a deep pit behind his garage and dispersed the dirt across the adjoining field. Then he'd covered it over with a concrete roof and turned it into an underground bunker. When he finished, he covered it over, laid a cement base, and erected a carport. He covered his tracks so well that neighbors were none the wiser. Nor was his former sister-in-law, with whom he shared the house. As a building contractor, Esposito was always coming and going with building material, and he frequently worked late into the night. Below ground, the bunker was decorated with ceiling hooks, chains, and other restrains. Blood spots that were later found on a sheet indicate that sadomasochistic practices had gone on there.

Esposito picked up Katie, carried her down to his office, and locked the door. She tried to dial 911 on the office phone, but he grabbed it from her hand. Then he unbolted a bookcase and moved it from its position on a dolly. He rolled back the floor covering to reveal a two-hundred-pound concrete slab. Then, with a block and tackle, he raised it. Beneath it was a six-foot shaft. Esposito carried Katie down a steep flight of steps to the bottom. A circular passageway, wide enough to crawl down, led off it. He used an electric wrench to raise three barriers along its length, and forced Katie through the crawl way.

It led to the concrete bunker, which was now lined with cork and foam rubber. The floor measured six feet by seven, and it was barely high enough for Esposito to stand up in. It contained a portable toilet, a dehumidifier, a radiator, and an air duct for ventilation, all illuminated by the blue glow of the TV monitors. These were connected to closed-circuit TV cameras around the house, so he could watch what was going on.

A smaller metal chamber running the length of the chamber was suspended from the roof. Katie was shoved in there. It contained a bed. She noticed the red stains on the sheets. Had someone been kept in here before, she wondered? There was also a TV and a radio. Esposito gave her a remote control. He explained that he was rescuing her from the bitter custody battle between her mother and Aunt Linda. She would be safe there. But first she had to record a message.

He bought her some sodas and junk food, then left her locked in. Now he had a detailed timetable to follow. Setting off at 4 p.m., he headed for Nesconset, stopping at a gas station to call Linda. The phone was busy. He tried repeatedly until he got through about half an hour later.

At 5:06, Linda's phone rang. Confined to her wheelchair, she did not get to the phone before the answering machine cut in. She heard Katie's voice. It said: "I've been kidnapped by a man with a knife... Oh my God! He's coming back."

Esposito headed on to the Spaceplex Family Center, Long Island's largest indoor amusement park. When he arrived there, he told security that he had lost a little girl named Katie Beers, last seen at around 4:30.

Linda knew that Esposito and Katie were going to Spaceplex. She called and had Esposito paged. Then she called 911. Twenty minutes later, she called Spaceplex again. This time she spoke to the manager, who handed the phone to Esposito. He said that Katie had gone to get change when she disappeared. Then he began sobbing.

She then took the time to go through what Katie had been wearing with Esposito. He then said that Katie had left her purse, coat, and hat in the pickup. Linda thought this was strange. Katie would never leave her hat. She was embarrassed to be seen in a public place with a shaved head.

The police arrived with sniffing dogs, and around fifty officers and cadets began searching the area. They brought in a mobile command post and searched every dumpster along a seven-mile stretch of Route 25.

Esposito was taken to the precinct to make a statement. As he had been the last person to see Katie, they grilled him for eighteen hours. He consented to having his home searched. From the bunker, Katie could see the detectives on the TV monitors. She screamed and pounded, but nothing could be heard outside. The detectives found Katie's coat in Esposito's pickup. They also recovered the Toys "R" Us receipt. Strangely, Katie's purse was found in Esposito's bedroom. But if he had something to hide, why wouldn't he have hid it?

There was no indication that the girl had run off and no body had been found, so the following day the case was handed over to Detective Lieutenant Dominick Varrone of the Kidnap Department at Suffolk County Police. When he heard the message Katie had left on Linda Inghilleri's answering machine, he was immediately suspicious.

If Katie had been in the throes of the abduction when she phoned, wouldn't she have said: "I'm being kidnapped…" And why did she use the word "kidnapped"? It was a grown-up's word. Wouldn't she have said "taken" or "grabbed"? When a person is grabbed, they do not immediately know they are being kidnapped; that only becomes apparent later. However, while the words Katie used sounded like they had been dictated, the fear in her voice was all too real.

Varrone also noticed that there was a certain amount of time unaccounted for in Esposito's story. The detectives who had questioned him found him strange and childlike. He had also mentioned that Katie had sat on his lap, helping him with the steering when he drove. One question sprung to Varrone's mind: Was Esposito a pedophile?

Varrone was eager to speak to Esposito before lawyers got involved. As Katie seemed to have managed to break away from her captor long enough to make a phone call, she might do so again. Varrone asked Esposito if Katie had his phone number. She did. In that case, they would need to put an officer in his house to intercept the call. Esposito agreed. Failure to cooperate with an investigation would have looked bad for him. However, he was insistent that Katie's disappearance was not a kidnapping. When asked why, he said her family did not have any money. Instead, he said, something "dirty" must have happened. How did he know? Before Varrone had a chance to ask, lawyers were on the phone. Esposito's family had called them.

Esposito had already agreed to let the police department listen in on his phone. But when they reached his house, he changed his mind. He wanted his privacy, he said. However, the apartment upstairs shared the same line, so the detective listened in from up there. Meanwhile, Varrone arranged to have Esposito tailed. Varrone was already convinced that Esposito was guilty. If the pressure was kept on him, Varrone was sure he would crack.

By the following day, WABC/TV Eyewitness News had picked up the story. At noon, they broadcast an interview with Linda Inghilleri and Marilyn Beers, who also happened to be at Linda's house. With Katie missing, the two women had agreed to a temporary truce. In the bunker, Katie was watching.

Varrone pulled Esposito's police record. In 1977, he had approached the seven-year-old son of a friend in a shopping mall and tried to drag him into a car. The security guards at the mall recognized him a month later. Esposito claimed that the boy was planning to run away from his family and Esposito only wanted to be his friend. His lawyers plea-bargained the charge down to unlawful imprisonment, and Esposito got off with a year's probation.

However, there was another suspect in the frame. Marilyn Beers had accused Salvatore Inghilleri, Linda's estranged husband, of sexually molesting Katie that October. The case had yet to come to trial. Might he have killed Katie to prevent her from testifying against him? He had certainly violated the court order that prevented him from coming in contact with Katie; he had been at Linda's house when Esposito picked her up and would have known where he was taking her.

But Varrone's instinct told him that Esposito was his man. He applied for a warrant to search his house again. The idea was to keep the pressure on him. As it was, having his house searched again caused Esposito considerable inconvenience. He had planned to visit Katie twice a day to take her food and toiletries, and it took between ten and fifteen minutes to get in and out of the bunker. When the cops left and he finally got down to the bunker, he found that Katie had climbed down from the upper compartment. He put her back with a chain and padlock around her neck.

While most of the officers on the case thought they should be looking for a shallow grave, Varrone stuck to his guns. It struck him that no one had called in saying they had seen Katie at Spaceplex. Perhaps she had never been there. He was convinced that Esposito had lied. This gave him cause for hope. The detectives who had contact with Esposito thought him incapable of homicide.

Examining the telephone records, detectives discovered that the call made to Linda Inghilleri's house had come from a pay phone at an Amoco station near Spaceplex. In fact, according to phone company's records, numerous attempts had been made to call Linda's number from that pay phone. How had Katie been able to escape her captor for so long? Varrone began to suspect that the stilted message left on Linda's answering machine had come from a tape recorder. That meant that Esposito had hidden the child somewhere before he went to Spaceplex.

Varrone upped the tail on Esposito in an attempt to rattle him. This amounted to harassment. Esposito's lawyers called a press conference where Esposito denied having anything to do with Katie's disappearance. His attorney pointed out that, if Esposito had abducted her, she would have said in her message to her aunt: "John kidnapped me…"

The press conference was televised, so Katie watched that too.

Esposito was kept so busy that he barely had time to visit Katie. As a result, she had soiled her panties. He kept women's panties in his bedroom, but they were too big for her. However, with the police following him, he could not risk going out to buy children's underwear.

Katie was a resourceful child. Distracting Esposito with requests for more soda, she stole one of the two keys to the padlock. After that, when he left, she would undo the chain around her neck, locking it again when she heard the sound of the electric wrench. However, that did not mean that she could get out of her metal compartment. He wedged the door closed with a piece of wood so she could not get out. Katie would spend her birthday locked in this metal prison. She shut her eyes and went to sleep singing "Happy birthday to you."

Varrone obtained another warrant and had Esposito's house searched again. This time the police found the instruction manual for a new GE tape recorder.

By then there were other people on the case. Lou Telano of the Long Island Society for the Prevention of Cruelty to Children, a former Brooklyn cop, had his volunteers out searching. Meanwhile, Marilyn Beers employed a psychic and former housepainter from Massachusetts named John Monti, who said that Katie was alive and underground, behind a red door. This helped keep the story in the news.

The constant surveillance of Esposito was taking its toll. He had to restrict his visits to Katie to once a day. She begged him to visit more often and started screaming. He threatened to seal her mouth with duct tape if she did not stop.

Varrone sent the tape from Linda Inghilleri's answering machine to the FBI. Their labs could not be certain, but they were fairly sure that the message had been prerecorded. Not only had Katie not been at Spaceplex, she had not been at the Amoco station when the call had been made. No one had seen her there either. The net was closing on Esposito.

Although Esposito claimed that he was protecting her, Katie's situation was becoming increasingly desperate. While he provided a plastic bag for her to pee in and another for excrement, which he then disposed off upstairs, they were only available when he came downstairs and let her out of her metal compartment. Sometimes she could not wait and had to pee under the TV in the box. The place was beginning to smell.

She was also tired of the diet of fast food and demanded a proper meal. He could not risk that. The police might become suspicious. She had now been held for six days and she began to wonder how long Esposito was going to keep her—a year? Or forever?

While the Suffolk County police were searching the area around the Spaceplex and the Amoco station for a grave, Varrone persisted with his theory that Katie was being held somewhere and he began to take an interest in the custody battle over Katie between Marilyn Beers and Linda Inghilleri.

The two women had been friends on and off for some time. They had met years before, around the time Marilyn had fallen out with her adoptive parents after she refused to tell them who the father of Little John was. She had left home and gone to work as a cab driver to support herself. She then got pregnant with Katie. This time she did not even know who the father was; he was just some guy she picked up in a bar. By the time she had Katie, Marilyn was on welfare and Linda helped, taking care of the little girl when Marilyn could not manage.

Linda was no angel either. A heavy drinker, she had gotten into scrapes with the law. She complained that her husband, Sal, had a low sperm count due to the medication he was taking for his blood pressure. Consequently, she had no children of her own. By the time Katie came along, Linda had dried out. Katie was the apple of her eye, and she was prepared to sacrifice anything for the child.

Katie went to live with Linda when she was one. Linda insisted that she be baptized. Marilyn agreed, but she did not want her child baptized as a Catholic as Linda wanted; rather, it would take place in the local Presbyterian Church. Linda became Katie's godmother. She took Katie to visit Marilyn regularly. However, the house where Marilyn lived with her now widowed mother was a mess. Marilyn's mother had twenty-two cats and a dog that was not properly housebroken. The place was crawling with cockroaches. Dead rats were a common sight. Linda once found a dead cat riddled with maggots behind the sofa. Katie contracted impetigo from dirty clothing. Then there was the lice in her hair.

Linda went to the Children's Aid Society to see if she could get permanent custody and was told that the birth mother would have to agree. While Marilyn was happy for Linda to look after her child, she would not take that final step. The situation grew more complicated when Katie started kindergarten. To establish residency in her school district, the child had to live with her mother during the week, but she was constantly calling Linda to come and get her. And, when her mother did not turn up to get her, she would roam the local mall on her own. At one point, the Child Protection Service was called in; over the years, they amassed a file four inches thick, but did nothing.

Eventually, Linda and Sal moved in with Marilyn and her mother in an attempt to tidy up their home. But they soon had a falling out over money. By that time Linda was bedridden with undiagnosed diabetes. Later, her leg was amputated. But still the struggle between Linda and Marilyn over custody continued.

As the search for Katie continued, Varrone was unable to sleep for several nights and his boss insisted that he take some time off. Instead of resting, he went to visit Linda's parents, Ann and Charles Butler. He had begun to wonder whether some concerned member of the family had kidnapped Katie for the child's own good. When he called at the Butler's home in West Islip, Ann was out. Charles said he did not know where his wife was. He appeared nervous and said he could not remember what he was doing on the day Katie disappeared. Then Ann turned up with her son Charlie. She was forthright and said she thought that Katie would be better off away from her mother. It was she who had arranged the pre-birthday party at Linda's. Marilyn had been against it. Ann was also vague about her movements on the day Katie went missing. Varrone took statements from them and he became so suspicious of Charlie Butler that he called in two detectives from homicide.

Meanwhile, one of Telano's volunteers reported seeing a small car driving up a back road in the early evening with no lights on. When Telano went to investigate, he was met by Monti, who took him to see a knife that he said he had found near the Amoco station. This had to have been the knife that the kidnapper had used to threaten Katie Beers, he said, and it was covered in blood. It looked like rust to Telano, but he gave it to the police.

In the middle of the night on January 4, Varrone woke with his head full of new theories. He had suddenly remembered that in the game *Home Alone 2*, which his son played, a figure on the phone is chased by a man with a knife. Could this be the origin of the message on the answering machine?

And had Katie seen the movie *Home Alone 2*? It begins with the boy played by Macaulay Culkin arriving in New York, when he should be in Florida. Had she been shown the movie to prepare her to take a flight of her own? A flight to a place of safety, say, away from her feuding mother and godmother? When Varrone outlined his theory at the precinct the next day, he was told he needed more rest.

To advance the investigation in a more logical fashion, the Suffolk County Police put a checkpoint on the highway by the Amoco station, causing huge tailbacks. They asked whether anyone had seen a small girl making a phone call from the pay phone in the gas station on the afternoon of December 28. But that was not what they were hoping to hear. They were really hoping to find a witness who had seen someone with a tape recorder in the phone booth. They found neither.

The investigation then broadened. While Suffolk country police interviewed local people—Katie's teachers, parolees in the area, and anyone who might have had contact with her—the FBI checked out relatives, especially those of the Butlers. Varrone still wondered if Katie had been sent somewhere for safekeeping.

At the same time, Varrone kept up the surveillance on Esposito, despite risking a lawsuit for harassment. If Katie was dead, as most of the police force thought, then Esposito had killed her. The purse found in his bedroom pointed to that. But if he had killed her, why had he stopped to get her make the recording?

Then Eyewitness News reported that the police thought the message on Linda Inghilleri's answering machine was prerecorded. At first, Varrone was furious, but in fact, the leak helped him. Esposito now figured that he had been found out. Once it was established that Katie's call had been prerecorded, doubt was thrown on Esposito's account. He was obviously a little paranoid at this point and, though the recording did not prove his guilt, he would imagine that the police were on to him. While Varrone had yet to close his case, he was becoming more optimistic that Katie would be found alive. He figured that, if Katie had been killed, her dead body would almost certainly have been discovered by then.

Linda Inghilleri was convinced that Esposito knew where Katie was. Esposito, she knew, worshiped his dead mother, Rose. She planned to phone Esposito and tell him that Rose had appeared in a dream and had told her that she could rest easier if he revealed where Katie was. But the police were monitoring their calls and she thought better of it. Instead, she too brought in a psychic who, when driving past Esposito's door—which he left open as if to announce he had nothing to hide—said that Katie was there. The feud between Linda and Marilyn was then taken up by their respective psychics.

The National Council for Missing and Exploited Children planned to put a poster featuring Katie on tractor-trailers coast to coast and to send out fifty-two million fliers. And Katie saw herself on *America's Most Wanted*. Esposito boasted that, as well as keeping her safe from the fight between Marilyn and Linda, he had made her famous. But *America's Most Wanted* only succeed in bringing in numerous bogus sightings, all of which had to be checked out.

Sal Inghilleri eventually submitted to a polygraph test and was cleared, as was Ann Butler. But Esposito, on the advice of his lawyers, refused to take the test.

By the sixteenth day of Katie's captivity, Esposito was talking about suicide. This scared Katie. If he died, no one would ever find her. He said he would leave a note. But what would happen if it got lost, or was overlooked?

Then on day seventeen, Esposito cracked. He told his family, then his lawyer that he knew where Katie was—in a bomb shelter under his home that only he knew how to open. At first, they did not believe him. It sounded like fantasy. After all, the police had searched the house three times. If Katie was "behind the wall," as he said, surely she must be dead. No, he insisted, she was alive.

This put his lawyer in a quandary. If he failed to tell the police and the girl died, he would be culpable. On the other hand, telling the police would be a violation of attorney-client privilege. First, he had to get Esposito to sign a paper waving his right to confidentiality. Then he called the DA, but not without tipping off *Newsday* first.

The media descended, but there were still delicate negotiations going on. The police had searched the premises and there was no sign of a bomb shelter. There was no record of the place even having a basement. If Esposito was telling the truth, they would need his cooperation to get her out. There was still a danger that he might kill himself. What's more, if Katie were there, behind the wall, the place was now a crime scene. It had to treated with the utmost care; otherwise, vital evidence would be destroyed.

When Esposito arrived home with his lawyer, the place was surrounded by cops, crowds, and cameras. Inside the office, he spoke into a hidden microphone and said: "Katie, I'm coming down."

Then he unscrewed the bookcase and moved it aside. He rolled back the floor covering and raised the concrete block. Detective Chris Zablocki, who had been monitoring the phones in the other apartment, climbed down the shaft with Esposito, who pulled out the power wrench.

"Hold it," said Zablocki, thinking it was a gun. Then, reassured, he let Esposito go about his business.

When Esposito was done, Zablocki crawled through. Reaching the dungeon, he called out Katie's name. She responded from the box. He let her out, helped her down, and hugged her. Then, sensing freedom, she scurried out of her prison.

Up in the office, Esposito had broken down. Katie did her best to comfort him.

Varrone turned up to take her to the precinct. On the way, she opened a plastic bag she was carrying. It contained $500 that Esposito had given her. At the station, she was interviewed. She revealed that, though Esposito had touched her between the legs, he had not violated her.

When Katie's family arrived, Varrone thought it might be a good idea for her to see Linda and Marilyn. He was overruled by social workers, who insisted that Katie should have counseling first. After all, Marilyn was a negligent parent. She had not denied Sal Inghilleri and John Esposito access to her daughter even though she had accused both them of sex crimes. As a result, Marilyn was forced to give the Child Protection Service temporary custody of her daughter.

Katie was taken to Schneiders Children's Hospital, where she was given a checkup and a hot bath, then put to bed. After that, her access to TV was strictly limited. She was not allowed to watch the news or any shows that might concern her kidnapping.

Esposito was charged with three counts of first-degree kidnapping, six counts of first-degree sexual abuse, one count of endangering the welfare of a child, and one count of making a false statement to the police. He pleaded not guilty.

After a plea bargain that spared Katie the ordeal of having to testify, Esposito was sentenced to fifteen years. Katie did testify against Sal Inghilleri, who was sentenced to twelve years for molestation. He was paroled in 2006, but was subsequently arrested for violating the conditions of his parole and returned to jail, where he in died in 2010.

While Marilyn Beers made money out of the media coverage of her daughter's kidnapping, she failed to regain custody of Katie and was later arrested for insurance fraud. Linda Inghilleri's application for custody also failed. It was judged that, as she was not a blood relative, she had no claim. Katie was raised by a foster family and went on to do well in school.

Chapter 9

Steven Stayner— The Subjugate "Son"

IN 1972, DELBERT AND KAY STAYNER and their five children lived at 1655 Shirley Street, Merced, California, not far from Yosemite National Park. Their middle child, Steven, was a regular seven-year-old with buckteeth and freckles. The family had moved into a ranch house with an almond orchard attached five years before so that the children could benefit from growing up in the countryside. They kept cows, goats, and pigs. Steven particularly loved this rural idyll, running free with his collie dog, Daisy.

Del would take the kids fishing at the nearby lake and go camping at least once a month. The kids also had a backyard swimming pool.

By September 1972, Steven had settled in at Charles Wright Elementary School. In the mornings, the eldest child, Cary, a sixth grader, would reluctantly shepherd her three younger siblings, Steven, Cindy, and Jody, the twelve blocks to school. However, at 2 p.m. each afternoon, Steven walked home alone. The others did not get out of school until later.

That November, Steven got into trouble with his parents for going straight from school to the home of a friend without asking permission first. The lecture he got had no effect. He continued to do it and, on Friday, December 1, he earned himself a whupping. That Sunday, he went to a Christmas party and told Santa that he wanted a GI Joe set, repeating the request to his father when he got home.

The following day, December 4, Steven went to school as usual. His mother, Kay, was going to the store to buy some auto parts that Del needed. It began to rain, and she decided she would pick her son up from school to make sure he went straight home.

Eighty miles to the east, Yosemite Lodge's kitchen cleaner Ervin Edward Murphy had missed the daily bus to Merced that left at 8 a.m. His friend, Kenneth Eugene Parnell, the night auditor at the Lodge, offered him a ride into town in his white Buick. While Murphy bought some Christmas presents in the Merced Mall, Parnell picked up some gospel tracts. He claimed he was studying to become a minister. They drove across town. Then they saw some children on their way home from school. Parnell stopped and told Murphy to give out the tracts.

Parnell claimed that there were a lot of battered children in the area. He wanted to take in underprivileged children, as he could do a better job of bringing them up than their parents, and he told Murphy to pick up one of the boys to be his son. Murphy was sympathetic. Both he and Parnell had been abused as children and had often talked about it.

Kay was held up at the auto parts store. When Steven came out of school at 2 p.m., it was raining. He was not expecting his mother to pick him up, and he started walking home alone. Parnell had dropped off Murphy, who was handing out the gospel tracts. Most of the kids just took one and rushed off. But Steven stopped to talk. Murphy said that he was gathering donations for the church and asked whether his mother might want to give something. Steven said he was sure she would. They lived about three blocks away. Murphy said that the minister would give him a ride there. Parnell pulled up, and Steven got into the car. Murphy got in the front, and they took off.

When they reached Shirley Street, Parnell drove right by. Steven mentioned this, but Parnell said they were going to his place first. He could call his mother from there to see if he could stay the night. Soon they had left Merced, and there was nothing Steven could do about it, except sit back and enjoy the ride. Murphy knew that there was something wrong, but Parnell was happy. He had spoken to two children in the Mall, but had said they were not suitable. Steven was perfect for what he had in mind. Besides, he had done nothing wrong, he thought. The child had gotten into the car perfectly willingly.

Later Parnell said that he had specifically picked Steven to be his "son." In a chance encounter with the mailman who delivered to Shirley Street, he discovered that Steven had been beaten. Parnell would rescue him from this abuse.

Kay Stayner had turned up at Charles Wright Elementary at 2:10 p.m. There was no sign of Steven. She drove home, looking out for him along the way. When she arrived home at 2:20, she asked Del if he had seen Steven. He had not. Perhaps Steven still had not learned his lesson.

At 3 p.m., Del and Kay went back to the school to pick up Cary, Cindy, and Jody. There was still no sign of Steven. As they drove home, Del grew angry, believing that Steven had disobeyed him again and gone to his friend's house. However, when they got home and phoned Steven's friends' parents, the boy was nowhere to be found.

By 4 p.m., the Stayners were scouring the neighborhood. At 5 p.m., when the search had proved fruitless, Del called the police. Meanwhile, Kay called Steven's teacher, got a list of the names and phone numbers of all the pupils in the class, and began calling each family on the list.

The police arrived and retraced the route Steven would have taken home. Then they began ringing doorbells along the way. Only an attendant in the gas station nearby remembered seeing Steven walk by sometime before 3 p.m. He was heading in the direction of home, and she had seen no suspicious characters hanging around.

At 6 p.m., reserve officers and the local Boy Scouts were called in to search the area. By then it was so cold and wet that there was hardly anyone on the streets. Local radio station KYOS put out a description of the missing boy. The Stayners' other children were sent to stay with friends, while Del was out with a flashlight searching a local junkyard, fearfully opening the doors of rusty fridges.

By then Steven was some fifty miles away in a small cabin Parnell had rented in Cathy's Valley. Inside, there were toys and Steven began playing with them. He asked whether he could take some of them home to his brother and sisters. This made Parnell angry, but then he got down on the floor and played alongside the boy.

At dinner, Steven ate the food he was given, including the green beans, which he hated, because he was afraid that he would be beaten otherwise. He was then told to take a shower. Afterwards, while Murphy dozed in a chair, Steven was told to drop the towel and climb into the cabin's one bed, naked, alongside Parnell. That night, Murphy recalled, Parnell had oral sex with the child.

When Steven could not be found, the police broadened the investigation. They asked Del whether he had killed his son. He said he had not and agreed to undergo a polygraph test. The following morning, a telephone extension was installed at the Stayners' to monitor any ransom demand, and Del and Kay were told to pick up their mail by the corners in case they were sent a ransom note; there might be fingerprints on the envelope. Missing person fliers were printed. Steven's picture appeared in the local paper, and an all-points bulletin went out across the state. That night, Del rode up to Cathy's Valley to tell Kay's father that his grandson was missing. Coincidentally, Del's father-in-law lived in a trailer park not two hundred feet from the cabin where Steven was being held. He might even have seen a white Buick traveling the other way, back down toward the highway. On the front seat there were two men. Between them was a seven-year-old boy, but his head would have been down below the level of the dashboard.

After driving Murphy home, Parnell took Steven to a remote spot where he forced the boy to fellate him. The crying child begged Parnell to take him home, but Parnell held his head in place. He informed the terrified boy that this was what he wanted him to do from now on. Then Parnell drove back to the Lodge where he worked. He undressed Steven and put him to bed in his room on the third floor of the Lodge, before going to work.

In the morning, when Murphy had finished cleaning the kitchens, Parnell sent him to check on Steven. When the boy awoke, Murphy gave him some food. Parnell then turned up. After Murphy had gone, Parnell fellated Steven once again.

While Steven suffered at the hands of Parnell, he did not blame Murphy. Indeed, he liked "Uncle Murphy," who bought him comic books. While Parnell made Steven go to the toilet in a bucket in the closet, Murphy sent him to the communal toilets, which felt much more normal.

The following Sunday, Parnell took Steven and Murphy back to the cabin. He had seen some of the TV coverage of Steven's disappearance, but was confident that little attention would be paid to it in Yosemite and Cathy's Valley.

Back in Merced, the police began checking on known sex offenders in the area. Parnell had a conviction from 1952. He had posed as a policeman, using a fake badge, to pick up young boys and sodomize them. He had served nearly four years. In the early 1960s, he went back to jail for a robbery in Utah. However, when he returned to California, he never registered as a sex offender as required by law.

Later, when the park rangers checked the payroll at Yosemite Lodge against the FBI's list of sex offenders, Parnell was overlooked. The Lodge paid employees on alternate weeks, and his name did not appear on the payroll the week they checked.

Had Parnell's name come up, it would have raised flags for plenty of other things on his record.

Parnell had been born in Texas in 1931. When his parents split up when he was five, he already showed signs of mental disturbance and tried to pull his own teeth out with pliers. His mother moved to Bakersfield, California. There, one of her lodgers induced the thirteen-year-old Parnell to perform fellatio on him. Soon after, the boy set fire to a field. The psychiatrist who examined him recommended he be sent to juvenile hall. When he was released, he stole a car. He was then sent to a secure school, where he engaged in homosexual practices with other boys. Released again, he was arrested for public sex acts of a homosexual nature—homosexuality was still a crime back then. He went back to jail for stealing another car. He escaped and made his way back to Bakersfield because he was attracted to a boy there, he said.

Back in jail, Parnell tried to kill himself by drinking disinfectant. This landed him in a mental hospital. There had been other suicide attempts. He escaped and stole another car to take him back to Bakersfield to see the boy he was so taken with. That landed him back in jail until he was seventeen. In May 1951, he abducted a nine-year-old boy, took him to a remote spot, and sexually assaulted him both orally and anally. It crossed his mind to kill the child so there would be no witness to the crime, he said. Instead he drove him back to the hospital where he had abducted him. The boy told his father what had happened, and Parnell was arrested.

Parnell admitted everything. He had stripped the boy naked. The child cried and fought back, but he sodomized him and ejaculated in his mouth. This was what he had planned to do from the start, he said. He even admitted that he considered killing the child, but decided against it. Parnell's wife was pregnant at the time, he said: "She was just too big for me, I guess, and I had to find another outlet." Before the case went to trial,

Parnell was examined by three psychiatrists, one of whom had seen him on six previous occasions. They found him to be a sexual psychopath who was a danger to others, and recommended that he be confined to an institution. He was sent to a psychiatric hospital for evaluation. They found him to be a sexual psychopath without psychosis—that is, he was legally sane. So he was returned to the county jail. In court, he was sentenced to five years to life. The judge remarked that he was dangerous and should be kept in jail for a long period.

Parnell was sent to San Quentin. When he came up for parole after three and a half years, he was released on the condition that he undergo psychiatric treatment. He went back to jail for violating the conditions of his parole, but was released in 1957.

Convicted for robbery in Salt Lake City in March 1961, he was sentenced to five years to life, but was released in September 1967 on the proviso he never set foot in Utah again. He then worked a series of jobs as a short order cook, before turning up at the Yosemite Lodge, where his application form mentioned nothing about his prison record or his spells in mental hospitals.

Parnell, Murphy, and Steven returned to Yosemite Lodge on Sunday night, then went back to the cabin in the morning. Murphy was to look after Steven there while Parnell went to visit his mother in Bakersfield. On the way, Parnell drove through Merced, even stopping at the gas station where the attendant had seen Steven heading home the week before. He studied Steven's description in the missing person flier for tips he could use to disguise the boy.

Parnell's mother gave him a Manchester terrier puppy. He took it back to Steven, who named the dog Queenie. Then Parnell put the boy on his lap and told him that he had been to see a judge who had given him custody of Steven, as his parents could no longer afford to keep him. From now on, Steven was to call Parnell "Dad" and the boy would be known as Dennis Gregory Parnell. Gregory was already Steven's middle name, one of the details Parnell had picked up from the missing person flier.

This was little comfort. Steven was confused and started crying. What about his brother and three sisters? Parnell said he should forget them. Parnell said that Steven must resign himself to the idea that his family did not want him anymore.

Parnell then quit his job, saying his mother had a heart attack. He spent the rest of the week in the cabin with "Dennis," whom he kept naked. With Murphy at work, Parnell was at liberty to molest the child at will. He cut the boy's hair and dyed it brown. He then dressed the boy in second-hand clothes and let him play outside, within sight of his grandfather's trailer.

Over the next week, Parnell frequently indulged in oral sex with his young captive. But worse was to come. On December 17, he removed the boy's clothes and explained what he was going to do with him. Then he lay the child face down on the bed, put Vaseline on his anus, and sodomized him.

He gave the crying child some sleeping tablets and crawled into bed with him. While the boy slept, Parnell fondled his buttocks and his genitals, and masturbated over and over again. In the morning, Parnell learned that Steven's grandfather lived nearby and decided to move on, first trading his white Buick for a Rambler American.

Parnell needed money. He got Murphy to bring his final paycheck over to him, then blackmailed the simple-minded kitchen-cleaner into paying part of his wages into Parnell's account by threatening to report him as Steven's kidnapper.

Passing through Merced again, this time with Steven in the car with him, Parnell headed for Santa Rosa, in Northern California, where they checked into a hotel as father and son. The following day, they moved into another anonymous motel where Steven spent his first Christmas away from his family. Parnell bought him a Hot Wheels race track set, a toy rifle, and a toy bow and arrow. Other presents were waiting for him at home where the Stayner family had the first of many bleak Christmases without their precious child.

Parnell had now saddled himself with the problems of being a single parent and had to hire a babysitter to look after his Dennis when he was out looking for work. But first he had to indoctrinate the child with a backstory he could relate if asked about his family background.

After Christmas, Parnell got a job as a front desk clerk in the Santa Rosa Holiday Inn, and a child named Dennis Parnell was registered at Steele Lane Elementary School. Parnell gave Steven's correct date of birth. His place of birth, he said, was Merced, but he put down Yosemite Elementary as his former school.

Steele Lane Elementary was in the Bellevue Union School District. That month, the school district's office received a letter and a sheaf of missing person fliers from Del and Kay Stayner. But Steele Lane Elementary never received any fliers; they were consigned to the trash at Bellevue Union School

District's office. When Parnell and his "son" moved on, the form sent to Dennis Parnell's next school noted: "Steele Lane did not receive any records from former school." Subsequent schools did not insist on receiving these records. Nor did they ask to see Dennis Parnell's birth certificate.

Steven was not happy at his new school, but this only made him more dependent on Parnell. Soon they made a pretty convincing father and son. Parnell even wrote to the California Department of Human Resources asking for financial assistance now that he had a son to support. The department checked out his previous employers, but in the end the request for financial aid was denied.

That February, they moved into a run-down trailer. Parnell allowed Dennis the run of the trailer park. He could take Queenie for walks, climb trees, and play with other kids. But he suffered nightly sexual assaults.

He eventually settled well at school, but teachers were concerned about the erratic behavior of Parnell. They never knew whether he was coming to pick the boy up, or whether the boy should be sent to a babysitter or travel home on the school bus.

Back in Merced, a pair of cowboy boots like those Steven had been wearing when he disappeared had washed up on the banks of Bear Creek to the north of the city. There was a tense time in the Stayner household until they discovered that they were not Steven's. Meanwhile they continued sending fliers to radio and TV stations across the nation. But by then, Steven's disappearance was old news.

Later Del found a sack in an irrigation ditch. He knew that there was something dead inside it. He cut it open to find a dead calf. Even so, he had to sit on the edge of the ditch for a quarter of an hour to compose himself. Then two Chinese brothers who ran a local supermarket accused each other of killing Steven, cutting up the body, and flushing it down the drain. The police had to dig up the sewer just in case they were telling the truth.

The longer Steven was gone, the harder it was for the Stayners to bear. They kept all his clothes, and sometimes Del would go and sniff them, just to remember what his son smelled like.

Steven's ordeal continued. One night after a particularly horrendous night of anal sex, he snuck out of the trailer while Parnell was asleep. He intended, somehow, to find his way home. But the eight-year-old had not gotten very far, when he became disorientated and started to cry. Somehow he found his way back to the trailer before Parnell awoke. Soon after, he began to play with matches and was frequently beaten for it.

By summer, Steven had saved enough out of his allowance to buy the GI Joe set he had wanted for Christmas. Despite Parnell's constant abuse of the child, he sometimes tried to give him some fun and would let Steven sit on his lap and steer the car while he operated the pedals when they were out driving.

After summer vacation, Dennis Parnell started third grade at Kawana Elementary, where he met Kenny Matthias. They soon became good friends and Dennis would head to the Matthias house after school. Parnell then formalized the relationship, asking Barbara Matthias to look after Dennis and give him his dinner each night after school so he could work late. Parnell also seized the opportunity to start an affair with Mrs. Matthias.

That fall, Dennis fell ill. Ken took him to the doctor and stayed with him during the examination, answering questions that were directed at the boy.

With the overtime he was getting at the Holiday Inn, Parnell had enough money to rent a large wood-framed house in central Santa Rosa. For Dennis, it meant another change of school. But he did not lose touch with his friend Kenny, whom Parnell invited to stay overnight.

Parnell and Kenny's father, Bob Matthias, joined forces for a number of doomed business ventures. The two of them went around drinking and losing money, while Barbara looked after Dennis along with her four other children. She had another two, but they were both in jail.

A lifetime smoker, Parnell lost his job at the Holiday Inn when they introduced a no-smoking policy at the front desk. He then got a job delivering the Santa Rosa *Press-Democrat* newspaper. For a while, he took Dennis with him on the delivery route, but soon started letting the small boy stay at home by himself.

Without Parnell's overtime from the Holiday Inn, he could not longer afford the house and moved back into a motel, where the two of them had to share a double bed. But the move meant that Dennis could return to Kawana Elementary. He could also spend more time at the Matthiases' house, where one of Kenny's sister's twelve-year-old friends offered to have sex with him. Dennis turned her down, and Kenny teased him when he found out about it.

When Bob Matthias got drunk, he would beat up his wife. Barbara fled to the Pelissier Motel where Parnell was staying with Dennis. She then moved into their room and the three of them shared a bed. One night Parnell and Barbara Matthias came home a little drunk. Dennis was still up watching TV. They took no notice of him, took their clothes off, and began having sex. Then Parnell called Dennis over. He got him to undress, then he played with his penis until it was hard, and got him to have sex with Barbara. Like so many things in his life, Dennis knew this was not right.

Parnell was rehired by the Holiday Inn on the proviso that he did not smoke while he was on duty. He then bought a sixteen-foot travel trailer and the three of them—Parnell, Dennis, and Barbara—moved into it. Again, there was only one double bed, and the three of them slept together. Steven/Dennis was now nine. Although he did not like Barbara, the new arrangement had its upside. Barbara took care of most of Parnell's sexual needs so, while she was around, Parnell left his "son" alone. However, Parnell continued to molest Dennis when they were alone and he indulged his appetite for voyeurism by encouraging Barbara to have sex with Dennis while he watched.

The police were called to this happy household when Bob turned up drunk one night and tried to pick a fight with Barbara. But no one scratched beneath the surface and asked what a child was doing in the midst of the mayhem.

Parnell wanted to take a trip out to Reno to gamble. Dennis was confined to a hotel room with a babysitter from a local service, while Parnell lost all his money at blackjack and craps. Back in Santa Rosa, Barbara got Parnell to install a makeshift single bed in the trailer for Dennis to sleep on. Then Parnell lost his job at the Holiday Inn again—he had continued smoking at work. He opened a stall in a flea market, which provided Dennis with clothes at least, though most of them weren't very suitable. Within two months, that had failed and he took a job as a cook in a diner. But Dennis was happy enough; he was now in the fourth grade with his best friend Kenny. However, the school was increasingly worried about Dennis's after-school arrangements. Parnell was warned that he needed to be careful, as "Dennis might be picked up by some weirdo on the street."

That Christmas, Parnell and Barbara turned up to see the school's Christmas play as man and wife. But something was simmering under the surface. During the vacation, the trio went to a shopping mall where Parnell looked for young boys. When he saw one who he thought was alone, he would send Dennis to approach the child and ask him to come with him. But as Parnell was too far away to hear what he was saying, Dennis would always ask some other question, one that would elicit the answer, "No." Then he would go back to Parnell and say the boy did not want to come. Parnell did not get angry. He just sent Dennis to approach another boy.

Barbara was used in a similar role. When Dennis joined the Santa Rosa Boys' Club, Parnell asked her to lure one of the other boys into the car. When the boy grew suspicious, Parnell shouted to Barbara. She scuttled back to the car and they took off.

A few days later after the Boys' Club incident, Parnell, Dennis, and Barbara towed their trailer eighty miles north to the town of Willits in Mendocino County. Dennis was registered at Brookside Elementary. The Stayners had sent fliers to the Willits Unified School District, but again they were not distributed to the schools.

Dennis began to get some sex education in school and learned, for sure, that what he was being subjected to was wrong. But he knew it made no difference. If he confronted Parnell with his knowledge, it would cause trouble—and that was the last thing he needed.

With money from his mother, Parnell bought a new Chevrolet Impala—he frequently changed cars—and opened a Bible store in nearby Fort Bragg. Parnell claimed to be a licensed minister. He said that he held a doctorate in Bible studies and knew the Bible by heart, though he never went to church.

Dennis changed schools again. On his enrollment form to Dana Grey Elementary, his mother was listed as Barbara Parnell. He was still playing with matches, and being beaten for it. Then he was caught shoplifting. The police were called, but Dennis did not seize the opportunity to tell them about the kidnapping. He was too afraid of Parnell. Once again, they did no background checks.

The Bible store failed. Around the same time, Barbara got her divorce from Bob and won custody of her kids. Parnell now had a family of seven to support.

He swapped his trailer for a converted school bus. This was not allowed on the trailer park in town. Instead, it had to be towed out to a site for similar wrecks down near the shoreline. One day, Dennis and Kenny went out fishing on a raft. When they did not return by nightfall, Barbara called the sheriff. However, the two boys turned up before the sheriff's office asked any awkward questions.

Now that they were living together, Parnell tried to sexually assault Kenny. Kenny told Dennis that his father had grabbed his balls and tried to fellate him. There were allegations that Parnell went even further. Dennis ignored what his friend had told him and nothing more was said.

To support the children, Barbara took a job washing dishes in a restaurant and promptly fell in love with another man there. Barbara and her brood moved out, leaving Parnell with his "son" Dennis. Parnell and Dennis took another trip to Reno. When they came back, the sexual abuse started again and Parnell had no one to inflict his libido on but the now eleven-year-old. Dennis/Steven had to submit daily to oral and anal sex. He had long accepted that he had to do this if he was going to survive.

Steven's parents had not given up on him, though, and the police were still pursuing every lead. When a mentally deficient young man said that he had murdered Steven out near Cathy's Valley, they dug up the spot where he said he had buried his body. Nothing was found.

Parnell got a new job in Comptche, thirty miles from Fort Bragg. They moved into a spacious trailer there. For once, Dennis had a room of his own. They stayed there for three years. Dennis went to school, played on the football team, and climbed trees. They kept their own pigs, chickens, and rabbits, and Dennis, for once, was relatively happy. His newfound freedom meant that he could avoid Parnell most of the time. He made some good friends there and took his first girlfriend, Lori Macdonald, out on a date. They went to the movies, though her parents came along as chaperones. The neighborhood boys were fond of swimming naked in a nearby water hole, but Dennis would not go skinny-dipping with Lori, even though she asked.

In Comptche, Parnell was thought to be a little standoffish. The only people whom he invited to the trailer were young male friends of Dennis. At Parnell's behest, Dennis invited Kenny to come and stay for a weekend. Parnell then arranged for Dennis to stay elsewhere and Kenny had to stay alone with Parnell overnight. Parnell grabbed the boy when he came out of the shower. Kenny said he fought Parnell off and, in the morning, persuaded him to take him home.

When Dennis found a new friend at school named Damon, Parnell invited him to stay too. Damon reported later that nothing happened, but Dennis never left him for a moment. Damon's mother was suspicious. She recalled that Dennis had told her that his mother lived with his brother and sisters in Merced, but she did not put two and two together. After all, years had passed since Steven Stayner had gone missing.

When Parnell was giving a ride to another friend of Dennis named Jeff, he asked the boy: "Can I put my dick in your hole?"

Confused, Jeff replied that he did not have a hole. Parnell gave the boy some money, perhaps to shut him up. Later, when Jeff came by, Parnell took photographs of the two boys in the shower, then got them to pose nude on the coffee table, but Steven said no sex took place.

When a boy named George came home with Dennis, Parnell gave them beers and got them to strip. Parnell took his clothes off, too, this time. He was aroused and took George in the bedroom. George later insisted that nothing happened, but his mother reported the matter to the police, saying that Parnell sodomized her son. Dennis admitted that he had sat in the other room, naked, reading a book while this went on. He was sanguine about Parnell's interest in other boys.

"I figured if he was fucking them he wouldn't be fucking me," he said.

No one followed up on the complaint.

At the age of thirteen, like much of his generation, Dennis began smoking marijuana. One night in the spring of 1978, he was drinking and smoking at a party when he started talking about his true past. He said, "I want to go home" and started crying. But no one understood what he was saying. Parnell had convinced everyone that he and Dennis were the perfect father and son.

As Dennis grew older, Parnell's sexual interest in him waned. With Dennis's help, he sought out younger boys. He got Dennis to call a boy named Ricky who lived in Fort Bragg and invite him over. Parnell then offered the child $5 for a sexual favor. The boy refused.

In 1979, they moved to Arkansas. Once there, Parnell insisted on having both oral and anal sex with Dennis again, though the frequency soon tapered off. Then when the bodies of a boy and girl were found in a nearby forest, Parnell moved on again and Dennis found himself in a squalid cabin fifty miles from Comptche. He had to change schools again, while Parnell got a night job in the Palace Hotel in Ukiah.

Parnell struck up a friendship with another of Dennis's friends, a boy named Sean Poorman. First Parnell asked Poorman to sell some marijuana for him. Then Parnell offered him

$50 to get him a five- or six-year-old child. He gave Poorman a bottle of sleeping pills to drug the kid. Later, Parnell offered him another $20 if he brought the child within a couple of days.

Dennis was also coerced into the plot to abduct another child, but Poorman complained he was no help at all. So Parnell and Poorman left him behind when they took off to Ukiah where Parnell had his eye on a five-year-old named Timmy White. They waited outside Yokayo Elementary School until they saw Timmy. Poorman was supposed to pretend that there was something wrong with the rear tire, solicit Timmy's help to hold the valve, then scoop him up and throw him on the backseat. But when Poorman asked for Timmy's assistance, the child said no.

Poorman went to get back into the car, but Parnell yelled at him: "Get the kid."

Timmy ran, but Poorman soon caught up with him. The child grabbed hold of a chain-link fence. Poorman pried his fingers free, threw the screaming boy in the back of the car, and covered him with a blanket. Then Parnell put his foot down and they made their escape.

Back at the cabin, Parnell paid Poorman off. Then he took off Timmy's clothes and dressed him in others he had bought. Later he dyed his hair to complete the disguise. Now he had two "sons."

In Ukiah, Timmy's parents were frantic. The police were on the case but, shockingly, given the drama of the abduction, no one had seen a thing. Dogs and helicopters were brought in. Appeals were broadcast; fliers were sent out.

Parnell slept with Timmy, but did not appear to molest him. He could not get a babysitter to come out to the remote cabin so when he went to work, Dennis had to look after Timmy. When Dennis had to go to school, he was supposed to give Timmy a sleeping pill. They seem to have had little effect and the child sat up most of the day, wondering how to get away, or playing with the toys that Parnell bought him. Meanwhile, Parnell hung out drinking beer with his friends, joining in the general speculation about what had happened to Timmy White. Several people noted the similarity been the picture of Timmy in the paper and the new boy Parnell sometimes had with him. But no one said anything.

Having Timmy around reminded Dennis painfully of his own kidnapping. As he got to know and like the boy, he began cutting school in the hopes that he could prevent Parnell from molesting him. He even started carrying a knife, but doubted that he had the courage to use it.

Timmy began to see Dennis as his big brother and asked him to take him home. Dennis became convinced that it was what he must do. But he could not get any help from his friends, as they were too afraid of Parnell. Meanwhile, Parnell had plans of his own. Dennis was now too old to fulfill his pedophile tastes. He was no good to him anymore, so he intended to kill Dennis and move to Arkansas with Timmy. But both Parnell's and Dennis's plans were thwarted by heavy seasonal rain.

On the night of March 1, 1980, Parnell went to work as usual. Dennis gave Timmy something to eat. Then he dressed him in warm clothes and they left the cabin. His one thought was to return Timmy to his family. After that, he did not know what he was going to do.

Around a quarter of a mile from the cabin, Dennis stuck out his thumb. They got a ride from a Mexican who did not speak much English. He took them to Ukiah and dropped them near where Timmy said his babysitter lived. There was no one home. Dennis was then depending on Timmy to find his way home. But it was dark and they got lost.

They stopped in a phone booth and Dennis looked up the address of the police station. The route there would take them past the Palace Hotel where Parnell worked. They risked it and passed by without being seen.

At the parking lot by the police station, Dennis squatted down and told Timmy to walk up to the front door of the precinct and give his name to the first officer he met. The officer would then make sure he got home safely.

As Timmy approached the station, an officer was coming out. Timmy was startled and ran back toward Dennis. The officer realized that something was up and quickly called up another unit to cut off the children's retreat. A patrol car skidded to a halt. The driver got out and grabbed Timmy. He recognized him immediately. Then he began talking to the other boy who said he was Steven Stayner who had been kidnapped from Merced seven years earlier. They went into the police station where Steven was locked in an interview room.

Timmy's parents were called and Steven was questioned. He gave the police a detailed description of Parnell and they went to the Palace Hotel to arrest him. Steven then had to identify him in person.

The Merced police were called and they sent two officers to collect Steven. Other officers were dispatched to tell Del and Kay Stayner that Steven was alive and well. They could hardly believe their ears.

Steven was asked to make a statement. In it he said he knew his first name was Steven, and he thought his last name was Stayner, though he could not remember how to spell it. It appears as "Stainer" throughout his statement. He denied that Parnell had sexually assaulted him, saying that his "dad" had been good to him and he did not know why he had kidnapped him or Timmy.

A doctor examined Timmy for signs of sexual abuse. There were none. Timmy's parents thanked Steven for bringing him back to them safely. Steven was then returned home.

In his statement, Steven had mentioned that a second man was involved in his abduction, but had not named him. On March 3, officers took Steven to the Merced police station for a second interview. After several hours of questioning, he told them that the second man's name was Murphy and he worked in Yosemite. Later, Ervin Edward Murphy was arrested.

Although Steven continued to maintain that he had not been sexually abused, the police began to suspect that he was not telling the truth. They had Parnell's record.

In April, Steven's parents took him to visit Timmy and then Steven's friends in Comptche. But then it was time to return to school in Merced. This was hard for Steven. Guessing the nature of the relationship between him and Parnell, schoolmates called him gay and the question was asked repeatedly: Why hadn't he run away from Parnell? He compensated by eschewing male companionship in favor of girls.

As investigations continued, the police heard of Parnell's alleged sexual assaults on Dennis's male friends in Comptche. Steven was then confronted with nude pictures Parnell had taken of him, and he admitted that Parnell had sexually assaulted him—not once but hundreds of times since he had kidnapped him. However, there was a statute of limitations on sexual assaults of three years in California. That meant they could not prosecute the early assaults in Merced County and the assaults between 1977 and 1980 would have to be filed in Mendocino County. The authorities there decided not to proceed with these charges to save Steven from having to testify about them.

There was also a three-year statute of limitations on kidnapping, but the Merced Country DA convinced a grand jury that the kidnapping did not just mean the original abduction. It also covered Steven's continued captivity. They returned an indictment for second-degree kidnapping. In California, first-degree kidnapping had to result in death or bodily harm to the victim. Sexual assault was not considered bodily harm in California.

On June 8, 1981, Parnell's trial for the kidnapping of Timmy White began in Mendocino County. Sean Poorman had already been convicted of false imprisonment in a juvenile court and was offered immunity from prosecution for kidnapping if he turned state's evidence. Both Steven and Timmy also testified. The jury took less than two hours to find Parnell guilty. He was sentenced to seven years, the maximum for second-degree kidnapping.

Then on December 1, 1981, Parnell and Murphy went on trial for Steven's kidnapping in Merced County. When Steven took the stand, he gave a detailed account of the sexual abuse he had suffered. Both Parnell and Murphy were found guilty of second-degree kidnapping and conspiracy to kidnap. Parnell was again given the maximum sentence of seven years, but it was to run concurrently with his other sentence, so it made little difference. Murphy got five years; it was a harsh sentence, as he was not the prime mover in the crime and had no prior criminal record. However, prosecutors pointed out that Murphy could have come forward at any time and rescued Steven from the clutches of Parnell.

Steven Stayner married in 1985 and had two children. He worked hard to support them. On the afternoon of September 16, 1989, he was returning home from work on his motorcycle in the rain when a car pulled out from a side road. He skidded to avoid it and struck his head. His helmet had been stolen a few days before. He died of his injuries in Merced County Medical Center, aged just twenty-four. Fourteen-year-old Timmy White was a pallbearer at his funeral.

More tragedy hit the Stayner family. The following year, Steven's uncle Jerry Stayner was shot and killed by an unknown assailant in his home in Merced. Then in 2001, Steven's older brother Cary was convicted for the murder of four women and sentenced to death. After his arrest, he claimed to have fantasized about killing women since he was seven, long before Steven's abduction. He asked for child pornography in exchange for his confession.

Kenneth Parnell served just five years before being paroled. By 2002, he had become a near invalid, requiring the assistance of social workers to deal with his everyday needs. Although he was in his seventies, Parnell had not changed. He offered one of his care workers $500 to get him a little African-American boy. The care worker did not take him seriously, at first. When he persisted, she reported him to the authorities, who told her to play along.

On January 3, 2003, she arrived at Parnell's home and told him she had the little boy he wanted outside in the car. Parnell gave her $100 for a forged birth certificate, and asked her to bring the boy in. When she went outside, police descended. They found the remaining $400 in Parnell's pockets. A search of his residence unearthed toys for his new "son," along with associated pornography and sex toys.

Parnell was charged with soliciting a kidnapping, trying to steal a child, and attempting to purchase a person. Tim White and Kay Stayner, Steven's mother, were called to testify at his trial to show that Parnell's attempt to purchase a young boy was a continuation of his earlier criminal behavior, though no details of his sexual abuse of Steven were permitted as Parnell was not charged with sexual offenses.

Parnell's defense had tried to quash any mention of the kidnapping or Steven Stayner and Timmy White, telling the jury that Parnell merely wanted to provide a nice home to a disadvantaged young boy. Parnell, they maintained, was too old to be a threat to young children. He had not mentioned the word "kidnap." He had merely asked the care worker to "get" him a child, though he admitted that it would be "risky."

The jury took just ninety minutes to find him guilty. He was sentenced to twenty-five years to life under California's "three strikes" law. Parnell died of natural causes in California State Prison Hospital in Vacaville on January 21, 2008.

Chapter 10

Charlene Lunnon and Lisa Hoodless— The Theft of Innocence

CHARLENE LUNNON AND LISA HOODLESS were best friends from school. But while Charlene had been in and out of foster care since she was young, Lisa came from a sheltered background. During their first sex education class, Lisa was shocked when she was told about the development of breasts and menstruation. Charlene, by contrast, had once woken up on her drug-addicted mother's lap to see a man trying to push his penis into her mother's mouth. Her mom had also watched pornographic movies with her friends when Charlene was in the room. For her there was no mystery. At ten, Charlene had already had her first period.

"I could get pregnant now," she said.

Lisa still had no idea how babies were made.

On the morning of January 19, 1999, the two friends were walking to school in the St. Leonards' district of Hastings, East Sussex, on the south coast of England. When they met in the street, ten-year-old Lisa had said that she thought a car was following her, but Charlene did not believe her.

A little way down the street, seagulls had ripped a trash bag open. Avoiding the spilled garbage, Lisa stepped onto the road. A turquoise car swerved and braked to avoid hitting her. The car stopped a little farther down the road. The driver got out and came back to speak to them. Charlene felt uneasy and made an excuse to hurry off, but the driver put his arms around their shoulders. His grip tightened.

"Get in the car and do as I say," he said in a menacing tone.

Lisa screamed. He put his hand over her mouth and bundled her into the trunk of the car. Charlene could have run away right then but, in shock, she froze. She could not abandon her friend Lisa. So when he told her to get into the trunk, she did. Then he slammed it closed.

In the darkness, Charlene could hear Lisa's sobs. She was little comfort.

"I know what he is going to do," she said. "He is going to rape us and murder us."

Lisa did not even know what the word "rape" meant. But it was stuffy in the trunk and it smelled of gasoline, and the thought of being murdered made her panic.

Charlene tried to take control of the situation. She told Lisa to keep quiet; everything would be okay. Then she started singing the Sade song "Your Love Is King."

To mask the sound, the kidnapper turned the stereo up.

They seemed to have been driving for ages when the car suddenly stopped. The trunk opened and the kidnapper grabbed Charlene. Lisa was thrust back into the dark and the trunk lid closed.

Charlene was shoved into the backseat of the car. They were in a remote spot and there was no chance of escape. The kidnapper got in too and sat her on his lap. He began asking her questions. What was her name? How old was she? What was her favorite color? What was her favorite subject at school? Charlene knew what he was playing at. At one of the foster homes she had been sent to after her mother died, there was a babysitter named Bert who took care of her when her foster parents were out. He liked to watch her having a bath. Then he played games with her, touching her, and doing things that he said she was not to tell her foster parents about—they would never believe her. He played mind games with her. The kidnapper was doing the same thing.

However, the kidnapper said that he had taken her for a ransom and got her to give him her father's phone number. He had kidnapped a girl before, he said. He had held her for just three hours and got a lot of money. But he had gotten caught and had gone to prison. This time things were going to work out better though, he said.

Charlene could hear Lisa sobbing and asked to be returned to her. The kidnapper obliged and put Charlene back in the trunk.

They were driven around some more. When they stopped, they were inside a garage. This time he wanted Lisa. The kidnapper produced a sports bag and told Lisa to get in. She refused, so he grabbed her and pushed her in. He zipped it shut and carried her into the adjoining house.

When he opened the bag, Lisa found herself in a dingy living room. The curtains were drawn. He began taking her clothes off. When she asked him why he was doing it, he said he had already told Charlene that he was holding them for ransom. She said that her parents would give him any money he wanted, but he continued taking her clothes off.

Once she was naked, she tried to cover herself with her hands, but he held her arms above her head, then bound her wrists behind her back with her panty hose. He picked her up and put her on his lap. She could feel him looking at her naked body. He began asking her questions; then he began stroking her between her legs with his fingers. She did not know why he was doing this, but it felt wrong and she asked him to stop. He took no notice. Behind his eyes, she said she saw an emptiness. It was as if there was not a real person there.

In the garage, Charlene was kicking and screaming. The kidnapper then left Lisa inside and came to ask Charlene what all the noise was about. She said she needed to pee. He offered her a bucket. When she refused to use it, he closed the trunk again.

Charlene not only knew about sex and what rape would entail, but she also knew about death. Her mother had died of a drug overdose two years before. Recently, Charlene had been reunited with her dad and had gone to live with him and his new wife. She was enjoying some sort of stability and happiness for the first time in her life, and this man was going to take it all away.

Then she heard him coming back. She figured that he had killed Lisa already. Now it was her turn. When he opened the trunk, she asked what he had done with Lisa. He said she was not to worry. Lisa was fine.

He got her out of the trunk and told her to take her pants off. Charlene, too, noticed his cold dead eyes. Then he told her to take her panties off as well. She knew what was going to happen next. She had been through it with Bert and she tried to cover herself with her coat. He pulled it off her and threw it in the trunk.

Then he got her to sit in the backseat of the car with her legs open. He stared at her, but did not touch her. Bert had done the same thing, sometimes. But she was much more scared of this man than Bert. Bert had done terrible things to her, but he was not a danger. This man, she decided, was quite capable of killing both her and Lisa just to prevent them from telling anyone what he had done.

After examining her private parts closely, he got her out of the car and told her to put her clothes back on. Then he returned her to the trunk. Lisa was then brought back to the car in the sports bag, but he took her out once she was in the trunk. In the trunk, the two girls told each other what had happened to them as the car drove off. After a while, the car stopped again and Lisa was returned to the sports bag while Charlene was left in the trunk. The man carried Lisa up the stairs to a small apartment and left her there while he went to get Charlene. He told her she was not to try to escape, as the man next door had a fierce dog that would tear her to pieces.

Charlene was too big to fit into the sports bag, so he carried her up the stairs wrapped in the trash bag with holes cut for her nose and eyes. He took the girls over to the window and opened the curtain. He said they would never be able to escape from that height. The fall would break their legs at the very least. The only other way was out was the front door, and it was securely locked.

They asked him his name. He wouldn't tell them. Then they asked him to call their parents for the ransom. He said he would do it later. He said he was now not sure what he was going to do with them; he would have to decide.

Lisa needed to pee. He took her to the bathroom, but would not leave and stood there watching.

When they pressed him again to call their parents, he said his plans had backfired and he did not know what to do with them. He might have to let them go. That was all right, they said. He did not have to drop them outside their homes. He could leave them nearby and they would walk.

Comforted by the prospect that they might be going home, they ate the packed lunches they had in their school bags. Charlene told Lisa what Bert had done to her. Soon they noticed it was getting dark outside.

The kidnapper bound Lisa's wrists and ankles with ladies' panty hose and took Charlene into his bedroom. There he took off Charlene's clothes. She quickly found it was pointless to struggle. He told her he was not going to hurt her and got her to lie on the bed. Then he took off his own clothes and lay down beside her.

He began rubbing Vaseline between her legs. Charlene let her mind go blank and distant, just as she had with Bert. She tried to think of nicer things—her hamster, Fluffy, her new bedroom, her father's wedding. The man got on top of her and tried to force his way inside her. The pain was unbearable. She screamed and begged him to stop. He put his hand over her mouth.

After he had finished, he gave her a T-shirt to wear and took her back in the other room. He gave Lisa a T-shirt too and told them to sleep on the couch. Once they were alone, Charlene explained what had happened to her. This was Lisa's brutal introduction into the facts of life. They tried their best to stay awake, but comforted by the thought that they might be going home, they drifted off.

In the morning, their abductor appeared almost contrite. He apologized and said he should not have taken them. He had gotten himself into a big mess and did not know how to get out of it. He said his name was Alan. This was his apartment. The other house he had taken them to belonged to his parents who were away in Australia.

The girls were eager to get going. Lisa suggested that he drop them off outside a police station then drive off.

"They wouldn't catch you," she said.

But he wanted to get caught, he said. He deserved to get caught. He should be in jail. He felt safe in jail. They gave him three meals a day and he did not have to worry about paying his bills.

He explained that he had kidnapped girls twice before. One had got away. When he had taken the other, someone had seen his car and he got caught. He had been out of jail for four years. Everything had been okay until his parents had gone away, now he had done this. It seemed he could not handle life outside jail. He was a bad person.

He asked them to hit him. They refused. He begged them. Eventually Lisa plucked up the courage to slap him. He thanked her and said he deserved that.

This gave her more courage. She asked him to promise to be nice to them and drop them off at the police station. He said he would and apologized to Charlene. He would not rape her again, he said.

Charlene asked whether he had called her dad. He said he had, but her father would not pay the ransom. Lisa's parents would not pay either. The girls were devastated. He told them not to worry. He needed to think and would leave them for a bit. Once he was gone, they agreed that their parents would have found the money if he had asked. They knew he had not called them and they hated him for sowing the tiniest seed of doubt in their minds.

After that, they realized that they could not believe a word he said. He did not take them and drop them off outside a police station as they had asked. Nor was his promise not to rape Charlene again any good. That evening, he dragged Charlene back into the bedroom. Lisa could hear her screams.

With Charlene, he pretended that he was being gentle and considerate. The man next door would not bother with the Vaseline, he said. He would tear her to pieces. It hurt Charlene more this time because she was sore. While he was raping her, Charlene wondered whether he would try and rape Lisa too. Or was he only doing it to her because she was bigger?

Afterward, she would not talk and spurned his attempts to cuddle.

"Be nice," he begged. She wouldn't.

Then he went and got Lisa. He got her to lay down naked beside Charlene and tied their hands above their heads. He watched them for a bit, then he untied Charlene and told her to go in the other room and watch TV. Lisa begged her not to go. She had no choice.

In the other room, Charlene wondered whether she could find a knife. She also wondered what it would feel like to stab a man. Then a news bulletin came on. The newscaster said: "The search continues for the two Hastings girls missing since yesterday."

Their pictures came up on the screen. The news program gave their names and showed footage of soldiers and policemen with dogs searching the area. Charlene wished Lisa could be there to see this with her. Instead, she could hear her screams from the other room, but there was nothing she could do about it.

In the bedroom, Lisa had turned away, so that she did not have to see the kidnapper's naked body, or his erection. He told her not to worry; he was not going to do anything. Lots of pretty girls her age came to his apartment to play on the computer. She was pretty too. Would she like to play on the computer later?

As he got on top of her, she said it was not nice to take people away from their homes. He said it was not his fault her parents would not pay the ransom. Who had he talked to, she wanted to know? Her mother, he said, and she said it was okay for her to stay. Lisa accused him of lying.

She begged him to leave her alone, but he took her hand and put it on his penis. She pulled away. He told her again that she was beautiful and reached for the jar of Vaseline. As he smeared it between her legs, she told him that she was not going to let him rape her. But he forced her legs apart anyway.

She was so small, she said. Would it hurt him? Why was he doing this? When he got on top of her, she realized that she would have to stop screaming and struggling or the sheer bulk of him would suffocated her.

Then came the pain. She made all sorts of promises in her head if it would stop. She would never be mean to anyone ever again. Tears were streaming down her face. Eventually it did stop and there was a sticky mess on her stomach. She did not know what it was.

When he tried to cuddle her afterward, it made her hate him even more. As she was uncooperative, he let her put her T-shirt back on and join Charlene while he had a bath. They seized the opportunity to search the apartment. They found only spoons in the kitchen drawers. He had hidden all the knives and forks. Charlene then found a letter with a name and address on it: "Alan Hopkinson… Kingfisher Drive, Eastbourne."

Eastbourne is just along the coast from St. Leonards. They were only fifteen miles from home.

When he appeared from the bathroom he told them he would take then home, but not until after dark. He asked them if they wanted to play on the computer to pass the time. Lisa did not want to accept any favors from him, but thought that the computer room might provide some more clues. When Lisa went with him, Charlene got up too, but he would only allow one of them at a time.

The first thing Lisa looked for in the computer room was a phone. He did not seem to have one in the apartment. He made Lisa sit on his lap as there was only one chair. She asked if he was married. He said he was, but his wife and son did not live with him.

There were maps on the floor, some hand-drawn with arrows on them. He said he had been watching her for some time. She asked him why.

"Because you're so pretty," he said.

She asked again whether he was going to take them home when it was dark. He assured her that he would. But first they had better have a bath. He let them do this without him watching, but told them that they had better be quiet or the neighbors would hear them. Once they were finished, he brought them their school clothes and they got dressed. But still it was not dark outside.

While they waited, they watched TV. There was another news bulletin. This time they saw Charlene's father and Lisa's parents at a press conference, begging them to come home. Alan beamed and said that they were famous.

When it was over, Lisa had to get back in the sports bag and he carried her downstairs. Meanwhile, Charlene wrapped herself up in the garbage bag. But when they went out onto the landing, they heard voices.

"Quick! Run!" said Alan.

They ran around down the stairs to the basement parking garage. Charlene peeled off the garbage bag and leapt into the trunk next to Lisa. This time he gave them a little flashlight.

Charlene knew that it would take about half an hour to drive back to St. Leonards, but they had not gone far before the car stopped. The trunk opened and he told them quickly to get in the backseat of the car. They were in a dark alley. Charlene figured that they could have made a run for it, but if he was taking them home, what was the point?

First, he said, he was going to feed them. He went to buy them sausages and fries, telling them to stay where they were because it was a bad neighborhood. They were less than ten feet from people walking by. Charlene wondered if they should ask them for help. But the thought crossed her mind that someone else might kidnap them too.

Lisa noticed a newspaper on the front seat. The front page was filled with the search for the missing girls.

They wondered again whether they should make a run for it and tested to see if they could open the door. But Alan was watching them through the window of the food shop. If they ran, he could easily catch them. Before they knew it, he was coming back with the food.

The girls had lost their appetites. But Alan ate his meal, then headed off again. After a while, Lisa spotted a sign for Brighton. This meant they were going the wrong way. When Lisa pointed this out, he said he knew a shortcut. Then he turned off onto a side road, saying he had gotten lost. The girls begged him to let them out anywhere.

He drove on. Then they realized they had left the road and were driving over grass. It was as if they were in a field. Lisa said she needed to pee. He stopped the car and pointed to some bushes. Charlene asked where they were. He said she should come and look. When they got out, she realized that they were on the top of a cliff. Suddenly Alan pushed her. She lost her footing and was about to fall over the edge when he grabbed her by her sweater and pulled her back. He could have killed her. Then he said that he had decided to keep them for one more day.

When Lisa came back, she could not see Charlene. Alan grabbed her and pushed her within two feet of the cliff's edge. She wondered whether he had pushed Charlene over already. But then she saw her a little way off.

He bundled the girls back into the trunk, and Charlene told Lisa what he had said. Then he started the car. Charlene wondered for a moment whether he was going to drive all three of them over the cliff, but soon they were back on the road. They had, it seemed, another twenty-four hours to live.

After fifteen minutes, they were back in the garage of his parents' house. Lisa had to get back in the sports bag and he carried her inside. Then he got Charlene and led her down the corridor. Suddenly, Lisa heard a scream and she ran down the corridor. Throwing open the door to a back room, she saw Charlene kneeling naked on the floor with Alan penetrating her from behind.

Lisa screamed for him to stop it. He had promised that he would not rape her anymore. He told Lisa to be quiet or the neighbors would hear. They were bad people and would do terrible things to them. She said he was a bad person and he was doing terrible things to them. He had lied, she said. He had promised to take them home.

Suddenly he stopped and looked at the two of them.

"All right, we'd better go then," he said and ordered Lisa to get back in the bag.

His eyes were cold and cruel. Lisa wondered whether she had made him mad and feared that he would take them back to the cliff and throw them off.

Back in the trunk, they decided the next chance they got to run away, they would seize it. They decided they would run in different directions. That way he could not catch both of them. They would run, even if they were on top of a cliff. Death was better than what they were being forced to endure.

Instead, he took them back to his apartment and let them sleep in his bed. He had to go and pick his parents up from the airport, he said.

When Charlene awoke the next morning, she was sure that it was her last day on earth. And she figured he would rape them again before he killed them. On top of everything else, she was humiliated that Lisa had seen her like that. Had she imagined that she had not fought back? She kicked herself for having gotten into the trunk with Lisa that first day. She could have memorized the license plate number and run to a nearby house and spared them both this agony.

Lisa awoke and went to the bathroom. It appeared that he had not returned, and they hunted around the apartment for a way out. The front door was locked and there was no handle on the inside. They searched for a phone, but could not find one. Instead, they found pictures of children torn from magazines. Examining the maps Lisa had seen in the computer room, they found that the arrows pointed to local schools. They also found a list of what appeared to be children's names and tortures he would like to inflict on them. They began to wonder whether he had tortured previous victims. Were things about to get even worse?

They decided that, if he had tortured other people, he must have killed them. Otherwise, the victims would have told the police and he would be in jail. Then they began to worry about what would happen if he did not come back. Would they starve to death? They feared shouting out the window in case it drew the attention of the man next door who Alan had said was even worse.

When Alan returned, he turned on the television. The news said that hopes of finding the two missing girls alive were fading. Charlene's father made an appeal to anyone who was holding his daughter. She looked at Alan's face. Plainly he was unmoved. Charlene could see that her father really thought she was dead.

Alan paced around the apartment. He told Lisa to come into the bedroom with him. She refused. He said he had something important to tell her. She said he could tell her out there. He stomped off.

Later he reappeared and ordered Charlene to go into the bedroom. When it became clear that he was prepared to drag her into the bedroom, she got up and went with him. Lisa felt guilty, but when she heard no noise coming from the bedroom she figured that nothing was happening.

The truth was that Charlene had been so brutalized that she did not put up any resistance. She was so sore and swollen that he could not do much. All she could offer was passive resistance. She refused to react to anything he did or said.

When he had finished, they went back in the other room and he told Lisa it was her turn. She did not dare refuse him twice. Afterward, he asked them if they were hungry. Lisa asked for pizza and chips, while Charlene continued to ignore him. When he went out to get it, they considered the possibilities of escape again. It was impossible.

When he returned with the pizza, Charlene decided that she had better have some.

"Don't say I'm not good to you," he said as he dished it up.

Why was he feeding them when he was going to kill them? Charlene wondered. But as darkness fell, she got more and more worried. Then he said: "Come on, Charlene. It's your turn." And the torment began all over again.

After he had finished with Charlene, he took Lisa into the bedroom. Then it was Charlene's turn again; then Lisa's. It went on all night. Eventually, after hours of trying, he managed to penetrate Lisa fully. The pain was excruciating. Lisa tried to do what Charlene had advised her to do and distance herself from the experience as much as possible, but the pain was so great that she could not help wondering whether it was possible to die from being raped.

When it was over, she went into the other room, where she hugged Charlene and they went to sleep in each other's arms.

They were woken by a loud, insistent banging on the door. Charlene feared that he had invited some friends over to have sex with them. But Alan did not open the door. Then they heard a man's voice say: "Police." Alan told the girls to stay quiet, while he cursed under his breath.

They began to fear that the police would give up and go away, but they were too scared to shout out. Eventually he opened the door. A policeman asked his name, said that there had been a complaint, and asked him to accompany him to the station. Alan asked if he could get a couple of things, then mentioned, as an afterthought, that he had the two missing girls from Hastings.

The girls reached for their clothes as the police rushed in. Once the police had identified them, they told them not to get dressed. They needed them as they were, wearing nothing but T-shirts, as evidence. Then they wrapped them up and carried them down to a police car.

At the police station, the girls each faced the ordeal of a painful, invasive medical examination. Then they were fed and allowed to put on clothes that their parents had brought them. In a comfortable room full of toys, they were asked to describe what had happened to them. Charlene said, straight out, that she had been raped, numerous times. But that was not good enough. The police needed a detailed break down, day by day, hour by hour. Little Lisa found it hard even to say the words. It was then that they learned that the Spice Girls had made an appeal for them. Both girls were fans.

At last, their parents were allowed to take them home. Both of their homes were besieged by the media, and they discovered that the police had been camped out there in case a ransom demand came through.

The girls and their families were assured that Alan Hopkinson would go to prison for a very long time. Then, after two weeks, they went back to school. Things were a little awkward at first, but they soon settled back into their routine. It helped that Charlene and Lisa had each other to rely on. Then a letter came to the school office for Charlene. It read:

Dear Charlene,
I think it is really good that you were abducted by Alan Hopkinson because you have learned lots of things about sex and you've lost your cherry. I'm going to find you and

abduct you myself now and we'll do much more things
than Alan ever did to you, just you wait and see.

Underneath there was a picture of a pregnant woman and the words: "This is what I am going to do to you."

Charlene was horrified by this. The girls' mail at home was being vetted, and the school had been told not to pass any correspondence on to them, but this one had been given to Charlene by mistake. The police managed to arrest the author two weeks later.

For Lisa there was another shock. Within weeks of her return, her mother left her father for another man.

Charlene was later encouraged to tell her father and the police about what Bert had done to her when she was six. However, when he was interviewed, Bert denied everything. Charlene could offer no proof and that case was dropped.

In court on May 28, 1999, Alan Hopkinson pleaded guilty, relieving the girls of the ordeal of testifying against him. He was given nine life sentences.

Lisa and Charlene gradually grew apart. Seeing each other brought back terrible memories. At secondary school, Lisa was bullied.

"Everyone knew what had happened to me, and some of the girls used to tease me by saying that I'd enjoyed it or had asked for it," says Lisa. "They also used to look up all the details of the attack on the Internet and then read it out loud for everyone to hear. All my classmates knew Charlene had been there, too, but because she was bigger than me and much more confident, no one said anything like that to her."

Charlene was never actually involved in bullying, but Lisa often wondered if she had encouraged it.

"She'd call me names on a regular basis, tell other people that I'd been rude about them behind their back, and she never stood up for me," said Lisa. "I used to dread going to school and nearly left before taking my GCSEs [General Certificate of Secondary Education] because I was so unhappy there."

However, following the death of a friend in a road traffic accident in 2005, Charlene held out an olive branch.

"I realized then that Lisa was the only person to truly understand what I'd been through," Charlene said. "I knew I'd been an awful person and had been cruel toward her, and I wanted to make amends. My hands were trembling as I picked up the telephone. As soon as she answered, I blurted out: 'I'm sorry.'"

Lisa accepted her apology. They got together and talked for hours, discussing for the first time the ordeal that they had shared. Despite everything, they discovered that they had a special bond. After that, the two friends began to see each other almost every day. Despite the passage of time, Charlene still does not like walking along the road alone.

Chapter 11

John Jamelske— The Miserly Slave Master

IN MOST CASES, SADIST KIDNAPPERS have taken one victim, sometimes two. Gary Heidnik managed to hold six, though two of them were killed, but his career as a kidnapper was short. John Jamelske succeeded in kidnapping and holding five victims as his personal sex slaves, one after the other, over a period of fifteen years. When he released his victims, some were so intimidated they did not report their ordeal. Others had no idea where they had been kept and could not lead the police there. It was only when Jamelske was caught red-handed with his fifth victim that the whole sordid story came out.

An only child, Jamelske was born in the village of DeWitt, now a suburb of Syracuse, New York, on May 9, 1935. At school in nearby Fayetteville, he was withdrawn and was given the nickname "Germs" for his terrible acne.

"He wasn't one to talk much," said one classmate. "You'd say hello and that would be the conversation."

Jamelske avoided sports and performed poorly in most subjects, though he did take an interest in history. His father was a horologist and collector of antique clocks, and encouraged him to go to college. He later graduated from a state university with a degree in watchmaking.

In September 1959, Jamelske married Dorothy Richmond, a schoolteacher who gave him three sons. They stayed in the vicinity of DeWitt, where the boys went to local schools and played little league baseball. But the children's relationship with their taciturn father was problematic.

"My father was always odd," one son told a journalist.

Jamelske supported his growing family by working in grocery stores; then he took a series of blue-collar jobs as a carpenter and handyman. Well-known for his miserliness, he was always ready to fight over a nickel. He scoured the area for bottles and cans, which he returned by the thousands for the deposit. He would also collect bottles that were not redeemable in New York from local recycling centers and take them to states where he could get money for them.

He also prevailed on local libraries to save coupons from the Sunday newspapers for him. He would get extremely annoyed if librarians did not put the coupons aside. On one occasion, he marched a librarian down to the janitor's office to find the coupons in a stack of newspapers that had been set aside for recycling.

"It was one of those things that made him our least pleasant patron," said one librarian.

However, Jamelske was not poor. He had persuaded his father to invest in the stock market in the late 1950s and early 1960s when it was booming. When his parents died, he inherited their nest egg. He also invested in real estate in Nevada and California. By 1988, when he began his career as a dungeon master, he'd sold a large area of land behind his house to a developer. By the time he was arrested in 2003, he was a multi-millionaire. No one would have guessed that he was wealthy by looking at him, though. He was recognized locally as the disheveled old man in the hooded sweatshirt and jeans who collected bottles and junk. His one redeeming feature seems to be that he went to church every day.

While the developer built an upmarket estate around Jamelske's dilapidated property, he let his blue-shingled ranch-style home fall to rack and ruin. His only concession was to build a six-foot fence around the acre he had retained. Even so, people who had spent hundreds of thousands of dollars on their modern mansions found themselves overlooking Jamelske's junkyard.

In the late 1980s, life for Jamelske began to change. His sons had grown up and left home. One was a high school vice principal; another, a college professor, who moved out of the state. Then his wife became bedridden.

Jamelske began to wear designer jeans and put his hair in a ponytail. It seemed he was going through a mid-life crisis. When he started bringing home a teenage blonde named Gina, his wife suspected that he was having an affair, but she did not pursue the matter.

Since his youth, Jamelske had spent his time cruising the streets of Syracuse and the surrounding area. He was out in his beat-up 1975 Mercury on September 17, 1988, when he saw a fourteen-year-old Native American girl named Kirsten walking along South Geddes Street, in downtown Syracuse. She was with some friends, drinking. He stopped and persuaded her to get into the car.

"We were going to have sex. There was no doubt," said Jamelske, who was fifty-three at the time.

It was late at night. Her friends told Kirsten not to go with him, but she wanted a ride to a friend's house. Instead, he took her home and chained her up.

"She didn't like that," he said. So he threw her down a well and kept her there.

"I woke up in there and I didn't have any clothes on," said the girl. "It was cold in there."

Jamelske did not consider her a kidnap victim.

"To me, somebody that's kidnapped is, you pick out somebody who has money and you grab them and you say I'm going to kill them...if you don't give me a half-million dollars or something," he said.

Kirsten's family reported her missing the day after she disappeared. The problem was that she had run away from home before. However, on those occasions her friends had always known where she was. This time, though, friends kept calling her home, asking where she was. The police interviewed her friends and family, but they had no idea where she might have gone.

Keeping the girl in a well was not very convenient, especially when he wanted to have sex with her, so Jamelske began building an underground bunker to keep her in. He told the neighbors that it was a bomb shelter. At the time, the Cold War was thawing, but Jamelske was known as an eccentric so this did not raise any suspicions. He brought in heavy machinery to dig a large hole in the backyard, lined it with concrete, then covered it over. Access was from his garage, via a series of steel doors.

One day, Kirsten woke up to find herself in the bunker. It had two rooms with no windows. There was no plumbing. She was given a bucket as a toilet. Electricity was supplied by a cable from the garage. Even though there was no escape, she was chained up in there. He intimidated her by telling her that he was going to kill her younger brother.

"He showed me a picture of my little brother, saying that he was going to hurt him," she said. "And he brought me a picture of my family and my house!"

Forced to submit to daily sexual assaults, she became compliant and submissive. As part of her humiliation, he made her keep a journal of her ordeal, recording every time she was raped, brushed her teeth, or had a bath. He crowed over his absolute power over her, but gradually softened. He began bringing her gifts and developed the delusion that they had a boyfriend-girlfriend relationship. She had to endure endless hours of emptiness and boredom, which she spent praying until her tormentor came to rape her again.

The concerns of her family were allayed by a series of letters he forced her to write. The first arrived in late September. It said that she missed her family and would be home the next month. Her family recognized her handwriting. The envelope was postmarked New York, so they put an ad in the personal section of the *New York Post*, telling her to come home and assured her that they were not angry with her. They included a phone number for her to call. There was no response.

Then in December, she left a message on a friend's answering machine. Again she said she was going to return home soon. There were more phone messages and letters, all mailed from different places. She even sent an audio tape, which said, "I can't wait to see you. I miss you." She was crying. None of these communications gave a clue to where she might be, but at least they knew she was alive.

Barely, though. At first, Jamelske fed her just crackers and water. Later she got Kool-Aid.

It is not clear whether he had developed some compassion toward the girl, or if she had become a burden, but in 1990 he decided to release her. He blindfolded her and put her in his car. Then, extraordinarily, he got his son Brian to drive them to Syracuse airport. Jamelske's strange and flimsy explanation was that the girl had a weight problem and her parents had asked him to look after her until she had lost some weight. After more than two years in the dungeon, the seventeen-year-old was well on the way to being emaciated. She was hooded, Jamelske, said, because she was going on a surprise trip. Brian said that he did not see the handcuffs. He was not prosecuted as an accessory, as by the time his father was caught, the statute of limitations had expired.

Jamelske and Kirsten then flew to Lake Tahoe for a vacation. They were seen around town and even visited a casino—which was not the miserly Jamelske's usual style. After a week, he gave the girl a ticket back to Syracuse and sent her home alone. Still frightened that Jamelske might hurt her younger brother, Kirsten pretended that she had simply run away from home and nothing of what had happened to her was reported to the police.

Jamelske then returned as if nothing had happened and resumed collecting bottles and junk. He had gotten away with his first kidnapping.

Against Their Will

He did not try to repeat the experience right away. But then, nearly five years later, on March 31, 1995, he was cruising downtown Syracuse again when he saw a fourteen-year-old Latina on Catherine Street. He stopped and talked to her, asking her to deliver a package for him. Naïvely, she got into his car and he drove her back to DeWitt. There, she went into the dungeon to get the package and found the door slammed behind her. He left her in the dark to intimidate her. Then he persuaded her to take some pills, which knocked her out. When she came to, she was naked and chained to the wall.

The girl fought back. She cursed him and spat at him, but it did no good. He took photographs of her lying naked and helpless on the floor. He also showed her pictures of her home and family. He knew where they lived, he said, and would kill them if she did not do what he wanted. He also boasted that he had sold other girls into sexual slavery abroad. She found she had no choice but to submit to him every day, while he fortified himself with Viagra and other performance-enhancing pills. Once a week, he hosed her down with cold water from a hose.

Her family reported her missing, but the girl had a history of drug use. The police went through the procedures. There was little they could do. Jamelske's new captive disappeared into the file with thousands of other runaways across America.

Again, after two years, Jamelske decided to release her. He blindfolded her, drove her to her mother's apartment block, and dropped her off. After a tearful reunion, she told her mother that she had been held in a dungeon and raped every day. She gave a description of the man who had held to the police but, still frightened that he might kill her, she did not report the full details of what had happened to her in the concrete bunker.

Because of her history of drug abuse and the inconsistencies in her story, the police soon dropped the investigation.

For weeks after her return, her mother noticed a gray-haired white man driving by their home. He appeared to be staring at her daughter. When she asked who he was, her daughter said that was the man who had kidnapped her. They felt too intimidated to report this to the police.

While Jamelske was now hooked on having a sex slave at his beck and call, he changed his modus operandi. Instead of picking a young waif, he chose an older woman—but someone who was similarly marginalized and, perhaps, whom no one would miss. On August 30, 1997, he was cruising an Asian neighborhood of Syracuse. On Lodi Street, he saw a fifty-two-year-old Vietnamese woman and stopped to talk to her. She was a refugee and spoke little English. He explained that he was lonely and needed a friend. She got into his car, but instead of driving her straight home, he cruised around town as if he was making up his mind whether to go through with it this time. Eventually, he took her to an abandoned house and raped her. Then he trussed her up in a cardboard box and took her back to DeWitt and locked her in the dungeon.

For days later, her boyfriend reported her missing. The police took the details, but there were no leads. As she was a full-grown woman, not an underage girl, they were under no obligation to make more than a cursory investigation.

Again, the woman was raped daily and made to do menial tasks such as poking holes in bottle caps and stringing them on a wire for six hours a day. He also made her sew quilts, pound metal objects with a hammer, and sort piles of screws. Once, she said, he dumped a military-style duffle bag full of money in the dungeon. He made her separate the loose bills into stacks of fives, tens, and fifties.

Jamelske's memories of this period differ from the woman's. He claimed that she sang to him in Vietnamese.

"She had the most beautiful a cappella voice with no accompaniment whatever," he said. "It was absolutely beautiful!"

Jamelske said that he was kind to her, giving her a TV so she could watch shows in the evening. She admitted that she was pleasant to him, but that was because she was so intimidated that she did not dare show any fear. She was determined not to show fear even when he placed a life-size plastic skeleton beside her on the mat where she was forced to sleep.

"I was so scared," she told police. "It was white. It had black eyes. It glowed in the dark."

And there was always the threat of physical violence. Once, when she cried after a rape that caused bleeding, Jamelske slugged her in the left ear, leaving her partially deaf.

"I cried and prayed every day of my captivity," she said. "I never cried in front of him again after he slapped me so hard and injured my ear, I did everything he asked, hoping he would release me. I tried to be friendly to him, and to make him laugh so that he would let me live. I would only cry when he was not around. I did not want him to hit me. I did not want to die down there in those rooms, because no one would ever find my body and my soul would remain in a cold place!"

She was in genuine fear of dying.

"When I thought I was going to die, when I was bleeding, he didn't have the humanity to save me, to take me to a hospital," she said.

And then there was the sex.

"I live with this every day because it's just horrifying that somebody could do that to somebody... Like some sex animal—for his pleasure."

On May 31, 1998, after nine months' captivity, he blindfolded her and dropped her off at the Greyhound station with $50 of the $70 that was in her purse when he abducted her. She went straight to the police and reported what had happened to her. However, she could provide few leads to Jamelske's whereabouts. She had no idea where she had been. According to the police, she thought that she had been held in a shed in Rochester.

She gave a description of her abductor. He was "a white male, forty-five years old, five foot eight inches, heavy build with a circular birthmark on his forehead." Jamelske was sixty-three, not heavily built for an American, and there was no sign of a birthmark on his forehead. She was convinced that the Syracuse police did not believe her story. She said they told her, "Usually if someone gets kidnapped they don't come home alive."

Jamelske, in his deluded way, believed he had been doing her a favor. If they had met under normal circumstances, he said, she would have dumped whoever she was with to be with him. Her abduction, he thought, was almost consensual.

"I think she would look at it as a positive thing," he said. "I do."

In August 1999, Jamelske's wife Dorothy died of colon cancer. She had been bedridden for years and there is no indication that she knew about her husband's crimes. Nor did he take advantage of her absence right away. He waited until May 2001, before he picked up his next victim.

On May 11, he saw a young woman walking home. Jennifer was twenty-six and the mother of two small children. According to her own statements, she had been drinking. Other reports say that she had taken LSD. She was on her way home from a friend's house. Jamelske offered her a lift. She took it.

"I was pretty messed up," she said. "I had been drinking and smoking, and I was walking to a friend's house on the west side of Syracuse. It was cold, it was raining, and it was a bad neighborhood. Some kids were kind of following behind me. So when this white old man pulled up and asked if I needed a ride, I figured it'd be all right. I guess I made the wrong decision."

Besides, he seemed like a nice guy, grandfatherly. She did not remember what happened during the ride, she said. But she did pay attention to which way they were going. They were heading toward her home in Bridgeport. DeWitt was on the way. However, she did recall arriving in Jamelske's garage. When she asked what they were doing there, he said he had to run into the house to get something. But when she tried to get out of the car, she couldn't. That was the last thing she remembered. Then she awoke to find herself naked in a cold room. It was pitch black.

He came to rape her. She fought back.

"I clocked him pretty good," she said. "He hit me a couple times. But I'm a tough girl, and it didn't really faze me."

Then he burned her on the back with a cigarette.

"I screamed and I pounded till my hands were raw," Jennifer said. But no sound made in the dungeon could be heard outside.

She thought she heard other screams and banging sometimes, and wondered if he had others locked away. There were drawings on the walls she imagined had been done by other women.

After a few days, she was reported missing. The police sent out a helicopter to search the area where she was last seen. But, again, they came up with nothing.

Meanwhile, she had to sleep on a piece of foam matting and go to the toilet in a bucket. He only fed her once a day and gave her a bath every two weeks in a bathtub did not have plumbing. He claimed he was part of a slavery syndicate and he threatened to sell her on the Internet for $30,000 if she did not do everything he said. The police were involved in it, he said, and he showed a fake sheriff's badge that he had found on the street years before.

He told her that the bosses of the syndicate would treat her far worse than he did. He was saving her from them. If she submitted to him sexually, they would eventually let her go. If not, they would ship her overseas.

"I was forced to have sex with him every day," she said, "It was part of a ritual. If I didn't have sex with him every day, then that would add on to the time that I was going to be there."

She said that he was skilled at brainwashing and made her read the Bible to him for hours on end. At one point, she thought of trying to knock him out and make her escape, but there was a combination lock on the door so, without him, there was no way out.

She considered suicide. That way, at least, he would have to go to the trouble of disposing of her body. But she did not want to die alone in a cellar, without her family even knowing of her passing.

He did afford her what he considered certain kindnesses. He gave her a television—cable, so that he could control what she watched. He would bring her food she liked, but she could only eat once a day—like a dog. This kept her weak so she could not fight back.

She said it was her belief in God that got her through the ordeal. She would tell him that God was watching and that what he was doing was wrong. One day, she said, God was going to get him. But it made no difference.

She worried about her two children and she begged him to allow her to write home to let them know she was alive. He permitted this. But she had to say that she was in a rehab clinic. When the letter arrived, it was postmarked Rochester. The police called every drug treatment center in the Rochester area, but all of them refused to say if Jennifer was a patient because of their confidentiality rules.

The cigarette burn on her back became infected. She could not stand up straight and it was painful to move. So after just two months, he decided to let her go.

On July 7, he came down to the dungeon with the clothes that she had worn when he kidnapped her. He threw them at her and told her that she was going home. She assumed that he was going to kill her and was terrified.

"I'm really thinking, I'm done for," she said. "I never thought in a million years that he would bring me home."

He handcuffed her and put a hood over her head, then took her out to his car. They drove around for around half an hour. Then he undid the handcuffs, took the blindfold off, and told her to get out. At last she could breathe fresh air. Then she discovered that he had dropped her off outside her mother's Bridgeport home, though she could not remember telling him where her mother lived.

Jennifer went to the police. Like previous captives, she could not tell them where she had been held, but she described the dungeon. There was a huge peace sign painted on the wall with the words "WALL OF THUGS" in red alongside it. But the story of her abduction was confused. The police drove her around Syracuse in the hope that she might recall something. They also tried to locate his car. She said that it was a 1974 Mercury Comet. The police searched the motor vehicle records. There was only one 1974 Mercury Comet registered in New York. It did not belong to Jamelske. She had made a mistake. Jamelske's car was a 1975 model. The police felt her story did not hang together.

"I was suspicious," admitted Detective Jack Schmidt of the Onondaga County Sheriff's Department Abused Persons Unit. "This sounded so remarkable. I don't want to say I didn't believe her, but at the same time I was thinking about the note from Rochester, the fact that she was a drug abuser…"

"They thought I was making up some story or something," she said.

Detective Schmidt showed his folder to a sergeant who advised him to close the case. They had no way to tell if Jennifer was telling the truth, and they had no more leads to follow. But the case nagged at Schmidt, partly because of the specific details she provided—the bathtub, combination lock, the graffiti on the walls.

Jamelske had kidnapped four women to use as sex slaves and had gotten away with it. So far he had abducted a Native

American, a Latina, an Asian, and a Caucasian. Now, to complete the ethnic set, he wanted an African-American.

In October 2002, he saw a sixteen-year-old black girl on the corner of Elk and Salina streets. She was alone. He stopped to talk to her and she got into his car. He claimed later that she was a prostitute. He asked whether she wanted to make money, and she said yes. Then they agreed a price for her to stay with him for a month. At least, that was his story. The girl denied it. She said he threw her in his dungeon, stripped her naked, shredded her clothes, and raped her. He told her there were vicious dogs that would kill her if she tried to escape.

She repeatedly told Jamelske she hated him, and demanded he set her free her. He said he could, first on November 17, then on Christmas Day. But when those days came, he said: "The people I work for say I can't let you go until you have more sex with me."

And the poor girl was in more trouble than she thought. Her family had not reported her missing and no one was looking for her.

Despite his maltreatment of her, Jamelske developed an affection for his latest captive, whom he decided to call Meikka. Unlike the other victims, she was allowed out of the dungeon. He let her walk around freely upstairs into the house, and she even slept in his bedroom. However, there were makeshift bars on the windows. Jamelske had taken the shelves out of an old fridge and nailed them to the window frames. She was even afforded the privilege of going to the toilet on her own as there were planks nailed across the windows in the bathroom.

But he still forced her to have sex every day. The rapes were often videotaped, and she was coerced into fulfilling his every fantasy.

"The only thing that got me through this horrendous nightmare was my strong faith in God," she said. She prayed every day that he would let her go home.

Jamelske began to think he could trust Meikka. He took her shopping in nearby towns. They would go out to play pool or go bowling. They were seen taking a stroll around the neighborhood and attending church together.

On April 3, 2003, they went to the karaoke night at Freddy's Bar and Grill in nearby Mattydale. Meikka wanted to sing and, when her turn came, she got up on stage and grabbed the microphone. She sang three numbers to a crowd of over one hundred.

They were a curious couple, to be sure. But no one would have guessed that she was his prisoner. Many people that night wondered why she did not scream for help. But she was young and her tormentor stood close beside her while she was on stage. She was, however, playing a longer game. He now trusted her completely.

On the morning of April 8, he took her with him when he made his regular run to the bottle redemption center in Manlius. While he was attending to business, she persuaded him to let her use the phone. She wanted to call the church, she said, to check on the times of the services. Instead, she called her older sister and told her what had happened to her. After Meikka hung up, her sister called the number back and got through to the bottle redemption center in Manlius. She persuaded the employee who answered the phone to call 911. Within minutes, the police arrived and caught up with the couple at a nearby car dealership. They asked Jamelske what he was doing with the young girl.

He told the police that they were friends. "We have a lot of fun together," he said. "We have a lot in common. The only thing that she likes that I don't is blue cheese."

The officers were not convinced.

"Is this a problem that I'm so much older than her?" Jamelske said. "I'd just like to get this straightened out so I can go home. I'd like to be with her tonight, if possible."

They planned to go bowling, he said.

Jamelske's story was that Meikka "moved into his house." He described their routine outings together—walking the dog, karaoke, dancing.

"We get on the dance floor and everybody's like, 'Wow, look at them, they're having fun.' Then everybody starts giving me high-fives," Jamelske said. And he planned to take her to his high school's fiftieth reunion.

He claimed he thought the sixteen-year-old was eighteen. The legal age of sexual consent in New York is seventeen. The sex, he said, was consensual. After her nineteenth birthday party on May 12, he said, they planned to go their separate ways. He had no intention of marrying her because he did not expect their relationship to last more than a few years.

"I know that one day she will want to be with someone her own age, and that's alright," he said. "I'm just gonna have as much fun for now as I can."

He was charged with kidnapping, rape, and sodomy.

But Jamelske was still unabashed.

"If this case went to trial, I think that the characterization of this as a kidnapping could be challenged," he said.

The police went to search his home. Outside it, Jamelske had erected a ten-foot pole in the front yard with the replica of a human head on it. From the ends of a cross beam dangled chains.

"We didn't know what it was supposed to represent," said Detective Schmidt. "It might have been some sort of omen for his victims."

Schmidt and his partner, Detective Eddie Bragg, found that the house, with its barred windows, looked like a prison. Inside, the place was full of garbage. It was strewn with old newspapers, half-eaten food, clothes, books, furniture, pots, pans, broken appliances, and all kinds of debris. Junk was piled almost to the ceiling. However, inside the closets, they found boxes of tissues, cereal, and cooking items all stacked neatly in rows. Every inch of space was taken up. It looked as though, if one item were moved, everything would collapse on the floor. In the basement, they found row after row of metal shelving units packed with bottles, all meticulously sorted by color, brand, and size. There were more than thirteen thousand bottles.

Behind another shelf unit full of bottles in the garage, they found a steel door, four feet by four feet. They opened it to find a short crawl way. Beyond it there was another steel door. When they opened it, they saw a bunker twenty-four feet long, twelve feet wide, and eight feet high.

"It was dark and smelled horrible, like some medieval dungeon," said Schmidt.

The passageway connected with the dungeon at ceiling height. Entering, you had to turn and climb down a small ladder. It was then that Schmidt saw on the wall a huge peace sign and the words, "WALL OF THUGS." Jennifer had been telling the truth after all.

There was more graffiti, too: the words "HATE" and "READY TO RUCUSS [sic], SO BRING ON THE PAIN" in a deep crimson. On the wall near the passageway, there was a crucifix and the words, "PEACE TO ALL WHO ENTER HERE."

Next to a yellow extension cord that ran out from a hole in the top of the walls was an eight-inch aluminum hose that pumped warm air from the house furnace, keeping the room warm and providing some ventilation. A clock radio sat on top of a filthy portable refrigerator. In the center of the room, there was a stained bathtub on top of a raised wooden deck. Victims were forced to bathe there, using a garden hose. It had a drain plug but no waste pipe. The water collected on the cement floor until it evaporated, making the room damp and moldy. An aluminum-frame chair with no seat was positioned over a pail to make a rudimentary toilet. They could also see the chain that Jamelske had used to tether his victims to a hook in the wall.

Speaking to the press, Sheriff Kevin Walsh said, "Our big fear is we don't know how many women he has taken over the years. Some were very young and some may have died down there; some may have even killed themselves."

The next day, ground-penetrating radar was brought in to search for buried bodies. None were found.

Inside the house, there were dozens of metal filing cabinets that were stuffed with papers, calendars, and business records. Jamelske had collected hundreds of issues of old magazines, such as *Popular Science* and *Popular Mechanics*, from the 1930s and 1940s. These were carefully arranged by date. Hundreds of manila folders contained old phone bills, fuel bills, receipts from grocery stores, gas purchases, car repairs. They contained a complete record of everything Jamelske had done in his life, and his painstaking record keeping made a remarkable contrast with the extraordinary mess that filled the rest of the house.

Police also found several videotapes. In some, Jamelske is seen dancing, singing, and exercising with one of the women as if they are friends—except for the sinister surroundings are macabre.

In the bunker, the police found a second room that contained a grimy foam mat sitting on plastic bread trays. This was what the women used as their bed. The mat had remained unchanged and uncleaned for years. Next to the makeshift bed were two blue cloth chairs that sat on top of pieces of ripped carpet. Several newspapers were strewn on the damp floor, and everything in the cell was rotting and moldy.

They also found a series of calendars with the letters "B," "S," and "T" beside the dates. Victims had been forced to write the letter S when they had sex, B when they bathed, and T when they had brushed their teeth. The calendar covered a period of fifteen years. The new visitors found the dungeon creepy. It was hard to imagine what it must have been like to be held down there, naked, in the dark, year after year.

Jamelske seemed to have no idea of the enormity of his crime. Sheriff Walsh reported:

> When he was first captured, he made light of it. He treated it like it was a joke. He was telling us that the young woman that he had with him—a sixteen-year-old African-American woman, who really broke this case—that she was just a friend and that they had a relationship and they were planning to have a birthday party for her. And he treated the whole thing as if he thought that he was going to get off, and worst-case scenario he'd get a slap on the wrist and maybe get some community service.

Jamelske insisted that he had never hurt anyone. Some of the girls had even benefited from captivity, he said. His lawyers spent days trying to make it clear to him that abducting women from the streets and holding them in a dungeon was kidnapping.

Eventually, Jamelske pleaded guilty to five counts of first-degree kidnapping, saving his victims from appearing in court to testify against him. However, when he appeared in a packed Onondaga County Court to face sentencing, the district attorney read the victims' statements into the court record.

Kirsten said she still felt the pain of being held as a sex slave in Jamelske's medieval dungeons.

"I am haunted every moment, even in sleep, by the thought of my months with Mr. Jamelske," she said. "The cold, dampness, darkness, and loneliness. I will never forget the constant hunger, thirst and fatigue. The thought of death… I cannot speak of the terrible things he did to my body and made me do to his… When I think of the things I have had to do just to stay alive, I cannot believe I am still here."

"The threats and intimidation… left her with great fears and anxiety that have impacted and directed her life for the many years that followed," the DA told the court.

Jennifer said:

> I have lived my life for two years knowing that sick old man has existed and has done to other girls what he has done to me. I have lived in fear ever since. John Jamelske is a sick and evil old man and should be punished. He has no right to take away my freedom, my right to breathe fresh air or my right to be treated like a human being. He made my children think I was dead. That hurts more than everything else in the whole world. They had to endure pain, so let his punishment be swift and just. Maybe then, I will at least be able to sleep at night.

In Meikka's statement, she said:

> I almost gave up hope when you brought my clothes to me in a million shredded pieces, telling me that these people trained those dogs to go after my scent. I felt completely stripped down to nothing… You will never be able to know the fear I felt, being raped every day, sometimes three times a day. The nightmares I have, remembering how I had to fulfill your sick fantasies, making disgusting videos, being humiliated, never having any privacy, not even to use the toilet or the shower. Being chained to a fence like a dog. I hope with time I will be able to forget the horrifying sex you forced me to have day after day after day, relentless, for six and a half long months, never leaving me alone, not for one day. You are the sickest man I have ever

known… I hope you die in a cold cement cell like you wanted us to do.

Throughout it all, Jamelske stood there impassive. He was a small, frail, harmless-looking man and, to those that knew him, the most unlikely slave master.

The judge was outraged by what he heard and by Jamelske's apparently indifferent attitude.

"You are a sick coward," he said. "You're an evil man. You're a kidnapper and a rapist and a master manipulator of people and the truth. You took your American dream and turned it into a nightmare for these five women. Your reign of terror is over!"

Jamelske was sentenced to eighteen years to life.

"Mr. Jamelske, there is no question in my mind you should die in prison for what you have done to these five women," the judge said.

Jamelske's attorney argued that the sentence should be reduced to fifteen years, But the DA thought eighteen years was hardly adequate:

In eighteen years, your honor, perhaps, perhaps, this
defendant may appear before a parole board. Those
members of that parole board may see a pathetic old man
in front of them who has lived in a cell for eighteen years
and they may say that he couldn't hurt anyone. The irony
is that the cell he will live in for the next eighteen years,
and probably for the rest of his natural life, was far more
adequate, will be far more comfortable, will have far many
greater creature comforts than is the hellhole that he kept
his victims for so long a period of time, and I truly believe,

judge, that that parole board will see this defendant for exactly what he is and never let him see the light of day.

Others sought harsher punishments.

"He should be tortured for what he did," said Kirsten's cousin. "As long as he kept them, each one of the victims should be allowed to torture him for that length of time… She was a baby when he took her. She had no teenaged life because of him."

Throughout the proceedings, Jamelske stood by the defense table, emotionless. He even appeared unmoved by the sentence. Asked if he had anything to say, Jamelske addressed the court.

"I'm just truly sorry for what I did," he said. "I've had a lot of time to think about it and I'm just sorry for what I did and how it's affected everyone and God bless all of them."

But no one believed that Jamelske really felt any remorse.

"I wanted to puke when he started to cry in court," said Kirsten's cousin.

From Onondaga County jail across the street from the courthouse, Jamelske was transferred upstate to Clinton Prison, better known as Dannemora, the end of the road for New York's worst criminals.

As part of Jamelske's plea agreement, his assets would be sold off and the proceeds divided among the victims. He was thought to be worth between $2 million and $8 million, though no amount of money could compensate them for the hell they had been through.

Interviewed in jail, Jamelske was unrepentant, claiming that his victims were prostitutes.

"We would just together like, you know: If you want to stay, this amount," he told the Syracuse *Post-Standard*. "When that time would come, sometimes I would say, 'If I give you so much more, would you stay another six months?' or this or that. If she said, 'No,' well, I'd say, 'How about if I double the money?' or 'How about if I add this or that or whatever?' They would say, 'Okay, we'll extend it.'"

The women, he said, were "buddies." He did, however, admit to being unconventional.

"I've always said, you know, I'm unorthodox, and I've said to hundreds of people, I'm a little bit crazy."

In the end, he said, he was unlucky. When the police turned up at Fayetteville Dodge, he said to Meikka, "We'll just get in the car."

According to Jamelske, she then said, "Go! Go! Go! Go!"

"And stupid me, I should have had the key in my hand. It was the darnedest thing. At the time I said to myself, 'Stupid me.' So, as I was reaching my hand in my pocket sitting down, which is very hard, you know, with tight jeans, I saw the gun point right at my head at the window. And then somebody opened her door, you know, said, 'Get out of the car.' And she's like, she's like, 'Go! Go! Go!' So this is her secret phone call."

Had police not arrived, Jamelske claimed, Meikka would have stayed with him until the date they agreed on for her freedom—May 12, her birthday.

"There's no question in my mind," he said.

After that, there would have been no more Viagra and no more captives, he claimed.

Chapter 12

Shawn Hornbeck— Hidden in Plain Sight

ON SUNDAY OCTOBER 6, 2002, eleven-year-old Shawn Hornbeck went out to ride his bike. When dusk fell at 5 p.m. and Shawn had not returned home, his mother Pam began to worry. Shawn was afraid of the dark.

Plenty of people in their town of Richwoods, Missouri, had seen him out that afternoon. He was hard to miss with his lime-green bike and the bright orange T-shirt he wore with the name of his little league team, the DeSoto Astros, on it. He was last seen at 4:30 p.m. near his elementary school, heading for home.

At 6 p.m., Pam called Shawn's best friend Patrick Reeves. Patrick said he had not seen Shawn all afternoon. At 8 p.m., she called the police. Shawn had vanished.

That day, thirty-seven-year-old Michael John Devlin had driven from his home in suburban St. Louis toward a parcel of vacant land in a development called Woodland Lake Estates in Washington County, just twenty-five miles from Shawn's home. Devlin often went camping there and kept a twelve-foot fishing boat, which he used on the area's thirteen lakes.

Devlin was a big man, six-foot-four, and he weighed three hundred pounds. But he liked little boys and he was carrying a gun. His route took him through Richwoods, where he spotted Shawn riding along a dirt track beside the church. The boy was just four-foot-eight and weighed ninety pounds—easy prey.

When Shawn turned onto the road, Devlin rode up behind him and nudged his bike lightly with his truck. Then he stopped and got out of the passenger door, pretending that he was concerned for the safety of the child. He grabbed the boy and flung him into the truck. Threatening him with a gun, he taped the boy's hands together, then set off back toward St. Louis, fondling the boy's crotch as he drove.

Back at his apartment, he sexually assaulted the boy repeatedly. Then he wanted to go to sleep, so he wrapped a rope around the boy's waist and tied it around his own wrist. For Shawn, there was no escape.

The following morning, Devlin went to work as usual at a nearby pizza parlor where he was manager. He left Shawn tied up on a futon with duct tape over his mouth. Every work day for the first five months, Shawn was left like this. During his lunch break, Devlin would return to feed Shawn and take him to the bathroom. He told his coworkers that he had to go home to look after a sick cat.

In Richwoods, there was not a single clue to Shawn's whereabouts. No one had noticed Devlin's truck. He had not left a tire track. Devlin had even taken and disposed of Shawn's lime-green bicycle. All the police made a fruitless search of the surrounding woodlands. Volunteers joined in. Fliers were distributed. Appeals were made. Shawn's picture appeared on *America's Most Wanted*. Searchers swore they would never give up.

A month after Shawn had disappeared, a woman came forward and said that a motorist had hit Shawn on Highway H, not far from where he had last been seen. Then he had tried to hide the boy's body in a grassy area near the road. Ten volunteers performed a fingertip search of the area. They found some blood and intestines. However, it was soon established that these came from a pig that a local home owner had slaughtered. Lakes were drained; abandoned mine shafts were examined. Nothing was found. But no one was searching the Kirkwood district of St. Louis.

Devlin lived in Unit D of a rundown apartment block at 491 South Holmes Avenue in Kirkwood. He had worked at Imo's Pizza since high school, graduating from delivery boy to manager. His friends had gotten married, developed high-flying careers, and moved on. By his own admission, Devlin was lazy. Short on ambition and personal hygiene, he stayed put. However, he had no criminal record, apart from a few traffic tickets. His only vice appeared to be smoking menthol cigarettes. He did not even drink beer when his boss bought a round after the night shift. To make a little extra money, he did a couple of shifts answering the phone at Bopps Chapel Funeral Directors. There, too, he was said to be a good worker—polite, efficient, and punctual.

At Imo's, Devlin was nicknamed Devo because of his occasional bad temper. No one knew much about his personal life. He did not talk about dating, though he sometimes cracked derogatory jokes about homosexuals. It was assumed he was shy, or asexual. His only known passions were playing computer games and 1970s rock bands. He was opinionated when it came to politics, and among the things he hated were child molesters. They were the scum of the earth.

While Devlin was a nice enough guy at work, the other residents at 491 South Holmes Avenue avoided him. He was known as a misanthropic curmudgeon. Consequently, he had no visitors.

When a brown-eyed boy turned up at Devlin's apartment, neighbors assumed he was Devlin's son. With a temper like Devlin's, it was not difficult to see why he might have broken up from his partner. Nor was it difficult to see why no one asked.

The sexual abuse of Shawn continued from the first day of his captivity. But Devlin could not keep missing work on account of a sick cat. A month after he had kidnapped Shawn, Devlin took him out to a remote area of Washington County to kill him. He later told the FBI that he did not shoot the boy because it would have made a mess and left too much evidence. Instead, he tried to choke him to death.

The boy had his arms bound and duct tape over his mouth. He cried, and Devlin found could not go through with it. He explained to the boy that he had to kill him, because he could not keep leaving work at lunchtime to feed him. Shawn then begged for his life. If Devlin let him live, he would feed himself at lunchtime. He would not try to escape, and Devlin could do anything he liked with him. It was a deal.

Despite the appalling abuse Shawn suffered, he lived up to his part of the bargain. He did not even try to escape when Devlin, who suffered from Type II diabetes, had to have two of his toes amputated and went to recuperate at his parents' home in nearby Webster Groves. Devlin called the apartment regularly to check that Shawn was all right. He had left the boy money to buy food and dropped by occasionally in case he had run out of cash.

When Devlin returned, life went back to normal. For Shawn, that meant a hell of physical and sexual abuse. Neighbors heard obscenities issuing from his apartment, along with the sound of thrashing. They heard whimpering, screaming, pleading. But they put it down to a father-son disagreement. Besides, when the young boy was seen out, he seemed normal enough. He told people his name was Shawn Devlin. Michael Devlin was his father, or sometimes he said he was his god-father. He said his mother had died in a car crash.

Shawn told a girl a similar story in a chat room on the Internet. Shawn's access to the Internet gave him another escape route that he did not take. His parents had set up the Shawn Hornbeck Foundation online. On December 1, 2005, a Shawn Devlin from Kirkwood posted the message on the Web-site: "How long are you planing [sic] to look for your son?"

He told some people that he went to private school, others that he was home-schooled. Though he lived in a squalid apartment, he was the envy of other kids because he had all the latest electronic toys: Xbox, iPod, cell phone, and a computer. And he could be seen out on his BMX and skateboard.

Shawn went to the library and the pool, and hung out with friends. And he slept over at friends' houses and went on outings with friends' families. Nobody thought that he was anything but a normal kid. There was only one thing strange about him. He did not like talking about his background.

One friend named Tony Douglas even stayed over at Devlin's one-bedroom apartment, sleeping with Shawn on a futon in the front room. It was far from pleasant. The place was a mess. Dirty dishes were piled in the sink. Devlin played computer games and rarely said anything. Occasionally, he exploded at Shawn, accusing him of messing up his game.

When Shawn's picture appeared on the TV, friends said that he looked like the missing boy. Shawn would tell them to shut up, or shrug and say: "Whatever."

Shawn even had contact with the police. When his BMX was reported stolen on August 15, 2003—ten months after he disappeared—an officer came to Devlin's apartment and spoke to Shawn and his "father." The officer suspected nothing and did not recognize Shawn, though no effort was made to disguise him.

On another occasion, a police officer who knew Devlin from the pizza parlor saw him in the street with Shawn and smiled and waved. And Shawn's friend Tony Douglas said that on at least three occasions, he had been out with Shawn when they had been stopped and given a ride home by the police. The *St. Louis Post-Dispatch* reported two other occasions when Shawn had been stopped by the police and had given his name as Shawn Devlin with a date of birth within a few days of his real one.

Devlin also traveled around with Shawn. They drove to Chicago. Then in June 2004, Devlin drove the 1,400 miles to Prescott, Arizona, to attend Devlin's brother's wedding. Shawn was with him in the pickup. They stayed at motels on the way together. The boy did not appear at the wedding, as it might have aroused suspicion. However, it was noted that Devlin was the only guest from the St. Louis area who had chosen to drive to Arizona rather than fly.

When he was fifteen, after nearly four years with Devlin, Shawn found himself a girlfriend. She took him to her school dance. Shawn remained a little reticent about discussing his background, and no one seemed to notice that Shawn did not go to school at all.

Now that Shawn was an adolescent and showing an interest in girls, Devlin was losing interest in Shawn. On January 8, 2007, Devlin went on the prowl again. In Beaufort, Missouri, he snatched thirteen-year-old Ben Ownby as he got off the school bus. He had already told Shawn of his plans to abduct another child. Shawn had become defiant in recent months, and Devlin thought that making him an accomplice in a major crime might make him more compliant. Shawn was in the pickup when Ownby was snatched. Devlin said, "Okay buddy, now that you are in the truck with me, you're in as much trouble as I am."

He told Shawn that his job was to keep Ben quiet, but Ben went quietly after Devlin showed him his gun. Shawn then distracted Ben with talk about food and TV, so it was not necessary to bind the young boy with duct tape. Back at the apartment, Shawn acted as a guard when Devlin was out. He and Ben played computer games. Ben even saw his parents on the TV, making an appeal for his return.

This time, though, Devlin had not snatched a child off an empty street. Ben's friend Mitchell Hults had been on the school bus with him and glimpsed Devlin's white Nissan pickup as it reversed into a ditch before speeding away.

The authorities immediately sent out an EPA—an Endangered Person Advisory. This alert system had been set up after one woman had cut a child out of another woman's belly to kidnap the premature infant in Skidmore, Missouri, in 2004. By that time, the America's Missing: Broadcast Emergency Response system had also been set up, following the abduction and murder of nine-year-old Amber Hagerman in Dallas in 1996. The next morning an AMBER alert was also sent out.

But this time the police had something to go on: Mitchell Hults's description of Devlin's white Nissan pickup. They even polygraphed the teenager in case he was involved in the kidnapping.

Devlin's boss at Imo's Pizza, Mike Prosperi, saw the story about the abduction of Ben Ownby on TV. He knew that Devlin had a white Nissan pickup. And Devlin had called in sick that day. When Devlin came in, Prosperi noticed that his pickup was caked with red clay; it was the color of clay that you found in the Missouri backwoods, not in the St. Louis area. Although Devlin had been a trusted employee and a friend for twenty years, Prosperi went to the police. He said that he was 99.9 percent sure that he was wrong. But nevertheless, he was there.

When questioned, Devlin's mother noted that her son had a white pickup like the one the police were looking for. Neighbors noticed the Nissan parked outside Devlin's apartment. They also noticed that Devlin had a new "son."

Although the white Nissan pickup was an important clue, the police were not looking for it when they visited 491 South Holmes Avenue. They were actually there to arrest one of Devlin's neighbors, but he was not in. Then they noticed the white Nissan in the resident's parking bay. It matched the description of the one they had been told to look for.

The officers asked around to find out who owned the truck. Michael Devlin then came out of his apartment to throw out the garbage. One of the officers recognized him from the pizza parlors and they got to chatting. Devlin was his usual friendly self. He admitted that the white Nissan was his. But when the missing child was mentioned, his attitude changed. He became defensive—"squirrelly" was the word the cop used at the time.

The police called the FBI; when they turned up, they asked to see inside Devlin's apartment. He refused to let them enter. However, through a curtain-less back window, they could see a child playing a video game. Devlin refused to tell them the child's name, though he said that the boy was his godson. Again, he refused to let them enter the apartment or talk to the child.

Eventually they persuaded Devlin to let them talk to Shawn in the doorway. He said his name was Shawn Wilcox. His mother was dead and Devlin was looking after him while his father was away in New York on a business trip. While the conversation was going on, Ben was hiding behind the door as he had been told.

The FBI were not looking for Shawn. Missing for four years, he had been all but forgotten. They were looking for Ben, and Shawn did not match his description. So they went away. However, the Kirkwood police continued their surveillance of Devlin's apartment.

The following morning, Devlin went to work as usual. About midday, the police and the FBI turned up to interview him again. During their interrogation of Devlin, an FBI agent mentioned that a tire track had been found at the site of Ben

Ownby's abduction. They were now going to check whether it matched the tires on Devlin's pickup.

Devlin was shaken. He knew the game was over. He blurted out that Shawn was not his godson. In fact, he was the missing boy Shawn Hornbeck. Then Devlin was asked whether Ben Ownby was at the apartment. He admitted he was. Both were alive.

"I'm a bad person," said Devlin.

They took Devlin back to his apartment. The two boys were there. Ben asked if they had come to take him home. He had been missing for four days.

The officers then asked Shawn who he was, this time out of Devlin's earshot. He said he was Shawn Hornbeck. He was finally returned to his mother after 1,558 days of captivity.

On Devlin's computer, the FBI found sexually explicit videos and photographs showing Devlin and Shawn. One shows Devlin torturing Shawn while the boy screams for him to stop. Devlin was charged with eighty-four offenses, including kidnap, forcible sodomy, producing child pornography, attempted murder, the use of a deadly weapon in the commission of a crime, and transporting a minor across a state line for the purposes of sex.

Prosecutors had evidence showing that Devlin tortured Shawn from his first days in captivity and made the boy promise not to flee in order to stay alive. It was a "devil's bargain" that kept Shawn under Devlin's control for more than four years, even as the boy had phone and Internet access, said Shawn's stepfather Craig Akers.

Devlin pleaded guilty. His attorneys said that he accepted his punishment because he knew what he did was wrong. This was dismissed by prosecutors and the boys' families.

"He pleaded guilty because he does not want the world to know the full extent of what he did," said St. Louis County prosecutor Robert McCulloch.

Devlin was sentenced to five life terms, plus a further 170 years.

Chapter 13

Zalina Israilova—
The Praetorian Plaything

STORIES OF ABDUCTION FOR SEXUAL slavery in war zones abound. Often these involve young girls in Africa whose male counterparts are fed drugs and forced to become child soldiers. On August 14, 2011, London's *Sunday Times* reported a chilling case from Chechnya, a country that has been in turmoil since it tried to secede from the Russian Federation in the 1990s.

Human rights activists eventually reported the plight of Zalina Israilova. Born in the village of Mesker-Yurt in central Chechnya, she lost her mother when she was ten. She was then raised by her grandmother but, when her grandmother died, she was sent to live with her father and her two brothers. Chechnya is a sternly patriarchal society, and Zalina was unhappy. After a few years, she ran away—a shameful act in a conservative Muslim country. She was jumping from the frying pan into the fire.

Zalina was a pretty woman, slim with large dark eyes. In 2006, she fell in love with a senior member of the Kadyrovtsy. This is the militia loyal to Ramzan Kadyrov, son of President

Akhmad Kadyov, who had been assassinated in 2004. In 2007, at the behest of Russian President Vladimir Putin, Ramzan Kadyrov took over as president of Chechnya. He had just turned thirty, the minimum age for the job. Ramzan is an advocate of polygamy. He has two wives—which is outlawed in Russia—and maintains that wives are the property of their husbands. The Kadyrovtsy has been accused of abducting, torturing, and executing suspected Islamic militants—allegations the Chechen president vehemently denies.

It seems that Zalina ignored the warning signs. Three months after she gave birth to her daughter, Elina, the militiaman dumped her. Then he married another woman and took Elina away from her mother. Zalina was distraught. She turned to relatives for support, putting them in a dangerous position. They did what they could, but she was considered a pariah. Being associated with her brought shame on their family.

Men from the Kadyrovtsy, colleagues of her former lover, came and took her away in cars with tinted windows. They used her as a sexual plaything, threatening to kill her if she resisted. There was nothing her family could do about it.

Then in late 2008, Zalina vanished altogether. She was taken to a militia base where ten girls were kept naked in one big room. Men would come and rape them at will. They would even rape them with bottles. Some girls simply disappeared. Young women were found dead in the fields outside Grozny, the capital of Chechnya. They each had a bullet in the head and one in the heart. The victims were condemned as prostitutes, and their executions described as "honor killings."

Zalina survived. After four months of captivity, she was released and she contacted human rights activist Natalya Estemirova and described her ordeal. She could not say where she had been held, as she was blindfolded when she was taken there and on her way back. However, she claimed that the abuse was sanctioned by the Chechen president himself. One girl had managed to steal the mobile phone of a senior militiaman who had raped her. It had the number of Kadyrov's private cell phone on it, so she called the president and begged for help. According to Zalina, Kadyrov was furious. He called the militiaman to upbraid him for allowing "one of your whores" to call him. As a result, the girl was shot.

Other girls got pregnant. Some miscarried. Others gave birth on the base.

Naturally, Zalina was traumatized by what she had gone through. But unburdening herself to Estemirova did no good. On the morning of July 15, 2009, Estemirova was abducted from her home in Grozny. Her body was found that evening in a wooded area a hundred miles away. She had been shot in the head and chest. Kadyrov denied any involvement and blamed exiled oligarch Boris Berezovsky, a former supporter of Vladimir Putin who claimed political asylum in the UK in 2003.

Zalina fled to St. Petersburg where the *Sunday Times* tracked her down in November 2010. They made contact through a Chechen intermediary.

"She was still frightened and emotionally scarred," the intermediary told the paper, "but she gave exactly the same account she'd given to Estemirova in Grozny. You could see she'd been through hell."

Zalina tentatively agreed to tell her story on condition that her name was not revealed. But the meeting never took place, as Zalina traveled to France and Turkey for treatment for internal injuries sustained during her captivity. Then the urge to see her daughter proved too strong and she returned to Chechnya.

A relative said that pressure been brought on Zalina's brother to lure her back. He assured her that she would be safe and could visit the daughter she had only seen twice in five years. Then four separate sources in Chechnya told the *Times* that Zalina was murdered by the men who had held her. She knew too much.

"Should anyone ever ask questions, it's easy to pin the murder on her brother and dismiss it as an honor killing," a relative told the *Sunday Times*. "But no one is even looking for her."

Zalina Israilova now lies in an unmarked grave.

So-called "honor killings" are common in Chechnya, and murders by the security forces are not investigated.

"Girls like Zalina simply vanish," said an activist. "No one will ever face justice for what happened to her. Officially, peace may have returned to Chechnya but terrible things are happening there still."

Scandals have surrounded Ramzan Kadyrov since 2006, when a video was posted on the Internet showing him with two prostitutes at an orgy in a sauna. According to a member of Kadyrov's entourage, "The people around him know that Kadyrov is a psycho who likes, for example, having sex while being observed by prisoners from his private jail, located in the village of Tsentoroi; the onlookers are forced to masturbate."

Kadyrov has also spoken out in favor of honor killings. Nevertheless, celebrities, including actors Jean-Claude van Damme and Hilary Swank, violinist Vanessa Mae, soccer-star Diego Maradona, and singer Seal turned out to celebrate Kadyrov's thirty-fifth birthday in Grozny.

Chapter 14

Tina Marie Risico— Dealing with a Killer

SOMETIMES A KIDNAPPING VICTIM is forced to become their captor's unwilling accomplice. This was the case with sixteen-year-old Tina Marie Risico. On April 4, 1984, she was in a clothing store in a shopping mall in Torrance, California, when she was approached by a balding, bearded man who said he was a fashion photographer. He was doing a shoot for a billboard that would be seen for miles around and he offered her $100 to pose for a few test rolls.

He took her to a nearby beach. But after he had fired off one roll of film, she grew uneasy and told him that she had to go home. Suddenly, he became angry.

"Your modeling days are over," he said, pulling a gun and sticking the barrel in her mouth.

He bundled her into a car and drove for more than two hundred miles to El Centro, California. In a motel room, he tied her to a bed and assaulted her. After a few hours, he put her back into the car and drove to Taos, New Mexico. There he tied her to the bed spread-eagle and raped and tortured her until he fell asleep. The next day, he tortured her with electric shocks all over her body and sexually humiliated her. He cut off most of her hair, telling her that he wanted all his victims to look like a short-haired actress in his favorite film, *Flashdance*. There had been many other victims. The day before he had abducted Tina, Wilder had made the FBI's "Ten Most Wanted" list.

The torture continued for several days. But Tina was lucky, though she did not know it. Her tormentor, Christopher Bernard Wilder, had killed his earlier victims. Tina was to be spared—at a price. If she was to survive, she had to help him kidnap fresh victims.

Wilder's career of sadistic kidnapping spanned two continents. Born in Sydney, Australia, on March 13, 1945, he was the son of an American naval officer and his Australian wife. It was a difficult birth and Wilder was immediately given the last rites. However, he pulled through. At the age of two, he fell into a swimming pool and almost drowned. A year later, he had convulsions and lapsed into a coma. But, again, he survived.

His father's career in the navy meant they moved frequently between Australia and America. In the U.S., he spent much of his boyhood in Alabama and New Mexico. A withdrawn child with a speech impediment, he seems to have been the victim of a pedophile; he told others that he had had sexual experiences from the age of nine. At home, though, his father was a stern disciplinarian and a religious man. Sex was totally taboo.

At age eleven, Wilder became a peeping tom. At twelve, he grew so nervous that he bit his nails until they bled. He blushed when sex was mentioned by other boys and suffered from a nervous stomach disorder throughout his teenage years. But in his fantasy life, he was omnipotent. He masturbated over the idea of turning girls into slaves.

When he was seventeen, he and a group of friends gang-raped a girl on a beach. He went first, and it was clear that he was the ringleader. However, he claimed that she had consented to sex with him. The others had coerced her afterwards. Nevertheless, he pleaded guilty and was put on probation with mandatory psychotherapy. As part of the course, he was given electric-shock treatment. The idea was to give him an aversion to assaulting women sexually. It failed. Instead, he turned the therapy on its head, forcibly administering it to Tina Risico and others.

Wilder also became obsessed with the 1963 novel by John Fowles, *The Collector*, in which a butterfly collector keeps a woman in his basement against her will until she dies. He memorized the text and owned several copies with large sections underlined. He had studied the book and clearly wanted to put some of what it described into practice.

On January 11, 1965, two fifteen-year-olds named Marianne Schmidt and Christine Sharrock were seen heading toward Sydney's Wanda Beach with a man answering Wilder's description. The two girls' bodies were found in a shallow grave on the beach the next day. Marks in the sand indicated that Christine had tried to flee, only to be caught and dragged back. Attempts had been made to rape both girls, and both suffered multiple stab wounds.

In November 1969, Wilder used nude photographs to extort sex from a student nurse. She went to the police but did not press charges. Then Wilder fled to Florida. Along the way, he married, but the marriage lasted just eight days. His wife could not cope with his sadistic desires and complained of sexual abuse. She also found that the trunk of his car was full of pictures of naked women and underwear that Wilder had stolen from clotheslines. It appears that he liked dressing up in women's clothing. In March 1971, Wilder was arrested in Pompano Beach, Florida, for soliciting women to pose nude for him. He pleaded guilty to disturbing the peace and escaped with a small fine.

At the time, Wilder was working as a carpenter. With a partner, he set up a building firm that won a lucrative contract to build a housing development. Soon they were employing dozens of men. Wilder became a millionaire. He lived a playboy lifestyle, took up racing driving, and slept with numerous attractive women. However, his taste was for very young women. He would behave inappropriately toward them, but was often contrite afterward. Some sixty teenagers later reluctantly admitted that they had been sexually humiliated by Wilder. Usually he forced them to show him their breasts and perform oral sex on him.

Early in January 1976, he was carrying out some building work for a couple in Boca Raton, Florida, and got to know their sixteen-year-old daughter. He discovered that she was looking for secretarial work and said he knew of a suitable job. He would drive her there.

She got into his pickup carrying a spare blouse. Afterward, she said, she was going to hang out with her boyfriend and wanted to change. Wilder realized that he had an excuse to get her to undress and suggested that she change her blouse before the interview as the spare one was much prettier. He pulled over.

When the truck stopped, he slapped her and tore off her clothes, telling her that she must do whatever he wanted. Then he forced her to masturbate and fellate him. Afterward he was apologetic and asked her if she wanted him to drive her to the police station. Fearing for her life, she said no. She promised not to tell anyone what had happened and he dropped her off at her boyfriend's.

However, three months later, she went to the police and Wilder was arrested. When interviewed by a psychiatrist, he wept copiously and admitted that the fantasized about rape, though he knew it was wrong. The psychiatrist said that he was not safe "except in a structured environment and should be in a resident program geared to his needs." But a second psychiatrist pronounced that he was not a danger to others.

Wilder went to trial for the oral rape of the sixteen-year-old, but was acquitted, possibly because she had consented to change her blouse in front of him. He refused therapy and made no effort to change his ways.

On June 21, 1980, he posed as a photographer and told a young girl from Tennessee that he was making a pizza advertisement. He had laced a pizza with drugs. When she ate it, she began to grow drowsy. He took her to his truck, where he persuaded her to take her top off, assuring the semiconscious girl that it was part of the ad. At the sight of her naked breasts, he grew aroused and viciously raped her. Impaired by the drugs, she was in no state to fight him off. However, she managed to note down his license plate number and he was arrested for rape the following day.

By then the drugs had cleared her system and the girl admitted that she had taken her top off voluntarily, so the charge was reduced to sexual battery. He was given five years' probation with mandatory therapy. His probation officer reported progress. But secretly, Wilder was drugging young women and a number of prepubescent children and photographing them. Later, the police found numerous disturbing photographs hidden in his studio. At this stage, Wilder still knew that what he was doing was wrong. He told a girlfriend that his compulsion to take photographs was a sickness, but he had to do it. She also recalled that he had once told her to leave his house because he was frightened that he might harm her.

Wilder continued to indulge his compulsion to wear women's underwear and he joined a dating agency, looking for young girls. Sometimes he would disappear for two or three days at a time and return looking shaken. He told acquaintances that he had blackouts and could not remember where he had been.

While visiting his parents in Australia in 1982, Wilder approached two fifteen-year-old girls on a beach in New South Wales. He said he was a fashion photographer and offered them a modeling assignment. After photographing them on the beach, he forced them into his car and drove them to a deserted park where he forced them to strip naked and pose for pornographic photographs. Then he assaulted both of them; he tied them up in subservient positions and masturbated over them. But they noted the license number of his rental car. The following day, he was arrested for kidnapping and indecent assault. He was only allowed to return to the U.S. when his parents posted $350,000 bail. The trial was scheduled for May 7, 1983, then postponed until April 3, 1984, because Wilder was a no-show.

Back in the States, Wilder was still enjoying the company of attractive women. He threw late night parties and set up a small photographic studio in his garage where women would voluntarily pose nude for him. He could have had any number of consensual girlfriends. But that was never enough for him.

On June 15, 1983, he abducted two girls, aged ten and twelve, at gunpoint from Boynton Beach Park, Florida. He drove them out into the woods and forced them both to fellate him. Then he returned them to the park. A year later, when Wilder was on the run, the girls identified him as the perpetrator.

On February 6, 1984, Wilder was racing at the Miami Grand Prix track when he approached twenty-year-old Rosario Gonzales, who was giving out aspirin samples. She had posed for him before, so she had no reason to be apprehensive. She left without even picking up her paycheck. She was never seen again. Her body has never been found. But then Wilder had access to a number of construction sites.

Less than two weeks later, twenty-three-year-old former Miss Florida finalist Elizabeth Kenyon disappeared after leaving Coral Gables High School, where she worked teaching emotionally disturbed children. She had been a girlfriend of Wilder's and had posed nude for him. He was, she told her parents, a "real gentleman"—unlike the other photographers who asked her to pose. Wilder had even asked her to marry him. She had refused because she was not ready to settle down and he was seventeen years older than her. They remained friends, though.

The police took little interest when she was reported missing. She was an adult and there was nothing suspicious about her disappearance. So Kenyon's parents hired a team of private detectives. They found Wilder's name in her address book. He had been seen with her at a gas station on the afternoon she vanished, though he denied having seen her. They also linked her disappearance to the Gonzalez case, as Wilder had been at the track that day.

On March 13, 1984, Wilder celebrated his thirty-ninth birthday by buying himself a 1973 Chrysler New Yorker sedan Gonzales had seen at the track. Three days later, the *Miami Herald* ran a story linking the missing girls to a racecar driver. Wilder was not named, but he got the message.

He missed his therapy appointment on March 17. The following night, he met his business partner and said tearfully, "I'm not going to jail." Meanwhile, he stole his partner's credit cards, which he used while on the run. Then he put his three red setters in boarding kennels and wiped his house clean of fingerprints. Figuring he had nothing to lose, he put a homemade torture kit in the trunk of his car and drove north.

In Indian Harbor, two hours north of Boynton Beach, Wilder approached twenty-one-year-old Terry Ferguson in a shopping mall in Satellite Beach. She was pretty enough to be a model, so she was not surprised when a man with an expensive camera approached her. She went to the restroom and changed into some clothes she had just bought, throwing her old outfit into her car. Then, it seems, she disappeared with Wilder.

Soon after, Wilder called a tow truck. His car was stuck in the sand along a dirt road near Canaveral Groves. This was a well-known lovers' lane, but Wilder was on his own. The police believe that Theresa was tied up and gagged in the trunk of the car when the tow truck turned up to extricate him. He held her for several hours and beat her with a tire iron before strangling her. Four days later, her dead body was found floating in a snake-infested creek in Polk County, seventy miles away. She was identified from dental records.

On March 20, 1984, Wilder struck again when he approached nineteen-year-old Linda Grober, a student at Florida State University, in a Tallahassee shopping mall. He said he was a photographer and offered her $25 to pose for him. He seemed sincere and credible, and not at all pushy, she said. She went with him to his car, where he showed her some photographs in magazines which he said he had taken. However, she refused to pose for him. Growing angry, he punched her in the stomach and the face, and dragged her into his car. She was unconscious when they drove off. When she began to come to, he stopped and put her in the trunk, choking her until she was unconscious again.

With the helpless girl in the trunk, he drove across the state line to Bainbridge, Georgia, where he checked into a hotel, paying cash. The man at the desk had no reason to be suspicious of Wilder. He was calm and well-dressed. Wilder put his victim into a sleeping bag, zipped it shut, then carried her to his room. When she came to, he forced her to strip naked and fellate him. He shaved off her pubic hair and put a knife to her genitals to see how she would react. Then he tied her to the bed, beat her, and superglued her eyes shut. He raped her repeatedly while watching *Dallas* on TV, saying that he admired the male lead character J.R. Ewing because of the power he had over women.

When he got tired of raping her, he got out an electrical cable and, for the next two hours, administered shocks all over her body. She could not scream because she was gagged. Eventually, he dozed off. Seizing her opportunity, she managed to crawl into the bathroom and lock herself in. Then she pounded on the walls to alert other guests. Wilder awoke, realized what was happening, grabbed his clothes, and fled. However, no one came to Linda's rescue and she eventually had to open the bathroom door and seek help, blinded, naked, and covered in blood.

After a week in the hospital, Linda was taken out of the country for fear that Wilder might return and kill her. When she returned, she resumed her studies and went on to become a marine biologist. Nevertheless, the memory of what Wilder did to her has never left her. More than ten years later, she told an interviewer: "I still can't believe that one human being could do this to another."

The day after he had fled from Bainbridge, Georgia, Wilder was in Beaumont, Texas. Twenty-four-year-old student Terry Walden told her husband that she had been approached by a bearded photographer between classes and asked to pose for him. Two days later, the young mother visited a local shopping mall where Wilder had been approaching young women, asking them to model for him. They had all turned him down. When he saw Terry he approached her. Again she refused, but he followed her to her car.

Although the parking lot was busy, Wilder knocked Terry out with a blow to the head and bundled her into the trunk of her car. The abduction took place in full daylight. He drove her to a secluded spot where he sealed her mouth with duct tape and tied her up with a nylon rope and the cord from a Venetian blind. Then he tortured her with a knife, stabbing her forty-three times in the breasts. He did not rape her. Rather, he seems to have enjoyed the sadistic pleasure of inflicting pain. The knife fractured two of her ribs and eventually punctured her heart and lungs. She bled to death. He made off in her car. Three days later, her body was recovered from a canal.

That same day, the body of twenty-one-year-old Suzanne Logan was found floating in Milford Reservoir, near Manhattan, Kansas. A married woman from Oklahoma City who studied modeling and fashion, she had been approached in a shopping mall in Reno. Again, Wilder hit her in the face and bundled her into the trunk of his stolen car. He drove her to an inn and smuggled her into his room. He cut off her hair and raped her. Then he shaved her pubic hair and bit her breasts.

He turned her onto her stomach and began stabbing her. The torture continued into the following day, when he eventually administered a fatal blow above her left breast. Then he dumped the body where it would be found within the hour.

By now, the FBI was in hot pursuit and posters began appearing in shopping malls warning women about men who approached them purporting to be photographers. Wilder drove to Denver, then on to Rifle, Colorado. He doubled back to Grand Junction where, at midday on March 29, he approached a young woman, saying he was a photographer and giving her his business card. She refused to pose for him.

A couple of hours later, he approached eighteen-year-old Sheryl Lynn Bonaventura. This time, his MO seems to have changed. They were seen together having a meal in a restaurant in Silverton. They said they were on their way to Las Vegas. Sheryl insisted on giving the waitress a lot of information, including her name. The waitress noticed that Sheryl was very nervous.

Wilder kept Sheryl alive for the next two days. Tortured with a knife then shot, she eventually died on March 31. Her naked body was found at the foot of a tree in a scenic spot in Utah five weeks later.

On April 1, Wilder was photographed at a fashion show sponsored by *Seventeen* magazine at the Meadows Mall in Las Vegas. He approached nine of the miniskirted teenage models. Eight of them agreed to meet him back at Caesar's Palace to discuss a modeling assignment. But seventeen-year-old Michelle Korfman left with him, ostensibly to see his portfolio in the parking lot. He took her to a downtown motel, where he beat her, raped her, and tortured her with electric shocks. Her body was found in California the following month and identified on June 15.

Three days later, he abducted Tina Risico in Torrance. After surviving several days of torture, she signed a pact with the devil and agreed to become his accomplice. On April 10, Tina approached sixteen-year-old Dawnette Sue Wilt in a shopping mall in Merrillville, Indiana, introducing herself at Tina Marie Wilder. She offered Dawnette a sales job and introduced Wilder as the manager of the store. They asked Dawnette to accompany them to the parking lot to sign some papers.

Once there, Wilder pulled a gun and pushed Dawnette into the back of the car and tied her up. Then he raped her while Tina drove around looking for a motel. They rented a room near Akron, Ohio, where Wilder gagged Dawnette with duct tape, raped her repeatedly, and tortured her with electric shocks. The next day, Dawnette was tied up in the trunk of the car, while they drove to Syracuse, New York. There, Dawnette was raped and tortured again, while Tina looked on silently, on pain of death.

The following morning they saw Tina's mother on TV, begging for the safe return of her daughter. The newspapers were full of stories about Wilder, and the video he had filmed for the dating agency in Florida was being shown on the networks. Wilder told his two captives that if they tried to escape or did anything to draw attention to themselves, he would kill them. He also said that the police would never take him alive. Then he bundled the two women into the car and sped off.

While he had become strangely attached to Tina, Wilder decided to get rid of Dawnette. He tried suffocating her by pinching her nostrils, but she shook herself free. So he got out a knife. She begged him to shoot her rather than stab her, but he found using a knife more satisfying. He stabbed her twice, then dumped her body on empty land outside Rochester.

But Dawnette was not dead. She managed to wriggle free of her blood-soaked bonds and stagger to a nearby highway, where she was spotted by a passing motorist who drove her to a hospital. Meanwhile, Wilder was beginning to have doubts about whether he had actually killed Dawnette and decided to go back and shoot her. When he reached the place where he had dumped her, she was gone.

Realizing that Dawnette might identify the car, Wilder decided that they needed another one. He saw a Pontiac Trans-Am he liked in the parking lot of Eastview shopping mall near Victor, New York, and carjacked the owner, thirty-three-year-old Sunday school teacher Elizabeth Dodge. While Wilder and Dodge drove out to some nearby woods, Tina followed in the other car. Wilder then shot Elizabeth Dodge, leaving her body in a gravel pit, and took off with Tina in the Pontiac.

As Wilder was determined not to go to jail, he knew he was likely to meet his end in a gun fight with the police. He did not want Tina with him when that happened, so he stopped at Boston's Logan Airport and bought Tina a one-way ticket to Los Angeles. He gave her a generous handful of spending money and walked her to the gate. While she headed down the skyway to the plane, she still half-expected a shot in the back. When she arrived in L.A., she was in such a distressed condition, she decided she could not face her family or the police. Instead, she took a cab to her favorite lingerie store. After what she had been through, she felt dirty and she had not had a change of underwear for nine days. She purchased several items, and then she told the manager that she was the missing girl everyone was looking for.

But Wilder was not done yet. Just hours after bidding Tina farewell, he spotted a nineteen-year-old woman standing by her vehicle at the roadside near Beverly, Massachusetts. Wilder offered her a ride. When she got in, he pulled a gun on her and told her to keep quiet. But when he slowed down as he was approaching a red light, she jumped out and made a run for it.

Heading for Canada where he had friends, Wilder stopped at a gas station in Colebrook, New Hampshire, just eight miles from the border. There he was spotted by two state troopers, Leo Jellison and Wayne Fortier. When they approached Wilder, he retreated to his car and armed himself with a .357 Magnum. Jellison grabbed Wilder from behind. In the scuffle, Wilder's gun went off. A bullet entered his chest and came out of his back, hitting Jellison in the ribs and lodging in his liver. A second bullet hit Wilder in the heart, killing him.

Jellison was seriously injured, but made a full recovery and returned to duty.

After Wilder's death, more victims have been attributed to him. On January 16, 1981, seventeen-year-old Mary Opitz disappeared from the Edison Mall in Fort Myers, Florida. She was last seen heading to the parking lot. A parcel she was carrying was found near her car. No trace of Opitz has ever been found. Eighteen-year-old Mary Hare disappeared from the same parking lot on February 11. Hare's badly decomposed body was found in Lehigh Acres, Florida, fifteen miles away. She had been stabbed in the back.

The skeletal remains of two unidentified women were found near properties owned by Wilder in 1982. On July 6, 1983, teenage model Tammy Leppert disappeared from a parking lot in Cocoa Beach, Florida. She was thought to have been three months pregnant when she went missing. Nineteen-year-old Melody Gay was abducted from the graveyard shift of a 7-Eleven in Collier County, Florida, on March 7, 1984. Her body was found dumped in a canal three days later. Then on March 15, fifteen-year-old Colleen Osborne went missing from the bedroom of her home in Daytona Beach. Wilder had been seen propositioning potential "models" in the area the same day.

After Wilder's autopsy, the pathologist Dr. Robert Christie got a telephone call from a man purporting to be from Harvard University, asking for Wilder's brain. The caller explained that they wanted to see whether there was any abnormality that might explain his pathological behavior. The body was cremated and the ashes sent to Wilder's parents, while the brain was preserved. However, no one came to collect it and Harvard's medical school denied making any such request. Wilder left an estate of $2 million.

The authorities briefly considered prosecuting Tina Marie Risico for aiding and abetting Wilder in the abduction of Dawnette Wilt and Elizabeth Dodge, but a psychological assessment confirmed her own account that she was an unwilling participant in those crimes.

Chapter 15

Sharon Marshall—
Identity Unknown

IN NOVEMBER 1983, A MAN calling himself Warren Marshall
arrived at Forest Park High School in Georgia with his fifteen-
year-old daughter. She had an IQ of 132 and an impressive
report card. She had done especially well in math at other
schools in the state. But the man purporting to be her father
said that he wanted her to move schools because he was not
happy with the advanced classes she was being offered.

Marshall explained that he was a painter by trade and a
single father. Sharon's mother had died when Sharon was a
child, and he had raised her himself. She was a good girl, studied hard at school, went to church on a Sunday, and looked
after her daddy. She also presented herself well, and Forest
Park offered her a place. Marshall accepted on his daughter's
behalf. The next day she started at her new school.

Sharon Marshall was pretty with shoulder-length blonde
hair and blue eyes. She became popular at school and was soon
elected to the student council. The following June, she was sent
to a summer leadership workshop on the campus of Berry

College in Rome, Georgia. There she met Jennifer Fisher from Stone Mountain, and they became close friends. After the end of the week-long program, Jennifer asked Sharon for her phone number so they could stay in touch. Sharon said that she could not give it to her, so Jennifer gave Sharon her number and Sharon promised to call.

When several days had passed and there had been no call, Jennifer decided to take matters into her own hands. Perhaps Sharon had lost her number. Jennifer was determined not to lose touch with her new friend. She went through the paperwork she had brought home from the student council camp and found a directory that listed Sharon Marshall's number. She called it. Sharon answered. But instead of being happy that her friend had called, she sounded angry. Sharon wanted to know how Jennifer had gotten her number.

Jennifer could hear a male voice in the background. He, too, wanted to know how Jennifer had got the number. Sharon insisted that she had not given it to her. Then, abruptly, the phone was slammed down. Jennifer could not make out what had happened.

Five minutes later, the phone at the Fisher home rang. Jennifer answered. It was Sharon. She apologized for what had happened before, explaining that her father was upset. Sharon was not supposed to give their number out. Then, for the next hour, the two girls talked.

The next day, Jennifer called Sharon again. This time a man answered. He said he was Warren, Sharon's father, and this time, he was quite pleasant. He even invited Jennifer to stay over some night. Nothing came of the vague invitation for some time, but in August, Sharon was invited to come spend the night at the Fishers' home, a four-bedroom mock-Tudor in an upmarket residential area. Warren brought her over in his beat-up pickup.

When he met Jennifer's parents, Marshall complimented them on their home. He asked Mr. Fisher to think of him if he ever needed any painting work, and gave him his business card.

The next time Warren brought Sharon over to the Fishers he asked to speak to Mr. Fisher privately and tried to borrow money from him so that he could buy materials for a job. Fisher refused. Warren asked to borrow money again the next time he brought Sharon over. This time, he explained that he had been in a motorcycle accident a few years before but, even though he was in pain, the state would not help with the money for his medical treatment. As Sharon had lost her own mother, Mrs. Fisher did her best to stand in for her. But she noticed that Sharon experienced mood swings. When the topic of Sharon's father came up in conversation, Sharon grew nervous and started to stutter. Mrs. Fisher pried no further, but her husband made it clear that, under no circumstances, would Jennifer be allowed to stay over at the Marshalls'.

However, when the invitation was extended, Mr. Fisher was out of town. Jennifer begged her mother to let her go and, eventually, Mrs. Fisher gave in. But when she drove Jennifer over to Sharon's house, she was not pleased. The Marshalls lived in a rundown neighborhood and the house was surrounded by weeds. Mrs. Fisher did not even get out of her car when she dropped Jennifer off.

Inside, the house was no better. On a wall above an old sofa, Jennifer saw a photograph of a woman. Sharon said that it was a picture of her mother, Linda. Jennifer also noticed that none of the rooms had doors, only curtains that hung across the doorways. She saw into one room where there were stacks of videotapes. No one was allowed in there Sharon said.

That evening, on the way to have dinner in a nearby restaurant, Warren told Jennifer that she was very pretty. Then Warren suggested they go down to Peachtree Street to make fun of the prostitutes there. Sharon pointed out that the prostitutes were now on Stuart Street, but she just wanted to go eat.

After dinner, Warren said that he was going to take the girls dancing. At fourteen, Jennifer had never been to a club. It was not something her parents would allow. Besides, she said, she did not have anything appropriate to wear. That was no problem; Sharon would lend her something.

Back at the Marshalls' house, they went though Sharon's wardrobe. It was full of lingerie—tiny G-strings and crotchless panties. Jennifer settled on a pink minidress and Sharon donned a miniskirt with an off-the-shoulder blouse. Then they did their hair and put on makeup. Warren voiced his approval.

Jennifer did not like the look of the seedy club. It was clear that she and Sharon were underage, but Warren had a word with the doorman and they were allowed in. Warren left the two girls on the dance floor. Sharon's sexy dance moves attracted a crowd of scruffy-looking men, mostly in their late thirties and forties. They wanted to dance with Jennifer, but she waved them away.

At midnight, Warren took them home. As they were getting ready for bed, Jennifer asked Sharon about the lingerie in her wardrobe. Sharon said her father bought it for her. Then, with Sharon standing there naked except for a small pair of white panties, Warren burst in. He was holding a gun. There were tears in Sharon's eyes. Jennifer fainted. In the morning, Sharon apologized for her father's behavior, saying he was just kidding around. The incident was never mentioned again.

At school, Sharon excelled. She got top marks in class and signed up for the Air Force ROTC, math and computer clubs, and the Future Business Leaders of America, and she was the secretary of the junior prom committee. However, her extra-curricular activities were always curtailed because she had to go home early. She said she had to be home at 4.30 p.m. to cook and clean for her father. She often appeared inappropriately attired, as if dressed by someone else who had no fashion sense. While Warren turned up to watch Sharon drill ROTC cadets, he did not put in an appearance at other school functions. He only appeared at one parent-teacher meeting, where he volunteered the information that Sharon's mother had died from cancer. Sharon maintained that her mother had died in a traffic accident.

Although she was a friendly, outgoing girl, Sharon did not develop any close friendships at school. None of her classmates had been to her home. Sharon read voraciously and loved intellectual conversation, but anything personal or concerning her past was out of bounds. Often, when they spoke on the phone, Jennifer was conscious that Warren was listening in the background, monitoring his daughter's conversation. Sometimes he even butted in. He often asked Jennifer to come and stay again, but Jennifer knew not to go back there. Nevertheless, they stayed in touch and Sharon often stayed at the Fishers'.

One Saturday in the spring of 1985, the Fishers arrived home after a trip to the mall to find Warren's pickup in their driveway. Inside the house, Warren was asleep on the couch.

Sharon was sitting nearby with tears in her eyes. Warren awoke complaining about his back. When they had arrived at the house, he said, he was suffering such intense pain that he needed to lie down. He found that the garage door was open and let himself in.

As Warren continued his explanation, Jennifer led Sharon upstairs. The Fishers liked Sharon and did not want any unpleasantness with her father, so they said nothing. But they could not understand how he had got into the house. The doors had been locked. The alarm was on. After he and Sharon left, they checked the house, but nothing was missing.

In June 1985, Sharon Marshall scored 1230 on her SATs and set her sights on Georgia Tech, though she could have gone to any college that she chose. She was seen as an all-around outstanding student. She began dating a football player named Jason Anderson. But when they went out, they always seem to have been accompanied by her father.

Fortunately, Warren could not attend the junior prom, and Sharon and Jason seized the opportunity to spend time together in Jason's car in the parking lot—to the disapproval of the teacher in charge. Soon after, the couple broke up. That meant she had time for Jennifer again. But Jennifer had not done well on her exams, so her parents strictly limited her time for socializing.

In March 1986, Jennifer got a phone call from a jubilant Sharon: she had gotten a scholarship to Georgia Tech. She planned to study engineering. Her ambition was to work for NASA, and studying at Georgia Tech meant that she could continue living at home.

Then Sharon's mood changed. She had not told her father yet. Maybe he would not let her go. He had a bad back and arthritis. In addition to cooking and cleaning for him, Sharon had to massage him every night. Later that night, Sharon called again. This time she spoke in a whisper. She had told her father about the scholarship and he was going to let her go to college.

But before Sharon left Forest Park High, her appearance changed. She began to put on weight. When asked if she was pregnant, she denied it. But eventually, she had to confess. The father, she said, was her new boyfriend, Curtis Flournoy. When Warren found out, he insisted that she give up her place at Georgia Tech. He even forbid her from receiving her diploma with her graduating class. Sharon grew depressed. She ran away with Curtis. Warren caught up with them at a motel just over the state line in Alabama. He seized Sharon, leaving a note telling Curtis that he was not the father of her child.

When Sharon phoned Jennifer to tell her about her pregnancy, she said there would be no abortion and no college. The following Saturday, Warren dropped Sharon off at the Fishers' and sped off. Sharon told Jennifer and her mother that Warren had decided to move to Arizona. The dry weather there would be better for his arthritis, and living was cheap there. Sharon was toying with the idea of going to Arizona State the following year. After a brief conversation, they heard Warren beeping his horn outside and said their farewells.

In mid-July, Jennifer got a letter from Mesa, Arizona. Sharon was working as a hostess in the restaurant of the Marriott Hotel near the airport in Phoenix. She had given birth to a son and had given it up for adoption. She asked if she could visit Jennifer. Two weeks later, she arrived by Greyhound. Sharon was her old self again. She and Jennifer pricked their palms and became "blood sisters."

Later Sharon drew Mrs. Fisher aside and asked whether she could move in with the Fishers. She did not like Arizona. Mr. and Mrs. Fisher said that, if her father approved, she could stay. But Sharon did not think it was a good idea to ask him. Disappointed, she phoned her father and told him she was coming home.

The following day at the airport, Sharon wept copiously. Mrs. Fisher thought something must be terribly wrong. She asked Sharon if she was sure that there was not something she wanted to tell them. But that was not Sharon's way. The problem, whatever it was, had something to do with Warren, the Fishers thought. They kissed her and said good-bye. Sharon begged them not to forget her, but they knew little of what happened after that.

The Fisher family later learned that Warren and Sharon moved to Tampa, Florida. There they lived as man and wife, under an alias. Warren called himself Charles or Clarence Marcus Hughes. Sharon was Tonya Dawn Hughes, née Tadlock.

Warren's real name was Franklin Delano Floyd, and he was a psychopath. Sharon's real name has yet to be discovered. The first record of her was in 1975 when she was in school in Oklahoma City under the name "Suzanne Davis." That does not seem to have been her real name either. Floyd had abducted her sometime before, when she was just a toddler, and pretended that she was his daughter.

They fled from Oklahoma City after he was accused of sexually abusing the child, though no charges were filed. In 1980, they turned up in Louisville, Kentucky, where they began using the names Warren and Sharon Marshall. After another two years, they suddenly moved to Atlanta.

In 1988, in Tampa, they had a child named Michael. They left Florida in November 1988 and moved to Louisville, Kentucky. On Christmas Eve, Sharon was found unconscious in her car and was taken to a hospital. She had overdosed and was found to be pregnant. She refused to say why she was suicidal, or who the father of her child was. Warren was notified as next of kin. After he picked her up from the hospital, they moved back to Florida. It seemed that every time she formed an attachment—or became pregnant—they moved on.

During her travels, Sharon managed to stay in touch with Jennifer. In sporadic phone calls and letters, she volunteered patchy details of her life. She told her friend about Michael and working in various clubs—though she said she was a waitress. When she was living in South Carolina, Sharon tried to get Jennifer to come for a visit. Remembering the last overnight visit, Jennifer refused the invitation and Warren got angry.

Eventually, they moved to Tulsa, where they were known as Clarence and Tonya, and lived in a trailer park with baby Michael—now Michael Anthony Hughes. Tonya supported the family by working as an exotic dancer in a seedy strip joint named Passions. Her body showed signs of incompetent plastic surgery. Her breasts were conical and hard, while her hips and thighs were large for her short body. But she made up for it with her dancing and the sexy schoolgirl outfits she wore at the start of her set. Tonya did not drink or take drugs, which were freely available in the club. Instead, between sets, she would read.

She worked seven days a week and her "husband" Clarence insisted that she bring home $200 a day. If she didn't, the bruises on her body were all too obvious the day after. The other girls at the club did not like Clarence. He was at least twice Sharon's age and seemed creepy. He would bring her to work and be waiting for her in the parking lot at the end of the night. In between, he would call the club nearly every hour to check up on her. Her friends at the club urged her to leave Clarence and flee town, but she was scared and told her boss, J. R. Buck, that things were not as they seemed.

Her fears were not unreasonable. Clarence had friends in the local sheriff's department. He had a number of guns at home and told anyone who wanted to hear it that he would kill Tonya if she ever tried to leave him.

Sharon's closest friend at the club was nineteen-year-old college student Karen Parsley, who used the stage name Connie. Karen figured that the solution to Tonya's problem was to find her a boyfriend. She fixed her friend up with one of Passions' bouncers. When Clarence found out about it, Tonya turned up to work with bruises all over her body. Her new beau wanted to confront Clarence, but Tonya forbade it.

Next Tonya got close to one of the customers, a college student named Kevin Brown. They began dating surreptitiously, and Kevin offered to take Tonya and Michael away, out of the state. She declined, fearing that Clarence would kill all three of them.

Although Connie and Tonya grew close, Connie learned little about Tonya's private life. Tonya said she was from

Alabama and had started dancing in Florida. Connie could see for herself that Tonya doted on Michael, while the boy shied away from Clarence.

Eventually, Kevin convinced Tonya that she could escape from Clarence. Her mood changed. She talked of going to college and studying to become a nurse. She even said that she knew things about Clarence that could put him in prison for life, but would not say more.

Then Tonya took a rare day off. That evening, Connie got a call from Clarence. Tonya had been in an accident. She was in a hospital in Oklahoma City. He claimed that she had a gynecologist's appointment there and had been hit by a car.

Three men had been driving down a poorly lit exit road from Interstate 35 toward a Motel 6 just outside Oklahoma City, when they saw a shoe in the road. Then they spotted a body in the gutter. It belonged to a young woman. She was still alive and her body was contorted with violent convulsions. The sped off to the Motel 6 and told the night watchman to call 911. An ambulance rushed Tonya to a Presbyterian hospital. When the police arrived, they found her groceries strewn across the road. There was also a portable radio and headphones, a broken windshield wiper, radio aerial, and a fleck of red paint that was thought to be from the suspect's vehicle. The road was wet and there was a forty-foot skid mark leading up to what was thought to have been the point of impact. From what they could piece together, it looked as if the woman had been walking along the road with the headphones on, listening to music, and had not heard the car approaching in the dark from behind.

The clerk in the mini-mart in the truck stop a few hundred feet away said a young woman had come into the store to buy groceries at around 12:30 a.m. and had set off back toward Motel 6 when she was hit.

In the hospital, the victim cried out, "Daddy! Daddy!"

She was given medication to stop the convulsions. When the medical staff removed her clothing, they found her body was covered in old scratches and bruises. There were fresh bruises on the back of her legs and a large hematoma on the back of her head. It seemed as if the car's bumper had hit her on the back of the legs and she had fallen backward onto the hood. Curiously, there were no broken bones, no cuts, and she had lost very little blood. This was rare in a road traffic accident.

The next morning, Clarence arrived at the hospital. He explained that he had driven from Tulsa the previous day with his wife and their two-year-old son and had checked into the Motel 6 at around 3 p.m.

Around midnight, Tonya was walking down the road to the mini-mart at the truck stop. A quarter of an hour later, she called from a pay phone, saying that they did not have any baby food but she was returning with what she could find. Clarence said that he had then fallen asleep. His wife was a stripper in a club in Tulsa, and she liked men, so he was used to her being out all night.

In the morning, he had gone to the mini-mart, where the clerk told him about the accident. He called the police and they came to the motel. They asked to see his car. He showed them his dark blue Oldsmobile, which was undamaged. Both the windshield wipers and the radio aerial were still in place.

In the hospital, Clarence showed little concern for his wife, though the doctors said that they believed she would pull through and come out of the coma in a day or two. Before he left, he put a sign on her door that read, "No Visitors."

Connie and Kevin drove to the Presbyterian hospital in Oklahoma City. They ignored the "No Visitors" sign and went in to see Tonya. The nursing staff reported the mysterious theft of all Tonya's belongings, including her clothes. When Connie commented that there were no marks on Tonya's face or arms, a doctor pulled her aside and said, "This was no car accident."

Connie said that she had already had doubts and believed that Clarence was trying to kill Tonya. The medical staff advised Connie to contact the police.

Tonya had seemed to react to Connie's presence, so Connie took a motel room nearby. Clarence still forbade visits, but the staff would phone Connie whenever the coast was clear. When Clarence heard about this, he phoned Connie and yelled at her. But Connie held her ground, telling him that Tonya was her friend and no one was going to stop her from seeing her.

Clarence then changed his tune. Without Tonya stripping, he was short of money and offered to sell Connie the trailer, saying he was planning to move to Oklahoma City.

The prognosis was good and Tonya was expected to come out of the coma the next day. But the following morning, Connie got a call, saying that Tonya's condition had suddenly deteriorated. By the time she arrived that the hospital, Tonya was dead. She learned that Clarence had visited the night before. Then in the morning, her life had slipped away without her ever regaining consciousness. Clarence had left instructions that Tonya's organs were to be donated and her body was to be cremated. Connie protested that Tonya had said she wanted to be buried. Clarence eventually backed down when Connie and J. R. Buck agreed to pay for a funeral back in Tulsa.

The one remaining problem was Michael. At two, he did not talk. Left in the care of Clarence, he was unwashed and smelled of urine. Connie contacted social services. Clarence agreed to allow Michael to go into temporary foster care for a week until after the funeral and after he had completed his move to Oklahoma City. An autopsy noted the implants in Tonya's breasts and buttocks. The cause of death was given as "head injury," and under "manner of death" the medical examiner ticked "homicide." As far as the police were concerned, Tonya's death had been a hit-and-run. However, with no clue to the identity of the driver, there was little they could do about it.

Michael's foster parents Ernest and Merle Bean, said they had never seen a child in such emotional distress. He beat his head on the solid floor on the foyer of their home and would not stop crying. Nevertheless, they did what they could.

Connie told the social services of her concerns. She believed that Tonya had been killed by Clarence and that Michael was not safe in his hands. As a result, Michael was made a ward of the court.

Clarence was furious. He turned up at Tonya's funeral, with two burly sheriff's deputies, then vented his anger on the mourners. He told them that Tonya had taken her secrets with her to the grave. Now they should let it be. Then he turned his venom on Connie, blaming her for depriving him of his son.

And he put a picture of a man of about thirty years old with a five-year-old girl on his lap on top of the coffin.

The street outside the chapel suddenly filled with police cars. Clarence went to speak to the cops. Connie and the others hoped that they were going to arrest him for Tonya's murder. But he shook hands and walked away. However, the police did impound the corpse for further investigation.

Clarence had taken out two life insurance policies on Tonya worth a total of $80,000 just weeks before her death. Right after the funeral, he called to see how the claims were progressing. He was asked for his social security number. However, the number he gave did not match their records. Nor did a second. A third number was accepted, however; it was for a Franklin Delano Floyd. A fugitive who had been on the run since 1973, Floyd was wanted for attempted kidnapping and a parole violation. The insurance company immediately informed the federal authorities.

When the U.S. Marshals turned up at Clarence's apartment, he had already fled. When they checked his background, they found that neither Charles nor Clarence Hughes existed. Neither did Tonya Hughes, née Tadlock. She had obtained her driver's license with a phony birth certificate. However, Franklin Delano Floyd most definitely did exist.

Born in 1943 in Barnesville, Georgia, the youngest of five children, he was the son of an abusive drunk who died when Floyd was one. Unable to bring the children up on her own, his mother took them to a children's home in Hapeville where she was not allowed to visit them.

Although he was the baby of the family, Floyd was forced to sleep in a separate room from his siblings. The regime was strict, and beatings were frequent. Food was sparse; clothing was second-hand. And, after a morning's schoolwork, the children would be sent to work in the fields.

Floyd was a sensitive boy. Perceived as feminine, he was bullied and claimed he was raped by a group of boys with a broom handle when he was six. His behavior and school grades rapidly deteriorated. He ran away repeatedly. At sixteen, he left the home and moved in with his sister, but her husband threw him out, saying he considered him dangerous.

Floyd went to Indianapolis, where he found his mother. She was working as a prostitute. Then he joined the army, saying that he had her permission. He was discharged after five months when it was discovered that he had forged his mother's signature on his enlistment papers.

Drifting from city to city, he broke into a Los Angeles branch of Sears, where he opened a gun case, setting off an alarm. When the police arrived, there was an exchange of gunfire. He was arrested after being shot in the stomach.

After a year he was released, but was re-arrested for a parole violation. Released a second time, he returned to Hapeville, Georgia, where, a month later, he abducted a four-year-old girl who it seems he knew from the children's home. Semen stains and teeth marks where found around her vagina. He was sentenced to ten to twenty years. A few months later, he escaped, stole a car, bought a pistol, and robbed a bank. This earned him another fifteen years. He got a further five years for another attempted escape. This time he was sent to the federal penitentiary at Lewisburg, Pennsylvania.

A convicted pedophile, Floyd was regularly beaten and raped by the other prisoners. He tried to kill himself. After a period in the hospital wing, he was returned to the general population, where the beatings and rape resumed. He became a serious disciplinary problem and had to be transferred to the new maximum security prison at Marion, Illinois. There, he settled for being the bitch of a prisoner who could protect him. The sexual abuse continued, but the beatings stopped.

He was returned to Georgia to complete the balance of his sentences for the sexual molestation and bank robbery in Reidsville State Prison. Again he was forced to seek the protection of another prisoner, career criminal David Dial.

Released in January 1973, Floyd was arrested again for trying to abduct a woman at a gas station. Dial, who had since been released, posted bail for him. Floyd then disappeared. Ever since, he had been on the run.

When Floyd disappeared from his apartment in Oklahoma City, the Beans were informed. As there was no way that Michael would be returned to the custody of a fugitive from justice, they volunteered to keep Michael.

While she had worked at Passions, Tonya had told some of the girls that her parents had been killed in a car accident. Others were told that she had simply been estranged from her family. Connie and J.R. Buck decided that, if her family was alive, they should know of their daughter's death. Buck began calling phone numbers listed to anyone named Tadlock in Alabama. After two or three calls, he reached a woman who said she was the mother of Tonya Dawn Tadlock. He braced himself and informed the woman that her daughter was dead. Mrs. Tadlock said she knew she was. Tonya had died of pneumonia twenty years ago when she was just eighteen months. It seems that the name of the girl who had worked at Passions had been lifted from a gravestone.

Six weeks after he had fled from Oklahoma City, Clarence Marcus Hughes, aka Franklin Delano Floyd, was arrested in a trailer park in Augusta, Georgia, after a tip-off. He was using the name Trenton B. Davis. It was one of his many aliases, most of which were taken from gravestones.

Once in custody, Floyd called social services in Oklahoma, explained the situation, and asked them to look after his son until he was released. A court recognized Floyd as Michael's father. The Beans were horrified. Floyd was a convicted pedophile and they knew something terrible had happened to Michael. At two years old, he could not speak. Nevertheless, when Floyd was transferred from Atlanta to the federal prison at El Reno, near Oklahoma City, he was granted visitation rights.

Floyd remained a suspect in the murder of Tonya, but the police could find no material evidence against him. They did not even know who she was. All Floyd would say was that he had met her in Chicago. They had had a child together in Alabama in 1988 and married the following year in New Orleans.

Michael made slow progress with the Beans. There were often problems after he was taken on his monthly visits to see Floyd. Meanwhile, Floyd underwent everything the courts required in order to get custody of the boy when he was released—except one. He refused to take a paternity test. Eventually, he was forced to. It came back negative. Franklin Delano Floyd was not the biological father of Michael Anthony Hughes, and Floyd's visitation rights were rescinded. The Beans then put in an application to adopt Michael.

Floyd was released on March 30, 1993. As legal wrangles over the custody of Michael were ongoing, Floyd was given a parole officer in Oklahoma City. Floyd would talk openly about his early life and his concerns over Michael, but he would reveal nothing of what he had been up to between 1973 and 1989. He maintained that Tonya had been the victim of a hit by organized crime, but would volunteer nothing to fill in her background. It was also clear to those who dealt with him that he was still dangerous.

Then in July 1993, Floyd's visitation rights were restored. A court decided that he had been denied the right to challenge the paternity test. What's more, he had had a two-year custodial relationship with Michael and his mother.

Floyd got a job as a janitor in an apartment block. When one of the tenants returned home, she found Floyd rummaging through her drawers. In his hand, he held a pair of her panties. He punched her in the eye and attacked her with a knife, cutting her arm. But her boyfriend, who appeared soon after, managed to subdue him until the police arrived.

Despite the severity of the attack, Floyd was released on bail and sent to a halfway house. He knew if he was convicted on the assault charge, he would lose all hope of regaining custody of Michael, so he took matters into his own hands.

By this time, Michael was going to elementary school in Choctaw. On September 12, 1994, Michael took the bus to school as usual. At 9 a.m., Floyd entered the school and walked into the office of the principal, James Davis. He had a gun and threatened to kill Davis if he did not help him.

Floyd forced Davis to go to Michael's class and ask the child to come out into the corridor. The teacher told Michael

341

to get up and follow the principal. Floyd, Davis, and Michael went out to the principal's pickup. Davis was then forced to drive them out of town. Floyd left Davis handcuffed to a tree in a field, with duct tape over his mouth. He told Davis that he would call someone to free him after two hours and left the key to the handcuffs out of reach. Davis eventually managed to remove the duct tape from his mouth and cried for help.

Two hours later, the FBI were on the case. Special Agent Joe Fitzpatrick of the Oklahoma City office sent details of the kidnapping to bureaus across the country. He was convinced that Floyd would flee the state. An All Points Bulletin was issued to police agencies throughout the region.

Agents were dispatched to interview Mr. Davis, the Beans, and anyone who had known Floyd, under his many aliases, over the years. In a lockup behind the halfway house in Oklahoma City that Floyd used for storage, photographs were found of Floyd's "wife" Tonya in provocative poses. In one, Fitzpatrick thought she looked about fourteen.

After a week, FBI agents tracked down an Oklahoma school district employee who had known Trenton Davis, aka Franklin Floyd, in the 1970s. He had a photograph of Davis with a young girl named Suzanne, who he said was his daughter, perched on his lap. Floyd had reappeared a few weeks earlier to reclaim the photograph, but at the time he could not find it. The girl appeared to be about five or six. Then Fitzpatrick realized that she was a younger version of the girl in the pictures found in the lockup. Tonya was Suzanne. Floyd's daughter had become his wife.

Agents tracked down David Dial, who had helped Floyd over the years. He was asked about the little girl Floyd had taken with him when he was on the run. Dial said that Floyd had told him that the girl's mother had been a crack addict. He had taken the child to keep her away from the drug scene. She had been four at the time.

Fitzpatrick obtained a copy of Floyd's phone records in Tulsa. Soon after Tonya's death, Floyd had called Greg Higgs in Phoenix. At the age of twenty, Higgs had worked as a waiter in the Marriott Hotel to put himself through college. He had dated Sharon Marshall, who said she planned to study aerospace engineering at Arizona State. But when local businessmen had offered to sponsor her, her father put a stop to it, trying instead to get them to invest in his painting business.

Suddenly Sharon disappeared, but eight months later, she was back at her old job. She and her father had been in Texas and elsewhere, but things did not work out. Six months after that, she disappeared again. Then in May 1990, Higgs got a call from Warren Marshall, saying that Sharon was dead. Warren also said that Greg was the father of Sharon's two-year-old son, Michael, and asked whether he was prepared to look after him. Greg said he would. Warren said that he would call back to make arrangements. That was the last Greg heard.

Six weeks after Michael's kidnapping, Davis's pickup was found in a parking lot in Dallas, Texas. But Floyd was nowhere to be found, so Fitzpatrick contacted the offices of the department of transportation in all the states Floyd was known to frequent—Oklahoma, Georgia, Arizona, Louisiana, Kentucky, Texas, and Florida—to ask police to watch for driver's license applications under any of the aliases Floyd was known to use. After two weeks, Fitzpatrick got a call from officers in Florida, saying that a man named Warren Marshall had applied to renew his driver's license. The application had come from an address in Louisville, Kentucky.

On November 9, 1994, an FBI agent posing as a Federal Express employee delivered the driver's license to Floyd at the used car lot where he worked. When Floyd signed for it, he was arrested by seven armed FBI agents. The area had already been sealed off. Fitzpatrick was taking no chances.

When Floyd was searched, agents found that he was carrying the current address of a woman he had raped in 1962 when she was four years old. Her name was Rebecca Barr.

When questioned about Michael, Floyd said he was fine, but would not say where he was. And Suzanne? He said he had taken her from a prostitute named Linda Williams in Indianapolis in 1974 because she was a drug addict, but he would not confirm that the child's last name was Williams.

Floyd boasted about his ability to evade the law and blamed Sharon for ruining her life by going with boys. He would not say what had happened to her first child. He said that, after Michael, she had had another baby that was adopted by a family in New Orleans. When asked if he had ever had sex with Sharon, he denied it and refused to answer any further questions if asked again.

Floyd's neighbors and colleagues at work were questioned. No one had seen Michael. There was no sign of him in Floyd's apartment. However, Floyd had with him a single bus ticket from Atlanta to Louisville, dated September 30. Fitzpatrick checked and discovered that Michael had not traveled with Floyd on that day. Whatever had happened to the child had happened before Floyd left Atlanta.

Fitzpatrick discovered that Floyd had checked himself into Grady Memorial Hospital on September 21, and discharged himself on the 29th. On the 20th, a man answering Floyd's description had attacked a woman while taking a test drive in a Dodge Shadow she was selling. She escaped and he drove off in the car.

The FBI office in Atlanta contacted Rebecca Barr. Fitzpatrick thought Floyd might have a soft spot for her. She agreed to help. After contacting Floyd by phone, she surmised that Michael was probably dead.

A fellow prisoner reported that Floyd had said he had thrown the boy off a bridge. Another said Floyd admitted killing Michael and hiding his body in a drainpipe. His sister said Floyd had told her that he had drowned Michael in the bathtub when they were having a bath together in a motel, after Floyd had asked Michael if he loved him and Michael had said no. He had then put his body in the trunk of his car and disposed of it.

When the Dodge Shadow stolen on September 21 was found, dogs trained to locate corpses showed an interest in the trunk. This all but confirmed that Michael was dead, but his body was never found. Without a body, Floyd could not be charged with murder.

Instead, he went on trial for kidnapping the child. Floyd chose to defend himself. He was found guilty and sentenced to fifty-two years in jail.

While the trial was going on, a mechanic working on school principal James Davis's stolen pickup found an envelope taped to the side of the tank. It contained nearly a hundred pictures of young girls—from teens to toddlers—many nude and being exploited sexually. A series of them showed Suzanne as she grew from a child to the brink of womanhood. This confirmed that Floyd had sexually abused the child since he had abducted her at the age of four—and throughout her short and tormented life.

Another set showed a young woman who had been bound, beaten, and tortured. Sexually explicit pictures showed burn marks around her anus. In some pictures, she appeared near death. When Fitzpatrick saw the photographs, he was convinced that Floyd had killed this girl too. However, further investigation was interrupted by the Oklahoma City bombing on April 16, 1995.

Then in July 1996, the FBI's office in Tampa tied a photograph of the bound and beaten girl found in Davis's pickup to a Jane Doe who had been found in a swamp along I-275 near St. Petersburg on March 29, 1995. The body had been there some time and had completely decomposed, leaving only the bones, hair, fragments of clothing, and some jewelry. There were two small bullet holes in the back of her skull, indicating that the victim had been murdered. But no further progress had been made in the case.

In the photograph, the girl was only wearing a striped shirt and a white bikini top that had been pushed up to expose her breasts. These two items of clothing matched the fragments found with I-275 Jane Doe.

Fitzpatrick had sent the photograph to Tampa because the girl had appeared tanned, and Florida had been one of Floyd's stamping grounds. He had been there in 1988 and 1989. The police reviewed the missing persons cases in the area at that time and came up with nineteen-year-old Cheryl Ann Commesso, who had last been seen in April 1989. She had been reported missing in June after her red Corvette was found, apparently abandoned in the parking lot of the St. Petersburg–Clearwater International Airport. Her dental records confirmed that the I-275 corpse was indeed Cheryl Commesso.

Cheryl had had a short and troubled life. After dropping out of school at the age of sixteen, she began working as an exotic dancer in Orlando. Before she disappeared, she had been working in the Mons Venus strip club in Tampa under the name Stevie. Another of the strippers had been Sharon Marshall, and some of the staff who had worked there back in the 1980s, remembered that Warren had been barred from the club on the grounds that only a weirdo would come to watch his daughter perform.

Sharon, Warren, and Michael had been living in the Golden Lantern trailer park. Michael's babysitter said she had seen Cheryl and her red corvette at the Marshalls' trailer.

Sharon had found a boyfriend named Cary Strukel at the club. Strukel found Warren peculiar; plainly he did not work and lived off of Sharon's earnings. He would talk to himself and shovel down handfuls of pills, and he kept a shotgun by the door. The babysitter also discovered a stun gun behind the Marshalls' sofa.

When Michael cried, Warren would yell for Sharon to shut the brat up. He also wanted Sharon to have breast implants like Stevie's so she could have a career in adult movies. As he said this, Warren would pull on Sharon's nipples. Warren was into adult movies. As a screen test, he had filmed Sharon and Stevie wearing string bikinis on the beach rubbing oil over each other's bodies.

It became clear to Strukel that Sharon had no interest in dancing at the Mons Venus, performing in adult movies, or the cheap boob job Warren had foisted on her. She had been coerced. Warren also drove Sharon to bachelor parties and gave her condoms before she went in. The rumor was that he was her pimp. At bachelor parties, Sharon did a lesbian act with another stripper. The other stripper sometimes stayed at the Marshalls' trailer and reported to the other girls that she thought Warren was sleeping with Sharon. Sharon, of course, had little to say about it.

Cheryl Commesso also stayed at the Marshalls'. Warren boasted that he had contacts in the adult entertainment industry and with *Playboy* magazine. She was happy to have him film her engaging in sexual acts with Sharon in the hope that he could further her career. She even slept with Warren. But once, when they took a boat trip and she refused him, he hit her in the face and tried to strangle her. She leapt out of the boat and swam to shore.

To get Warren back, Cheryl called Florida social services and told them that, while Sharon was collecting welfare, she was also earning thousands of dollars as a stripper. Warren was livid. He lay in wait for Cheryl in the parking lot of the Mons and grabbed her. She screamed and was rescued by the bouncers. A week later, she disappeared.

By then, Sharon was clearly pregnant. In May 1989, Warren Marshall had sunk a boat in an attempt to make a fraudulent insurance claim, then he set fire to his trailer, and fled with Sharon and Michael. They had headed to New Orleans where they had married. Detectives reasoned that they had done this to prevent Sharon being forced to testify against Floyd if he was charged with the murder of Cheryl Commesso.

The authorities also believed that as Sharon had grown older she had become less desirable in his eyes. Her only purpose was to support him financially through nude dancing and prostitution, while Floyd's erotic interest began to focus on Michael.

The detectives investigating the murder of Cheryl Commesso went to visit Floyd in Oklahoma City County Jail. He denied knowing Cheryl, though he said she could have been a friend of his "stepdaughter" Sharon. He then told them a rambling story about Sharon stealing money from the mob. That's why they had left Florida.

Later they interviewed one of Floyd's cell mates, who said that Floyd had told him that he had killed someone and covered the body in lye to get rid of it. Floyd had also told the cell mate that he had killed his wife. Once Floyd had said that he had hit her over the head and left her by the side of the road. Another time, he had said he had run her down. When asked about Michael, Floyd's cell mate said that Floyd had again said that he had thrown the boy off a bridge and the child had screamed all way down until he hit the water. But then, Floyd had said a lot of things. His cell mate thought he was just trying to make himself look big.

Although this information did not help move the case forward, a grand jury in Florida returned an indictment for first-degree murder in the case of Cheryl Commesso.

In jail, Floyd was caught with child pornography. Another cell mate said that he admitted to killing Cheryl Commesso and, said that in regards to Michael, Floyd said: "If I can't have him, no one will."

After some legal wrangling, Floyd was found mentally competent to stand trial for the murder of Cheryl Commesso. The trial lasted just nine days. The jury took four hours to find him guilty. It took them another hour to unanimously recommend death by lethal injection. Floyd will likely go to his death without having revealed the whereabouts of Michael Anthony Hughes, or the true identity of Sharon Marshall.

Chapter 16

Lena Simakina and Katya Martynova— The Russian Demographic

ON SEPTEMBER 30, 2000, seventeen-year-old Lena Simakina and her fourteen-year-old friend Katya Martynova, set off from their homes to a disco in Sobornaya Square in the center of Ryazan, 150 miles south of Moscow. There was a party there to celebrate the Russian Orthodox holiday of *Vera*, *Nadezhda*, and *Lyubov*—faith, hope, and love. When their evening out was over, they accepted a lift home from forty-eight-year-old Viktor Mokhov, a metalworker at the Skopin car factory, and his girlfriend, twenty-five-year-old Yelena Badukina, who introduced herself at "Lyosha." The girls thought they were safe because there was a woman in the car.

In the car, Mokhov gave them vodka that had been laced with sedatives. He drove them to his hometown of Skopin, where they woke up in a dungeon. It was nine feet underground, and their screams were inaudible to anyone outside.

The cell, which measured eight feet by ten feet, had taken former army officer Mokhov three years to build. He excavated

351

about sixty tons of earth by hand and spread it around a lot nearby. The subterranean prison was hidden under his rusting garage, but could not be accessed directly from it. The entrance was carefully hidden. Around to the side, it was screened from the garden by a wooden fence. Behind a metal panel that had to be pried back with a screwdriver, there was a steel door about six inches thick that was held down by magnets. Beyond that was a secret ground-level room that was only three feet high; a trapdoor and wooden ladder led to another chamber below. That chamber contained a padlocked steel hatch at ankle height, measuring just twenty by fifteen inches. Mokhov could only just squeeze through.

Beyond the hatch was the door to the girls' cell and the entrance to the "sex chamber." Mokhov had drilled ventilation holes in the concrete ceiling, and wired it up to provide electricity. He would lower a bucket to be used as a lavatory and another with water for washing. Later, he allowed them a small electric stove and let them cook rice to supplement the meager rations he provided.

Mokhov beat the two girls with a rubber hose and demanded sex every day. If they tried to resist, he would starve them or cut off their electricity—their only source of warmth during the cold Russian winter. He would limit the supply of oxygen so they could hardly breathe and spray tear gas into the cellar.

Once the girls had been forced to comply, he would take them one at a time into the smaller room, where the walls were covered with pictures from pornographic magazines. There he would act out his fantasies with them.

This was not Mokhov's first offense. In December 1999, a sixteen-year-old girl and her boyfriend visited him. He gave them alcohol, then began to make advances toward the girl. She rejected him and left, so he followed her out into the street, hit her in the head, and dragged her back to his bunker. For the next two weeks he kept her in the dungeon and raped her, until she managed to escape. However, she did not report the incident.

But Mokhov had learned a lesson and had tightened security.

"We tried everything to get away," said Katya. "We tried to kill him once, a month after we were kidnapped. We attacked him and tried to strangle him with a heater cord. But he threw it off his neck."

When that failed, they tried to persuade him to let them go.

"We promised him we wouldn't go to the police," Katya said. "And we meant it. But he said, 'I'll only let you go in twenty years, when each of you has given me ten kids.'"

Lena gave birth twice in the underground dungeon with only Katya and a medical manual Mokhov had given them to help her.

"I just helped Lena with everything," said Katya. "The first boy, Vladik, was much healthier than the second, Oleg, who was small and blue, and did not cry. I was washing and cleaning the baby after tying up his tummy button and Lena collapsed on the bed. Could I ever imagine I would deliver two babies successfully? I don't know how I managed."

Both babies were taken away by Mokhov and abandoned on doorsteps in the small town of Skopin. Later, the two boys were adopted.

Katya was determined not to suffer the same fate.

"I was terrified," she said. "Every day I would pray that I wouldn't be pregnant. If I had been, I would have exercised my stomach so hard that I aborted the baby."

For Katya, this brutal, humiliating experience was her first introduction to sex.

"I was a virgin when I went in there," she said. "It was my first time. Just think how that makes me feel. He ruined something that should have been so special for me."

Lena had a boyfriend at the time of the abduction, but after she disappeared, he assumed she was dead and married another woman.

There was little to do in the dungeon except await the next sex attack, though after the three years and eight months they spent in the cellar, Mokhov's demands tailed off to twice a week. As the girls became more cooperative, he rewarded them with paints, pens, and paper, and some books. They also passed the time learning English. An exercise book they found on the floor was filled with neat handwriting in blue ballpoint pen. One entry read, "The remains of an extinct hippopotamus have been found by a party of Soviet and Mongolian paleontologists."

The conditions they lived under were appalling. The walls were slimy and damp. They had two bunk beds with moldy mattresses, a small table, and a stool. To brighten their dull existence, the walls of the main chamber were decorated with posters of Madonna and Pamela Anderson, along with a religious icon and a landscape painted by Katya showing a woman standing by a river. Katya also built a castle out of matchsticks, which she took with her when they were let out of the cellar.

"There were two bunk beds, but we slept together," said Katya. "At the beginning, we just lay on it with our arms around each other and cried all the time. During the first six months we were apathetic. We did nothing. It was only later that we started making our bed, cooking, keeping busy. We needed to make our life as bearable as we could to survive."

They clung to each other and to the routine they built.

"Katya and I prayed every day," said Lena. "We never gave up. We lived in fear of death but still hoped. We wanted to believe that one day he'd let us go, though he said, 'Why should I? It is easier to kill you.' But we planned it anyway. We always had a note ready with our addresses and what had happened to us. We tried to hide notes in the clothes of my second son but that bastard must have found them all."

They certainly couldn't reconcile themselves to being Mokhov's sex slaves.

"He was a cruel, poisonous, sly, stupid coward—cruelty and cowardice were his nature," said Katya. "Contact with him was the worst thing. He was old, smelly, and so ugly. Don't think either of us got used to it."

The girls started exercising every day, while Katya wrote poems and read. Then on May 1, 2001, Mokhov bought them a small black-and-white TV.

"We watched it for hours on end," Katya said. "We even watched the ads with the same excitement."

They saw Sabine Dardenne on TV after she was freed from Marc Dutroux in Belgium. That gave them both hope.

"We saw her smiling and saying she wouldn't let this experience ruin her life in the future," said Lena. "I remember turning to Katya and crying, like we did hundreds of times. I remember asking, 'Will we ever give interviews and smile like this?'"

Later he bought them a tape recorder.

Eventually Mokhov began to drop his guard. He boasted to drinking companions about the "mini-harem" under his garage, and people became suspicious of the amount of food his mother, eighty-year-old Alisa Mokhova, was buying. Occasionally, he let them go up to the trapdoor and smell the air. It was their biggest treat. But then in the last few months of their captivity, he allowed them outside one at a time to exercise after dark.

Of course, he had an ulterior motive. He hoped they would help him seduce a female student who had moved into the house as a lodger. Katya was introduced to her as a relative. Then Katya was able to give the neighbor girl an audio-cassette tape, ostensibly as a gift, and asked her to give it to the police. Inside was a note that read: "This person knows where we are."

The plan worked. On April 26, 2004, the police, who had long since given up on finding the girls, assuming they were dead, went to Mokhov's home and found them.

After being deprived of sunlight for 1,320 days, Lena could not walk more than a few yards without help. She smelled of mold, and her skin was light green. When she was released, Lena was eight months pregnant, but her third child was still-born. She still didn't know what had happened to her two other children.

"When they were inside me, I didn't think of them as my children," she said. "They were his babies, implanted against my will."

But she could not suppress her maternal instincts. When the police finally rescued the two girls, her first words were, "Please, please find my babies and bring them back to me."

She remained torn between her love for them and the feeling that they could never have a normal mother-child relationship.

"I don't want to see them now, because I know I will only cry and get distressed," she said after six weeks of freedom. "They will always remind me of him, and that's not best for them. They deserve the chance of a decent life and I don't know if I'm strong enough to give them what they need."

Mokhov told investigators, "I wanted to have many children. I wanted to improve the demographic situation of Russia."

Mokhov was sentenced to seventeen years in a labor camp plus two years in jail.

"Nothing is enough for him," said Lena.

Badukina was jailed for fifteen years, but no charges were filed against Mokhov's mother, who does not seem to have known what her son was doing.

Although Lena thought she would never trust another man, less than two years after she was released she married Dima Isaev in a Georgian ceremony. They had been introduced by Katya in 2004.

"I thought it was utterly impossible that I'd ever be able to love or even trust a man," she said. "My wedding day felt like a miracle. It was as if I was watching a film. When I was in the cellar, I stopped dreaming of the future. I didn't think I would ever get out. I thought I would die down there and never love again. If I'd imagined having someone to love me, I would have gone crazy. Instead, I focused purely on survival. I knew which thoughts it was safe to have and which ones were too painful to cope with… It still seems surreal that I have a normal life ahead of me."

She also went to college to study journalism. She hopes to have children with her husband.

"I would like two or three," she said.

When Natascha Kampusch was freed, Lena sent her a message.

"My message to Natascha is private, for her only," it was reported. "I hope it will help her with what lies ahead. Back then I never would have thought that I could have a normal life ahead of me, so when my family and friends toasted us at our wedding last year it felt like a miracle."

And when Elisabeth Fritzl was released, Lena and Katya sent a message of hope, saying, "We want to tell Elisabeth, it can be all right. Not all men are monsters. You can find true love, as we have. We know something of what you went through and will go through in the future as you try to recover."

Katya added, "Elisabeth, please know you will recover and you will learn to trust again. Love can conquer anything, however horrific. Our lesson is that you can put all this ordeal somewhere at the back of your mind and get on and live a completely new life."

Bibliography

Birkbeck, Matt. *A Beautiful Child: A True Story of Hope, Horror, and an Enduring Human Spirit*. Berkley, 2005.

Cawthorne, Nigel. *House of Horrors: The Horrific True Story of Josef Fritzl, the Father from Hell*. John Blake, 2008.

Dardenne, Sabine. *I Choose to Live*. Virago, 2005.

Davis, Carol Anne. *Sadistic Killers: Profiles of Pathological Predators*. Summersdale, 2007.

Donnelley, Paul. *501 Most Notorious Crimes*. Bounty Books, 2009.

Dugard, Jaycee Lee. *A Stolen Life: A Memoir*. Simon & Schuster, 2011.

Echols, Mike. *I Know My First Name Is Steven: The True Story of the Steven Stayner Abduction Case*. Pinnacle Books, 1991.

Englade, Ken. *Cellar of Horror: The Story of Gary Heidnik*. St. Martin's Paperbacks, 1992.

Fass, Paula S. *Kidnapped: Child Abduction in America*. Oxford University Press, 1997.

Green, Jim B. *Colleen Stan: The Simple Gifts of Life*. iUniverse, 2008.

Grievens, Perry. *True Crime: The Kidnapping of Jaycee Dugard*. York Publishing Group, 2011.

Haberman, Maggie, and Jeane MacIntosh. *Held Captive: The Kidnapping and Rescue of Elizabeth Smart*. Avon Books: 2003.

Hall, Allan, and Michael Leidig. *Girl in the Cellar: The Natascha Kampusch Story*, Hodder, 2007.

Hall, Allan. *Monster*. Penguin: 2008.

Herzog, Arthur. *17 Days—The Kate Beers Story*. iUniverse: 1993.

Jaeger, Marietta. *The Last Child*. Pickering Paperback, 1983.

Kampusch, Natascha. *3,095 Days*. Penguin, 2010.

Lunnon, Charlene, and Lisa Hoodless. *Abducted*. Penguin, 2009.

Mariotte, Jeff. *Criminal Minds: Sociopaths, Serial Killers & Other Deviants*. Wiley, 2010.

McGuire. Christine, *Perfect Victim*. Morrow, 1988.

Newton. Michael, *The Encyclopedia of Kidnappings*. Checkmark, 2002.

Sauerwein. Kristina. *Invisible Chains—Shawn Hornbeck and the Kidnapping Case that Shook the Nation*. The Lyons Press, 2008.

Smart, Ed and Louis Smart. *Bringing Elizabeth Home*. Doubleday: 2003.

About the Author

NIGEL CAWTHORNE is known for his best-selling Sex Lives series, including *Sex Lives of the Kings and Queens of England* and *Sex Lives of the Roman Emperors*; the books are available in 23 languages. He is also the author of *Serial Killers and Mass Murderers*, *Confirmed Kill*, *Warrior Elite*, *Canine Commandos*, and more than 60 other books.